Working Beyond 60

Working Beyond 60

Key Policies and Practices in Europe

Geneviève Reday-Mulvey

First published 2005 by
PALGRAVE MACMILLAN
Houndmills, Basingstoke, Hampshire RG21 6XS and
175 Fifth Avenue, New York, N.Y. 10010
Companies and representatives throughout the world

PALGRAVE MACMILLAN is the global academic imprint of the
Palgrave Macmillan division of St Martin's Press LLC and of
Palgrave Macmillan Ltd.
Macmillan® is a registered trademark in the United States, United Kingdom and other countries. Palgrave is a registered trademark in the European Union and other countries.

ISBN 1–4039–4796–1 hardback
ISBN-13 978–1–4039–4796–3

This book is printed on paper suitable for recycling and made from fully managed and sustained forest sources.

A catalogue record for this book is available from the British Library.

Library of Congress Cataloging-in-Publication Data
Reday-Mulvey, Geneviève.
    Working beyond 60? : key policies and practices in Europe / by Geneviève Reday-Mulvey.
      p. cm.
    Includes bibliographical references and index.
    ISBN 1–4039–4796–1 (cloth)
      1. Older people—Employment—Europe. 2. Social security—Europe.
  I. Title: Working beyond sixty. II. Title.

    HD6283.E8R43 2005
    331.3'9812042'094–dc22

                                                          2004062717

10   9   8   7   6   5   4   3
14   13   12   11   10   09   08   07   06

Printed and bound in Great Britain by
Antony Rowe Ltd, Chippenham, Wiltshire

Contents

List of Boxes

List of Figures

List of Tables

The Geneva Association

The International Association for the Study of Insurance Economics, or the 'Geneva Association', is the world's leading insurance think-tank. The Geneva Association serves as a catalyst for progress in this unprecedented period of fundamental change in the insurance industry and its growing importance for the further development of the modern economy. It is a non-profit organisation.

Its main goal is to research the growing importance of worldwide insurance activities in all sectors of the economy. Its research team identifies fundamental trends and strategic issues where insurance plays a substantial role or which influence the insurance sector. In parallel, it encourages various initiatives concerning the evolution – in economic and cultural terms – of risk management and the notion of uncertainty in the modern economy. Throughout the year, the Geneva Association organises or supports about a dozen conferences and seminars, gathering experts from all sectors and backgrounds to combine their knowledge.

The Geneva Association publishes leading insurance journals, newsletters and books and monographs. The main ones are:

Geneva Papers on Risk and Insurance – Issues and Practice (four times per year) for insurance professionals and researchers/consultants, published by Palgrave.

Geneva Risk and Insurance Review (twice per year) for insurance academics.

Internal working paper series 'Etudes et Dossiers' (ten–fifteen per year).

Eight Geneva Association Information Newsletters published usually twice per year on its research programmes: The Four Pillars (Social Security, Employment and Retirement), Risk Management, Insurance and Finance, Insurance Economics, Regulation and Trade Issues, Health and Ageing, World Fire Statistics, and General Information.

www.genevaassociation.org

Foreword

Patrick M. Liedtke

Virtually since its foundation in 1973, the Geneva Association has worked on issues related to pensions, retirement systems and the work environment. However, in the mid-1980s, the Geneva Association, conscious of changing demographic and financial trends, became especially concerned with the crucial challenges of the future financing of pensions, which would require not a mere adaptation and gradual evolution of the (then) existing social security systems but a wider and much more comprehensive rethinking. A whole series of activities ensued and the dedicated research programme called 'The Four Pillars', which focused on this area, was inaugurated. Since that time the Geneva Association's activities have had an important impact on the research and policy debates on social security systems, particularly concerning issues of old-age security.

Today, there is a wider awareness that populations in OECD countries will decline over an extended period and that dependency ratios of non-active retirees to the active population are eroding rapidly. This was not always the case. Through earlier research programmes (conducted under the acronyms PROGRES and now ASEC), the Association was able, perhaps before most, to see that the tectonic shifts in demographic development and future financial constraints were occurring in a new economic context where four jobs out of five were in service functions. It was also becoming increasingly recognized that such service activities typically require less physical effort and greater mental abilities with the consequence that, in principle, workers could easily remain productive longer. This is especially the case where retirement regulations and conditions are more flexible and adequate continuing training, among other things, is made available. This means that the problems posed by demographics can be turned into opportunities and older workers could be kept working longer on a flexible basis.

In 1987 Professor Orio Giarini, Secretary General of the Geneva Association until 2000, and Honorary Member of the Club of Rome, formally launched the 'Four Pillars' research programme with the aims of studying the key importance in the new service economy of Social Security, Insurance, Savings and Employment. The programme has focused mainly on the future of pensions, welfare and employment. Some of the key issues for the programme have been the developing complementarity between social security and insurance, the changing perspective of the welfare state, employment and the life-cycle, and, of course, changing demography and its financial impact. The programme has been directed since its first days by Geneviève Reday-Mulvey, the author of this book.

Over the years, the Geneva Association developed the research through activities such as organizing seminars and expert meetings, encouraging research in the areas mentioned above, publishing new findings in newsletters, journals and monographs, and directly contributing to the research and publications of other organizations in the field. Over the last decade alone, over 20 conferences and seminars on social security issues were organized or co-organized, often with other prominent European and international organizations and networks. Four books, several issues of the Geneva Papers on Risk and Insurance – Issues and Practice, numerous working papers and special brochures were produced, and, last but not least, 35 issues of *The Four Pillars* Newsletter were sent to over 4,000 researchers and organizations throughout the world.

In the mid-1990s Geneviève Reday-Mulvey and one of her academic colleagues, Dr Lei Delsen from Nijmegen University, prepared a book on *Gradual Retirement – Macro and Micro Issues and Policies*, with the support of the European Commission and the cooperation of experts from seven OECD countries. The book had a significant impact and over the last few years, often under the advice of the European Commission, most governments of EU member states have adopted important reforms to their pension and social security systems and are in the process of launching a number of employment policies and measures to encourage higher employment for the 55–64-year-olds, and a later and more flexible retirement.

In the late 1990s, the Geneva Association engaged with the Club of Rome to address the growing problems of efficiently organizing work and employment systems, which are the economic and social basis of any modern society. Orio Giarini and I wrote a Report to the Club of Rome entitled *The Employment Dilemma and the Future of Work*, which was translated into eight languages and became an economic bestseller in some countries. It was prepared with the input of specialists around the world and a dedicated high-level working group of the Club of Rome comprising some of the most outstanding experts, including a former Prime Minister and leaders of important international organizations. Among other topics, the book further developed the issue of how to efficiently organize work and employment systems so as to assure sustainable solutions for social security systems in the future.

The Geneva Association's new book *Working beyond 60 – Key Policies and Practices in Europe* brings a number of answers to the problem of reversing the trend towards early retirement, and points to how new policies for extending the work life could be implemented in Europe. Geneviève Reday-Mulvey has been able to secure the example of a number of best practice companies, which have already benefited from new attitudes, measures and strategies in encouraging later and more flexible retirement.

The idea for this book emerged after we organized a joint conference with the Club of Rome in Vienna in March 2003, which was widely applauded as to its theme and the positive impact it had on the public debate. As Secretary General of the Geneva Association and member of the Executive Committee of the Club of Rome I had the honour of conducting the proceedings of this conference. It was then that we first used the title *Working Beyond 60*. It is a great pleasure to see how Geneviève Reday-Mulvey has been able to take the spirit of that conference further, combining it with the original ideas of Orio Giarini, the results of the Geneva Association's research activities and some Club of Rome initiatives, to achieve this excellent result.

I thank all specialists in the European Commission, national administrations and private sector companies (three of whom are members of our Association) who have cooperated in preparing this book.

Patrick M. Liedtke
Secretary General of the Geneva Association

Foreword

Professor Alan Walker

This book focuses on one of the most important policy issues confronting Europe as well as other developed countries: how to ensure the sustainability of pensions and social protection. The question is posed more sharply in Europe than elsewhere because, on the one hand, it contains nearly all of the world's most advanced social protection systems, some of which deliver higher standards of living and lower levels of poverty than anywhere else. These social protection systems are among the jewels in the crown of European civilization. However, on the other hand, during the second half of the twentieth century, Europe witnessed a profound revision of the relationship between old age and employment which, indeed, amounted to a redefinition of old age. Europe led the world in the 1970s and 1980s in the rise of early exit from the labour market among older workers. Governments, employers and trade unions encouraged this trend in what was a remarkable policy consensus. But overlooked at the time were the facts that population ageing means workforce ageing and that the social contract between the generations of workers and pensioners that underpins Europe's social protection systems would be put at risk by the decline in revenues and extension of payments resulting from early exit. Warnings were ignored, including those from Orio Giarini and his colleagues in the Geneva Association who have consistently pressed the case for a revival of the fourth pillar (employment) of retirement income. Instead the key players in Europe's labour markets continued to act as if there was no need to change practices based on a completely different era of continuous workforce rejuvenation. The realization dawned in the mid-1990s and consequently there was a rush to close the early exit gates. The new millennium is characterized by a common policy focus on extending working life by changing the European culture of early exit, although the details of the strategy necessary to achieve this have not yet been clearly formulated. If the strategy is simply a matter of raising the age of eligibility for pensions, that would have profoundly negative effects on many older workers who experience the psychological impact of age discrimination in the labour market and are forced to exist on social assistance.

That is where this book comes in very powerfully. Building on the pioneering work of the Geneva Association, Geneviève Reday-Mulvey outlines a detailed strategy to enable people to work longer, a strategy we might label 'active ageing'. As she demonstrates in this book, such a strategy must be multifaceted, including remedial action to overcome skill deficits among current generations of older people, as well as preventative measures such as lifelong learning, continuous vocational training, shorter working hours, anti-age discrimination legislation and general education about the benefits of continuing employment. The book shows that this strategy must be sensitive to occupational differences, because of the variable impact of jobs on physical and mental capacity, and be based on the principle of gradual retirement comprising part-time employment and partial pensions. Above all, the fourth pillar must be flexible, which echoes a proposal made in the UK some 15 years ago, for a flexible decade of retirement. To achieve this flexibility major changes will be required in employment and social protection and this book provides the necessary guidelines.

If Europe can successfully extend working life in the careful way advocated by Reday-Mulvey it would bring benefits to everyone: extending quality of life among older people, a reduction in wastage and an increase in production for employers and a route to social protection system sustainability for policy makers. For Europe as a whole the prize is a very big one: the maintenance of that unique combination of economic competitiveness and social justice that is its hallmark. In setting out clearly, with case studies, how it is possible to achieve the goal of extending working life, this book provides an invaluable contribution to the European debate about the future of employment and social protection and will be a substantial resource for policy makers, employers, trade unions and anyone else interested in one of the most important policy issues of the present century.

Alan Walker
Professor of Social Policy
University of Sheffield, UK

Acknowledgements

This book is dedicated to Michael Brendan Mulvey, my husband, who over my whole career has been interested in political, economic and social issues and progressive practice. His thinking, and his way of often asking key questions, has allowed me to sharpen and deepen my thinking on innumerable questions with which our societies are grappling today.

My thanks go first to Professor Orio Giarini who was one of the first academics to perceive the importance of recent and future changes in the process of ageing and the life-cycle, and of the fact that we need to work differently in order to work longer. Our numerous discussions over recent years have always been stimulating. I also thank Patrick M. Liedtke who provided a Foreword and who encouraged and supported me in preparing this book in the framework of the Four Pillars' research programme of the Geneva Association.

In preparing the book I was also privileged to be able to count on a number of experts who prepared a 'box' or provided me with their expertise on a number of topics. They are listed below, and my thanks also go to them, but the list cannot be exhaustive, and I apologize for any oversight.

James W. Vaupel, Max Planck Institute for Demographic Research
Jan Sadlak, UNESCO-CEPES
Orio Giarini, the Geneva Association
Alan Walker, University of Sheffield
Axel H. Börsch-Supan, Mannheim Research Institute
Roland Sigg, International Social Security Association
Wolfgang Gallenberger, BG Institute of Work and Health
Juhanni Ilmarinen, Finnish Institute of Occupational Health
Daniel Atlan, Human Resources Management, Arcelor
Renée Husson, Human Resources, Laboratoire Boiron
Martin Hutsebaut, European Trade Union Institute
Per Jensen, Aalborg University
Philip Taylor, Cambridge University
Kene Henkens, National Interdisciplinary Demographic Institute, The Hague
Lei Delsen, Nijmegen University
Karl Kuhn, Federal Institute for Occupational Safety and Health, Dortmund
Jean-Michel Brunet, CEGOS Consulting, Paris
Mara Tagliabue, Macros Research, Milan
Petra Huth, Credit Suisse, Zurich
Ritva Hyytia, John-Crane Safematic Oy, Finland

I would like also to thank all the international organizations – in particular the European Commission (F. Von Nordheim); firms – in particular the human resources departments of AXA France, CNP Assurances and Groupama; government agencies and professional associations who have willingly provided valuable information, a wealth of statistical data, and many suggestions.

Special thanks go to Professor Alan Walker who prepared a Foreword. He has been for me the inspiring 'guru' in the field for the last 15 years and has often contributed to the conferences organized by the Geneva Association and its publications.

This study could not have been completed, especially in the time framework, without the qualities in research and reflection of Dr Katalin Velladics, who has been our researcher over the last months. It has been a great pleasure for me to work with her and I am grateful for her hard, serious and excellent work in the preparation of this book.

Finally, this book owes a lot to the two revisers: first, John Sykes, now an active retiree from the International Labour Office who is a living example of how important it is to remain intellectually active and interested in the political and social debate; and second, Michael Mulvey, who has shown a sensitive understanding of the subject matter and has spared no effort in translating a number of texts into English and in revising the whole of the completed study.

Introduction

At the beginning of the twentieth century, pension schemes were set up to provide a replacement income during a well-deserved though short period of retirement (on average five years). After the Second World War, these schemes were substantially improved to provide more generous benefits over a longer period. At the time, however, nobody even dreamed of the extended life expectancy that we enjoy today – an expectancy that continues to rise.

Demographic projections in EU member states for the early years of the twenty-first century awakened policy makers in the early 1990s to the need for far-reaching reforms of pension and social welfare systems. In part initiated, these reforms are regularly updated and complemented. One of the main issues today remains, however, the lengthening of the contribution period to pension schemes so as to provide for an adequate benefit level to support a retirement which itself has lengthened considerably: in the EU of 15 member states retirement now lasts on average 20 years for men and 25 for women, compared with around ten years in 1950 (GINA and the Geneva Association, 2002).

Life and health expectancies, a major progress of the twentieth century

A lengthening of life was one of the most remarkable feats of the twentieth century, a century that in almost all fields was no stranger to achievement. Not only has life lengthened but the health of persons in their 60s, 70s and 80s has improved considerably. By comparison with 50 years ago, life has been extended by one or even two decades in good health. Not only does old age last longer, but adult life has also gained in length, and young people now benefit from a greater number of years devoted to study. Meanwhile, the extended time of retirement has given rise in richer countries to a whole new phase in the life-cycle, a 'golden' age, according to some, of rest, leisure and non-remunerated activity within the family or voluntary sector. Retirement, then, commences before the onset of old age, with the result that old age itself needs to be redefined as it is no longer coterminous with retirement and even less with the age of withdrawal from active life.

Paradox of early retirement

Meanwhile, during the 1970s and 1980s, thanks to sustained technological progress in most of the Organization for Economic Cooperation and Development (OECD) countries, industry was 'restructuring' and with it the demand for manpower was shrinking. This situation led to mass unemployment, especially among the young. The problem was becoming urgent and, in their attempts to address it, governments in consultation with employers and the unions began to encourage increasingly early exits from the labour force, a practice that became known as 'early retirement'. Frequently the state helped out financially by underwriting the replacement income. For the unskilled or semi-skilled worker early retirement was a significant development. For these were people who had started working at an early age and often in arduous circumstances, and for whom therefore the unions had long been militating for earlier retirement. However, early retirement was a more mixed blessing for higher qualified and managerial staff, since people in this category identified strongly with the life and culture of the enterprise. Many found themselves overnight outside the firm, something for which they were ill-prepared. Some were left with the feeling that they served no further social purpose and a fair number began to be beset by serious health problems. The absence of any proper transition between full employment and full retirement was for many an experience with which they simply could not cope, and few firms had made arrangements for some sort of gradual retirement.

Early retirement, a new social entitlement?

In a number of countries however, especially those in continental Europe such as Germany, France, Italy and Belgium, early retirement, far from being one option among others, was becoming a new social right, an entitlement to which people were beginning to look forward, and something substantial which needed to be planned for. This lengthening of life combined with an early exit from the labour force, often at age 60 or even earlier, was causing working life itself to shrink, frequently to 40 years or less, and thus to cover a period shorter than the years of training and retirement combined.

As early retirement schemes expanded, so governments began to realize that vacancies created by early retirement were much of the time not being filled by the young unemployed and, more often than not, enterprises were simply downsizing their workforce. It soon became clear also how exorbitant the cost of these mass exits really was. Enterprises which had parted with qualified staff before the statutory retirement age found it necessary to re-employ them as consultants to avoid the sudden loss of valuable know-how which the latter had taken with them into early retirement.

In certain countries, such as the Nordic countries (save for Finland) and Switzerland, and beyond Europe in Japan, firms were able, in spite of the enhanced productivity that came with technological progress, to retain their employees until the age of 65. Jobs frequently had to be adjusted for these not-so-young workers and work-time reductions put in place. In certain cases, where retirement benefits were too modest or when the employee in question was especially committed to the job, workers were able to remain in employment beyond 65, frequently on a part-time basis. In other countries, the UK and US among them, and in yet others to a lesser extent, firms were laying off numerous 50-year-olds whose future income was underwritten neither by the firm nor by the state. These workers in general faced enormous difficulties in finding fresh employment, more often than not less well paid and with less favourable work conditions and benefits. These jobs, many of which were part-time and temporary, were called 'bridge jobs' – they enabled the employee to survive until he or she was able to draw a pension at the age of 65. But at times also workers were unable to find any further employment and for several years had to make do with unemployment benefits or were registered for a disability benefit. In a number of countries, applications for disability benefit were filed by an increasing number of the over-50s leading to substantial invalidity insurance deficits.

Working beyond 60 – a new consensus

Over the last ten years or so, all actors – politicians, economists and sociologists alike – have begun to view the situation just described in an entirely new light. Gradually a new consensus has emerged regarding a radical reappraisal of social welfare and employment policy, with special emphasis on end of career and retirement.

First, budgetary constraints and demographic projections have forced states thoroughly to rethink and update their social welfare systems and more particularly their pension arrangements. Reforms have raised the pension age of workers, especially of women, and in relative terms have reduced benefits under the first-pillar pension and promoted the development of occupational pension schemes (the second pillar) and personal assets (the third pillar). They have led to greater flexibility regarding the age of retirement, to an increase in the years of contributory service and to the possibility of combining a pension with an occupational income. By limiting the generosity of social benefits EU member states have thus been able gradually to establish more manageable public debt levels. The paradox of the relatively early age of exit from the labour market became increasingly evident as life and health expectancies continued to rise and as more and more 60-year-olds remained active and in good health and yet almost entirely absent from the labour market. Debt-burdened unemployment and disability insurance schemes were being forced to limit the number of beneficiaries and, in some cases, even to limit the range of benefits provided.

For their part, employers were faced with an ever-increasing demand for profitability and flexibility and had on their hands a workforce that included a rising proportion of employees in their 40s and 50s who had frequently benefited from continuous training and had managed to build many of the new technologies into their skills base. Firms, accordingly, began to realize that it would probably be in their own commercial interest, among other things, to keep employees within the labour force later by making certain adjustments to work conditions and wages.

Indeed, some firms are already predicting a shortage of labour, given the expected sharp fall in the number of youngsters entering the labour market and the rise in the number of exits as baby-boomers reach retirement age.

The unions, meanwhile, have continued to struggle for more generous terms for early retirement in the sure knowledge, however, that in future the new conditions for pension entitlement will necessitate a fairly radical redesigning of the second half of occupational life. They are already beginning to realize that the main focus in future will be on career planning, continuing training until career end and adjustment of work conditions for employees between the ages of 50 and 65.

Media treatment of the future of pensions, while frequently alarmist, has served to bring home to workers that an extra effort will be required of them in terms of an extended work-life and pension benefits that are less generous than in the past. Surveys show that workers remain attached to the European social welfare model and would want a transition period between full employment and full retirement, preferring in general to work part-time if they must remain in the labour force until 65 or beyond, rather than as at present being able to quit at 60.

Working beyond 60 and a fourth pillar?

Having encouraged member states during the 1990s to reform their pension and social security systems, the European Commission has set as its main target for the first decade of the twenty-first century to increase the participation of 'seniors' in the labour market. More generally within the economy, but also socially and culturally, the concept and practice of 'active ageing' has been steadily gaining ground, and the World Health Organization and European Commission have both been at pains to promote the concept. Major publicity was given to it during the International Year for Older Persons (1999).

The Geneva Association (the International Association for the Study of Insurance Economics), for its part, has since the late 1980s been developing a research programme called 'The Four Pillars', essentially designed to do two things: first, to raise awareness of the need for multi-pillar pension arrangements which spread the financial burden hitherto supported mainly, where not exclusively, by the first and second pillars; and second, to promote the idea that a fourth pillar (which would combine a partial pension with income from part-time work) might, and indeed should, be added to the other three pillars after official retirement age (or slightly sooner in the case of early retirement). Conferences, workshops and a European network on the issue have accompanied the Association's research in this area leading to a number of publications. Around the mid-1990s and with the support of the European Commission, a major study was made of the key topic of gradual retirement in OECD member states, with contributions by experts from several countries.

From the very outset, the Association, contrary to the fears and predictions of many, has always considered that demographic trends – and particularly life expectancy – constitute a positive and formidable challenge for our communities and firms and the workforce within them. In working on the paradigms and variables of the new service economy (formerly through PROGRES (Programme de recherche sur l'économie de service) and now through its ASEC (Applied Service Economy Centre) research programmes) the Association realized early on that the predicted demographic and financial constraints would be occurring in a new economic context where four out of five jobs were in service functions. It was also becoming widely recognized that such service functions are typically less demanding physically and involve far greater mental skills so that, in theory at least, workers should be able to remain productive longer, especially if conditions governing retirement could be made more flexible and, among other things, continuous training provided. Problems posed by demographics could perhaps, then, be turned into opportunities if older workers could be kept working longer but preferably on a part-time basis. Those in the Association were also becoming aware that, over time, this new challenge would be affecting other continents.

Rethinking retirement and employment

The new challenge meant rethinking retirement in the context of a new design for employment across the entire life-cycle so that people, rather than being relegated to a role of passive consumers, could work later in life, remain socially integrated and continue to make a valid contribution to our service economy. The reorganization of the end of the career and the new age-management strategy of which it was part – where *gradual retirement* plays a key role – also dovetails with many of the changes elsewhere in the life-cycle and in the quality of work that are specific to our contemporary service economy. The nature of our life-cycle is changing. Vertical distribution of our main activities (education and training, work and retirement) as a function of age is gradually giving way to a horizontal arrangement better suited to the economic, social and family realities of our time, producing a more flexible and dynamic life horizon.

While the answer to 'Why work beyond sixty?' is now obvious, the how and for whom are questions that require more subtle responses. The aim of the present book is precisely to supply some of those answers. In attempting to suggest how exactly one can work beyond 60, our research has shown that an extension of working life (now part and parcel of almost all reformed pension schemes) must be primarily on a part-time basis. Indeed, extending work-life full-time would seem possible only for a minority of workers. Studies show work-time reduction to be a crucial component of all forms of extended work-life as indeed of end-of-career management in general. Significant benefits would seem to accrue to both workers and firms alike since frequently both require a transition period between full employment and full retirement. Indeed, in a number of countries, work adjustments at career end and gradual retirement have become viable alternatives to straight early retirement. Governments have chosen to finance partial pre-retirement as a first step towards extending work-life. As the career end approaches, part-time work patterns prevent a firm from suddenly losing an employee's skills and know-how, and at the same time make for a smoother staff turnover and a more satisfactory age balance within the firm. Gradual retirement, meantime, has already proved its worth and will increasingly enable workers to remain active beyond the statutory age of retirement. It is nevertheless essential that cumulation of income from work and from a pension become standard practice. This is precisely the idea behind the fourth pillar which, as of age 65, will make it possible for an individual to draw a partial as opposed to a full pension and thereby continue to increase the benefits available on total cessation of work.

Tomorrow's pension schemes must provide the majority of workers with an incentive to remain in the workforce longer. Such schemes must also make room for diversity and flexibility, for customization, for part-time work options and for the possibility of accumulating income from various sources. They must, moreover, be built into employment policy at the macroeconomic level and microeconomically into global strategies within the firm.

The book is divided into four parts through ten chapters.

Part I, 'Working Beyond 60 – Why? The Global Picture: New Constraints and Opportunities', comprises four chapters centred on two key issues: first, the major constraints which have engendered the challenges we face; and, second, recent changes providing answers to some of these challenges and which make a longer and more flexible work-life conceivable.

- Ch 1 summarizes demographic prospects
- Ch 2 examines the changes in social patterns and looks at the social opportunities
- Ch 3 addresses the economic constraints, pension and welfare reforms
- Ch 4 looks at change and opportunity in employment and work environment.

Part II, 'Working Beyond 60 – How? The Reduction of Working Time and the Promotion of Age Management', is divided into four chapters centred on two main issues: public policies and company measures with the aim of increasing the participation of workers beyond 60.

- Ch 5 examines the place of part-time work in work-life extension
- Ch 6 looks at the significant role of supranational organizations and of the social partners
- Ch 7 considers recent public policy in two groups of selected European countries: those with global policies, and those with partial policies
- Ch 8 analyses recent company measures and best practice in selected European firms: work-time reduction, career planning, continuing training, ergonomics, seniority wages, pension regulations, anti-age discrimination legislation and codes of practice.

Part III, 'Working Beyond 60 – For Whom? The Need for Fairness, Diversity and Flexibility', comprises a single chapter divided into two sections.

- Ch 9, first section, analyses the need for diversity and discusses the importance of fairness; the second section analyses the need for flexibility and discusses the importance of choice.

Part IV, 'Working Beyond 60 – Key Policies and Recommendations', comprises a single chapter in three sections.

- Ch 10, first section, provides a comparative country synthesis; the second section examines key policies for working beyond 60 and main recommendations; the third section looks at additional policies to face the overall demographic challenge.

Part I

Working Beyond 60 – Why?

The Global Picture: New Constraints and Opportunities

1
Demographic Constraints

Demographic factors and prospects are already very well-known and have recently been substantiated by international studies. We shall mention here only the main trends having significant relevance for employment beyond 60. This first chapter deals with three main aspects and their future evolution: (i) a longer life, health and retirement expectancy, (ii) changes in the population age structure and (iii) the consequent shrinking workforce and population.

Longer expectancy for life, health and retirement

Rising life expectancy

Over the last 50 years life expectancy at birth and later in life has risen considerably in all industrialized countries and elsewhere. In France, for example, since 1950, life expectancy for men has risen by twelve years to stand in 2002 at 75.6 years of age. For women this rise was even greater – by 13 years – to 82.9.

In Switzerland:

- at the beginning of the 1970s, life expectancy at birth was 70.1 years for males and 76.2 for females; 5.1% of males and 11.3% of females survived to age 90 (in the mortality conditions of 1968–1973)
- twenty years later, in 1990, life expectancy at birth was 74.0 for males and 80.8 for females; 10.1% of males and 25.1% of females survived to age 90 (in the mortality conditions of 1988–1993)
- in 2001, life expectancy at birth was 77.2 years for males and 82.8 for females. (Michel and Robine, 2004)

In the past, as a result of medical advances, increases in life expectancy tended to be due to falling infant mortality rates. Since 1970, however, these increases have mainly been due to survival into higher old age. The greater the age, the greater the relative gain in life expectancy. Changes in patterns of national health over the

11

years can be divided into several different periods. At first, it was mainly the young who benefited from a dramatic fall in the incidence of infectious diseases. Since the 1970s, treatments for cardiovascular conditions and cancer have improved the lot of all age categories, especially of adults over 50 years of age. Today, increased life expectancy is manifest at even the most advanced of ages – 80 years for women, only slightly less for men.

This trend started in the Nordic countries. In southern European countries, however, very rapid development has made up for the 'slower' start. In Spain, life expectancy at birth for women was for a considerable period four years lower than in Sweden. Today, it is somewhat higher. In Japan – the country with the highest score in this area – life expectancy in 2003 was 78 years for men and 85 for women, and there were more than 20,000 people aged 100 years or over.

Both the fact that people enjoy a healthier old age, dying later, and its impact have been very much underestimated with even the most optimistic of forecasts proving to be conservative. However, some experts believe that in future there might be a slowing-up of medical and economic progress and that an upper average age limit of about 85 years is close at hand and that thereafter the return on increasing health expenditure will virtually disappear. They point out that a catalogue of different problems might emerge, such as new diseases and infections, increased stress in the workplace, difficulties due to climate change and environmental degradation, food emergencies and industrial hazards, and that these could affect the rising trend in unexpected ways. The fall in life expectancy which some countries in Eastern Europe have recently experienced shows that such a reversal is indeed possible.

Other demographers point out that in developed countries the trend towards more educated older cohorts currently explains the disability decline of persons over 65 or 70 in countries such as France, the US and Finland (Michel and Robine, 2004) and that this trend will be even stronger with the baby-boom generation, which enjoys improved health status and displays enhanced health behaviour. Some experts even predict that within a few decades life expectancy will be close to 100 years.

Health expectancy

Nowadays a distinction is made between life expectancy as such and life expectancy 'in good health'. As early as 1984, the World Health Organization (WHO) proposed a general model making possible the evaluation of life expectancy in good health. The WHO insisted that health expectancy was more important than life expectancy, and their studies have shown that over recent decades, 'average incapacity-free life expectancy has risen faster than average life expectancy overall. The impact of disease is diminishing' (Dr A. Kalache, Ageing and Health, World Health Organization, in GINA and the Geneva Association, 2002).

In France, for example, serious studies show that between 1981 and 1991, life expectancy at birth increased by 2.5 years for both women and men but that incapacity-free life expectancy increased by 2.6 years for women and 3.0 years for men. Other more recent studies in the US and England suggest the same phenomenon (WHO, 2001).

Box 1.1   How quickly will life expectancy increase?

Is life expectancy approaching its limit? Many – including individuals planning their retirement and officials responsible for health and social policy – believe it is. The evidence suggests otherwise.

Consider an astonishing fact. Female life expectancy in the record-holding country has risen for 160 years at a steady pace of three months per year. In 1840 the record was held by Swedish women, who lived on average a little more than 45 years. Among nations today, the longest expectation of life – just over 85 years – is enjoyed by Japanese women. There is no evidence of any slowing of this long-term rise in best-practice life expectancy. ...

Given intelligent economic and social policy and continued investment in research, longevity and healthy longevity will continue to increase in coming decades. ...

If the rise in life expectancy continues for another 60 years, then females in the record-holding country in 2060 will enjoy a life expectancy at birth of 100 years. Knowledge flows so freely across national boundaries that advanced countries will be clustered within five years or so of the record. So my best guestimate of female life expectancy in 2060 in countries such as Germany, France, Japan and the United States is 95 to 100 years. Male life expectancy will probably be five years or so lower.

This forecast is much higher than most national forecasts. For instance, the US Social Security Administration predicts that US female life expectancy will gradually increase to a level of 83.9 in 2060 – compared with my prediction of 95 to 100. The Social Security forecast is, however, patently ludicrous because *current* female life expectancy in Japan is already 85.2 years. Is it possible that US females six decades from now will have a life expectancy that is less than current levels in Japan?

Progress in reducing mortality could accelerate as biomedical knowledge grows: instead of an increase of three months per year, an increase of four or even five months per year is possible. Economic and political instability and failure to invest in research, on the other hand, could slow progress to perhaps one or two months per year. A reasonable, middle-of-the-road forecast is an increase of three months per year.

James W. Vaupel – Director, Max Planck Institute for Demographic Research, in World Economic Forum (2004, p. 10)

While our health status depends on genetic inheritance and the quality of medical care received, it also – perhaps crucially – depends on our way of living or life-style. This is determined early in life for the entire life-cycle. Physical and mental exercise, for example, can be started at any age and can be highly beneficial for physical and mental health as well as for our ability to work and remain active and socially integrated longer.

The vast majority of the elderly remain in good health and fully capable of looking after themselves as they grow older. Studies show that objective health (measured according to precise criteria) and subjective health (an individual's personal perception of his or her state of health) have both improved significantly over the last 20 years and continue to improve. The activities that the elderly engage in, coupled with physical exercise, have transformed not only their lives but also their perception of their lives. As summarized by a well-known gerontologist, 'the combination of activities such as do-it-yourself, gardening, voluntary work and family and care activities reduce fivefold the risk of senile dementia' (Dr J.-Fr. Dartiques, Inserm, Paris, 2000).

Life expectancy at 65 and retirement expectancy

Clearly, for employment beyond 60 years, the most important factors are life and health expectancy at 65 and the number of years anticipated in retirement. Table 1.1 shows that any additional years of life expectancy have so far been integrated entirely into the retirement period and not as yet into the working period of life. The number of years in retirement has doubled in Europe over the last 30 years, while following the Second World War pension systems and retirement income had been designed for a retirement period of five to ten years, to be extended, but not to the extent currently required.

Table 1.1   Life expectancy at 65, average age of exit from work and retirement expectancy in selected old and new EU member states in 2002

	Life expectancy at 65		Average age of exit from work		Retirement expectancy	
	Men	*Women*	*Men*	*Women*	*Men*	*Women*
Old member states						
Austria	16.3	19.7	59.4	59.3	21.9	25.4
Belgium	15.8	19.7	58.6	58.4	22.2	26.3
Denmark	15.4	18.3	61.9	59.8	18.5	23.5
Finland	15.8	19.6	60.6	60.4	20.2	24.2
France	16.9	21.3	58.9	58.7	23.0	27.6
Germany	16.0	19.6	61.1	60.3	19.9	24.3
Greece	16.3	18.7	61.2	57.7	20.1	26.0
Ireland	15.3	18.6	62.0	62.8	18.3	20.8
Italy	16.5	20.4	60.2	59.7	21.3	25.7
Netherlands	15.6	19.3	62.9	61.6	17.7	22.7
Portugal	15.6	19.0	62.8	63.0	17.8	21.0
Spain	16.5	20.4	61.5	61.5	20.0	23.9
Sweden	16.9	20.0	63.4	63.1	18.5	21.9
United Kingdom	15.7	18.9	62.7	61.9	18.0	22.0
New member states						
Czech Republic	14.0	17.4	62.2	58.4	11.8	19.0
Hungary	13.1	17.0	59.6	58.8	13.5	18.2
Poland	14.0	17.9	58.1	55.8	15.9	22.1
Slovakia	13.3	17.0	59.6	55.7	13.7	21.3

Sources: Eurostat Population Statistics; European Commission (2004, p. 19); and author's calculations.

Financing longer retirement will inevitably bring about substantial increases in pension costs. In half the countries studied, men spend over 20 years in retirement and, if the education and training years are added – and these have also been extended – men are out of the labour force for over half their lifespan. For women the situation is even worse: in four countries, women not infrequently spend over 25 years in retirement and in no country of the 15 EU member states would women be spending less than 20 years out of work if current trends continued.

A key issue for this book, therefore, is how can this period of inactivity best be financed? The good news is, of course, that health expectancy has also increased considerably. New solutions and measures, then, will be needed to adapt working life to reflect this new lease of longer and enhanced health expectancy.

Changes in the population age structure

General outlook

The required fertility rate to maintain a population at a stable level is 2.1 children per woman and around 1.7 to 1.75 if given changing trends in life expectancy and immigration are taken into account. There have been various forecasts by the UN and Eurostat of population growth for the period 2000–50. For the EU as a whole, the forecast suggests currently a population decline of 3% as opposed to the decline of 11% forecast by the UN in 1998.

Fertility has declined to an unprecedented level in most developed countries. In Italy and Spain, fertility rates have plunged to very low levels below 1.3, while in Germany and Switzerland they hover between 1.3. and 1.4. France and Ireland have fertility rates approaching 1.9 and 2.0, while Sweden's fertility increase, for example, has not lasted (cf. Eurostat, 2004b, p. 78).

Larger proportion of over 60s

As a consequence of higher life expectancy and declining fertility, data relating to the European Union and Switzerland for the years 2000, 2020 and 2050 show that the proportion of persons aged 60 years and over relative to the rest of the population will grow substantially and rapidly over the next half century (Table 1.2). In contrast, that proportion has remained fairly stable over the last 50 years because the number of young people has risen.

Table 1.2 Persons 60 years and over as a percentage of the total population, 2000, 2020, 2050

Country	2000	2020	2050
Germany	23	30	41
Austria	20	28	40
Belgium	22	30	38
Denmark	20	28	36
Spain	22	28	44
Finland	20	30	36
France	21	29	38
Greece	23	29	41
Ireland	16	24	39
Italy	24	32	44
Luxembourg	20	28	36
Netherlands	19	29	37
Portugal	21	26	38
United Kingdom	21	27	37
Sweden	22	29	36
Switzerland	20	27	37
EU15	22	29	40

Sources: Eurostat and Swiss Federal Office of Statistics.

In the EU, 20% of the population is now over 60 and that figure is forecast to rise to 30% in the next 20 years. Countries such as Germany and the Netherlands, which in just 25 years will have over one-third of their population over the age of 60, will be subject to greater pressure than those with only 20% or 25% over-60s.

Between 2005 and 2010, the population of 60 years of age and over will become larger than that of the under-20s. Reference is often made to the effects of the baby-boom – children born at the end of the Second World War and in the 1950s who are now reaching retirement. This baby-boom phenomenon is likely to occur, depending on the country concerned, somewhere between 2005 and 2030, but in certain European countries the impact will be evident as early as 2006–08 when the numbers of those retiring will exceed those entering the workforce (see Figure 1.1). From 2020, the population of persons of 60 years of age and over is expected to outstrip the population of under-20s in absolute as well as relative terms.

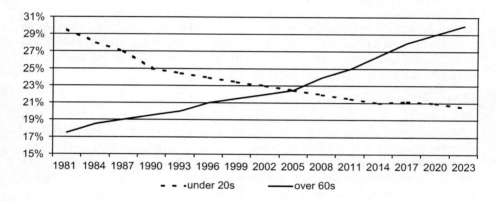

Figure 1.1   Predicated changes in the proportion of under-20s to over-60s within the EU: young and old – inverted representation

Source: *Demographic Status of the European Union*, Public Relations Office of the European Communities, Luxembourg, 1995.

It is not only the industrialized countries which see their populations 'ageing' rapidly. The trend can be observed in a number of less developed countries as well. Indeed growth is even more marked than in Europe in some countries like China, Argentina, Costa Rica and Uruguay, and they face the increasing problem of coping with large elderly populations. The situation which industrialized countries now face will also occur in many developing countries, though slightly later in the timescale (see Figure 1.2).

The forces behind demographic transformation – falling fertility and rising longevity – are causing China to age with unusual speed. In Europe the elder share of the population passed 10% in the 1930s and will not reach 30% until the 2030s, a century later, while China will cover the same distance in a single generation.

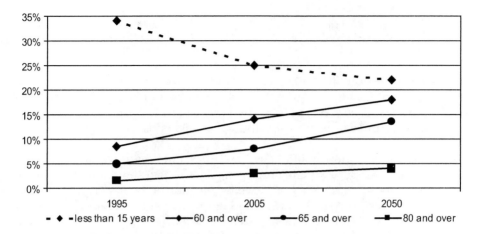

Figure 1.2 Proportion of elderly in the overall populations of developing countries

Source: UN Population Division (2002).

The median age in China will climb from 32 in 2004 to 44 in 2040 (in Germany it is now 42 and is heading for 50 by 2040) (Jackson and Howe, 2004).

Without doubt, ageing, for the population as a whole as well as for individuals, is an enormous step forward, provided, of course, that it is accompanied by reasonable health and decent living conditions. In the twentieth century, advances in medicine and hygiene coupled with economic and social progress have brought about an unprecedented demographic revolution, an achievement of which we can be justly proud. In the years to come, however, it is imperative that adjustments be made to our social security systems if we are to satisfy the needs of a population which is no longer young, and these needs will be very different to those which were only gradually, though successfully, met in the 20th century.

Dependency rate

In determining the financial resources needed to face this important demographic change, one needs to be mindful of the dependency rate. To find the dependency rate, the number of persons who are aged 60 (or 65 depending upon sources) and over and who are assumed to be inactive are calculated relative to the number of persons of 'active' age (that is, those between 20 and 60 years of age). Although somewhat imprecise since it does not take into account under-20s in the workforce, nor those studying beyond that age (already numerous and set to increase in the future), nor those who are in the workforce yet who are over 60 years of age, nor again, of course, those who are simply unemployed, this figure nonetheless gives a rough and ready but useful picture of the difficulties to be faced in financing pensions in the future, especially if certain key changes and adjustments are not made.

In France, for example, there were two retired persons for every ten of active age in 1970. By 1995 this figure had risen to four in every ten. By 2020, the ratio is likely to be five in every ten, by 2030 six in every ten and by 2040 seven in every ten. In certain countries, such as Germany, Italy and Japan where population ageing has been particularly rapid, these dependency rates will be even higher. In today's European Union, overall less than 3.5 workers on average contribute to the pension of every retired person. By 2020 this figure will have fallen and there will only be 2.5 wage earners making a contribution to the retirement of each individual. The situation in some countries is even worse; for example, in Spain for every retired person there are three persons in activity, and by 2035 this will have dwindled to 1.4 persons.

Naturally these figures should be treated with some caution since they take no account of current or possible future changes to pension and employment conditions. Thus the dependency rate itself is a function of the activity rate of those who are aged between 20 and 60 years and not merely of the number of persons over 60 years of age. Furthermore, the situation will depend on the *activity rate of those who are 60 years of age and over*. And, in the final analysis, activity rates are also a function of economic growth and immigration, and also, in the longer term, of changes in the birth rate.

Shrinking workforce and population

As a result, the proportion of people of working age is currently starting to diminish and with it the size of the active population. Between 1995 and 2025 in the EU15,

- the number of young people aged under 20 will fall by 9.5 million or 11%. This will have a direct impact on the organization of services destined specifically for the young (for example, education) and attention will have to be paid to ensuring that their life quality and opportunities for fulfilment are preserved despite their decreasing number
- the 'adults of working age' group will also decline, but to a lesser extent (6.4%). Nevertheless, this age group will lose 13 million people, significantly altering the human resources available
- the over-60s and retired adults will see their numbers increase by 37 million, a rise of some 50%. This spectacular increase will be the result of 'baby-boomers' progressively reaching retirement age, and it is against this background that we have to rethink our social and employment policies
- the median age of the general population will increase at a very rapid rhythm: for example, in France the median age which was 32.5 in 1980 and 37.6 in 2000 should be 42.2 in 2020 and as high as 45.1 in 2050 (see Figure 1.3); in Italy, the median age of 38 in 2000 could reach 52 in 2050 (UN Population Division, 2002).

Significantly, as we shall be seeing later, a key resource in facing this challenge will be the older persons themselves. Not only are most workers in Europe able to remain productive long past labour-market exit ages, but new patterns of consumption could stimulate the emergence of 'aged'-service sectors that provide impetus to

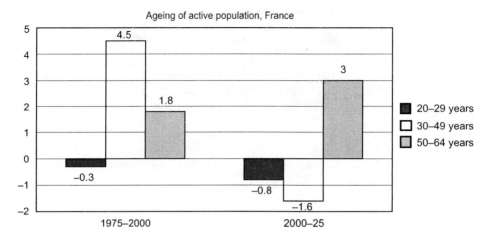

Figure 1.3 Ageing of active population, France

Source: Godet (2003, p. 210).

growth in those economies that effectively adapt to changing demographics. The ability to mobilize the older workforce in pursuit of new economic opportunities may well become one of the yardsticks of success by which societies will be judged in the future.

Shrinking population

According to a report published by the Population Reference Bureau (Washington, DC) in 2004, the population of Europe is forecast to fall from 727 million today to

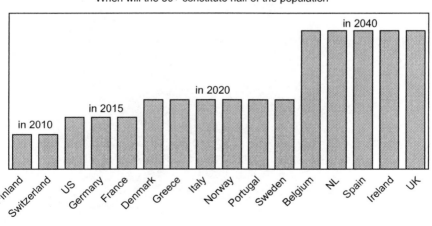

Figure 1.4 Ageing of population in selected OECD countries

Source: 'The Demographic Transition', International Monetary Fund, September 2004.

668 million by 2050; a decline of 8%. While some countries may experience a slight increase (for example, the UK +10%, France +7%, Belgium +5%), most countries are expected to show a drop: Portugal −11%, Italy −10%, Germany −9%, Spain −3% (Figure 1.4 shows the changing demographics in some OECD countries). The decline is projected to be even steeper in the countries of Central and Eastern Europe: Bulgaria −38%, Romania −27%, Hungary −25%, and Poland −15%. Japan is also expected to experience a significant loss, equivalent to 20% of today's population by 2050.

On the other hand the report predicts that India will become the world's most populous country, increasing to 1.6 billion from 1.1 billion today. In so doing it will overtake China, whose population is expected to increase by 11% to reach almost 1.5 billion by the same date.

2
Social Changes and Opportunities

Over the last two or three decades, economic and social development has been marked by a number of important changes. These changes have transformed significantly the way we learn, work, combine work with family life, retire, age and organize our various commitments throughout the life-cycle. Thus they have transformed our lives and the way we think, even if most people and workers are perhaps largely unaware of them. As a result, our modern society is more dynamic, more flexible, more unstable and requires new solutions to current and future problems. A proper understanding of the changes is essential as we prepare to work longer and retire later and more flexibly. We shall see that they often constitute opportunities for extension of work-life. This chapter will describe and analyse five distinct areas: the new life-cycle, training and education through life, a new definition of old age, active ageing and the need for a transition between work and retirement.

The new life-cycle

A new activity pattern

Observation of change in our modern societies reveals that the work life-cycle which was traditionally divided into three periods – training, work and retirement – has altered significantly in recent years. We find that today continuous training is often a standard feature of the workplace. Career interruptions due to unemployment or a change in occupation and/or employer (a second or third career) are now commonplace. Women, and increasingly men, who cease working or work less in order to raise young children, will often return to the workforce after a period which might include retraining or the updating of skills. Nowadays many retired people spend time with their families or doing voluntary work, but even so some continue, or would like to continue, doing professional work. It is our life-cycle that is changing, then, and the compartmentalization of work-life into three age-based vertical periods is gradually giving way to a horizontal arrangement which is more in tune with the realities of modern economic, social and family life – a life pattern that is at once more diversified, more flexible, and more dynamic and where responsibilities and benefits are more evenly apportioned between men and women. Figure 2.1 summarizes this new life-cycle which most of us are now experiencing or envisage for the future.

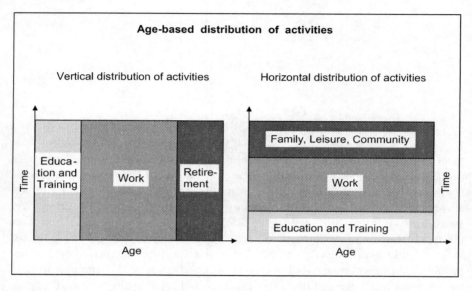

Figure 2.1   Evolution of life-cycle or age-based distribution of activities

Source: Reday-Mulvey and Giarini (1995).

Lifetime allocation of labour and leisure across OECD countries

In the OECD in 2000, men worked on average 55% of their lifetime, spent 26% in childhood and education before entering the labour force, and 18% in retirement. These proportions vary widely, however, from country to country. They are below average for work in continental Europe (France, Germany, Italy) and in Eastern European countries (Hungary, Poland). Countries with above-average lifetime activity rates include the United States, Japan and some European countries (such as Iceland, Portugal, Ireland, Denmark and Switzerland). Women worked proportionally less than men, but the ranking of women's lifetime activity rates across countries is similar to that of men (Figure 2.2).

During the past decades, lifetime allocation of labour and leisure has changed substantially. The proportion of lifetime that men dedicate to work has declined in all OECD countries. Part of the explanation for this decline is quite simply the increase in life expectancy. But in many countries also, this trend has been reinforced by a lowering of the effective average age of retirement (for example, France, Germany). This reduction of the working time proportion for men has been accompanied by an important increase in the proportion spent in retirement (see Figure 2.2).

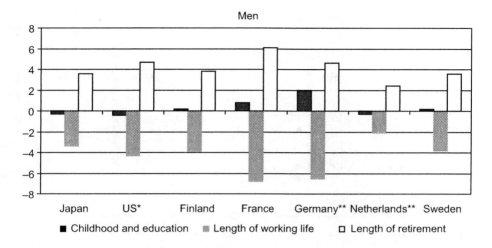

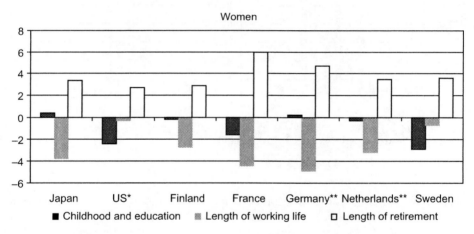

Figure 2.2   Changes in lifetime allocation of childhood/education, labour and retirement, in selected OECD countries over the last three decades (%)

*1965–2000, **1975–2000
Source: OECD (2003a, p. 69).

Workers who have retired over the last 30 years had usually begun what proved a long and arduous working life at an early age. They have been part of the long pattern of post-war economic growth and, while largely benefiting from exceptional material well-being, they have often had little time to devote to activities outside the workplace.

Retirement comes, then, as a well-deserved rest, a kind of golden period with time to enjoy the leisure a good pension makes possible. However, numerous surveys have already revealed that overnight or 'guillotine' retirement has proved a difficult experience for many retirees who have not had time to adjust before entering it.

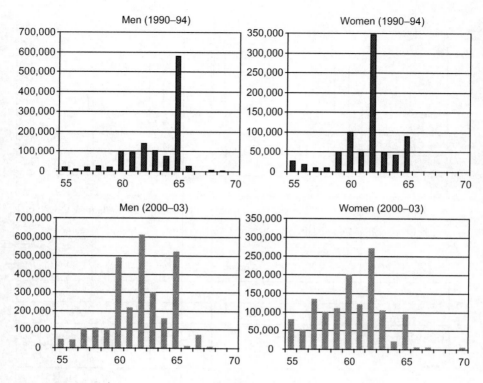

Figure 2.3   Changes in the exit age in Switzerland

Source: *Neue Zürcher Zeitung*, 9 June 2004, p. 71.

Many have switched from a position of social prestige and integration within their company into what has been called 'social oblivion' (Guillemard, 1990). Hence a fair proportion of retirees wish to continue to enjoy a little longer the mental alertness and social integration that the workplace affords.

A key cohort effect

People retiring today, and even more so in the coming years and decades, will, for the most part, have enjoyed much longer periods of education and training. Their working life will often have been interrupted by unemployment or part-time employment, by training and, for a few, by sabbatical leave. On the whole, most of them will have experienced much more flexible work patterns than their parents' generation. Indeed, growing categories of employees nowadays – other than parents of young children or young people in training – are concerned to organize their work in new ways and frequently quite simply to work less. These new categories include young workers who need to work while studying, workers in the mid-life period who wish to combine regular work with meeting other requirements (for example, self-employment, a return to training, community service of one sort or another, caring for elderly parents, and so on) and workers at the end of their career who wish gradually to move from a full-time work-life into healthy retirement. Since youth, this latter category of workers has had much more leisure and a majority has had continuing training in service or outside the firm. Often, these workers have had two or three different careers (Gaullier, 2003).

A significant 'cohort effect' is therefore likely to obtain, which means that people retiring in the next ten or fifteen years are very different from those currently in retirement. Not only have they had greater opportunities to study and to benefit from improved working and living conditions and from the 'leisure society', but they have also in all probability experienced greater risk in employment, marriage and family life. They have often had to adapt to new values and norms, new technologies, and their perception of life and retirement has changed significantly – change, incidentally, is precisely what has characterized their occupational and personal lives. They will be familiar with pension problems and reforms and they will know that they cannot entirely count on the welfare state to provide their pension income. Many of them will already be used to the idea that from now on work and retirement will have to be organized in new ways.

A new conception of work and retirement

When these workers, these baby-boomers, are questioned about what they want in retirement, many – particularly if they are qualified and have pride in the contribution they make – would wish to keep a foot in the occupational door for some years after the legal retirement age. As was so aptly observed some time ago, the relative utility of leisure and retirement to that of work will tend to diminish in the years to come (Kessler, 1990). However, a majority of baby-boomers will wish to alter their work rhythm and will therefore be attracted by part-time work as part of a gradual withdrawal from full-time employment.

In the Netherlands, two surveys of employees conducted in 1995 and 2000 (Delsen, 2002) revealed significant changes in people's perception of the life-cycle. In 1995 half of those surveyed hoped to be able to retire before the age of 60; in 2000 this proportion had decreased to one-fourth. In 2000, if a little less than half of those surveyed hoped to be able to retire before the age of 65 (27% before 60, 38% between 60 and 65), over a third believed that they might have to continue working after 65 (29% until 69 and even 6% after the age of 70).

A recent survey in Switzerland, a country well-known for the high value it attaches to work, shows that the importance of work compared to that of family and leisure/ friends has decreased: 89.4% believe that family is the most important value in their life, as compared to 55.2% who opted for friends/leisure and 45% for work. Regarding work itself, 47.3% would like to reduce their work time, and only less than 30% (29.3%) identify chiefly with work as opposed to 46.9% who identify with culture and leisure (*L'Hebdo*, 29 April 2004, Lausanne). These new perceptions are more pronounced in younger people and women.

What these surveys show in depth is not that work has ceased to be important for most European citizens but that most people wish to work according to a different life-cycle pattern: perhaps the same amount of work overall but distributed differently over the ages in the life-cycle, with a diversity and flexibility that enable people to manage different tasks simultaneously – family, work, leisure, voluntary commitments, and so on.

Training and education through life

General outlook

The globalization of our economies implies that a country's competitiveness largely depends on the quality of its supply-side activities. Investment in human capital becomes a *sine qua non* condition for future competitiveness. Employment adjustments that are too rapid and rely to too great an extent on the external labour market may not prove as satisfactory in the long run as the lower transaction-cost 'employment retention' model. What appears to be increasingly important is the functional flexibility which the new technologies have made necessary. The modern enterprise requires the development of higher level skills and performance of a much broader mix of tasks and functions than did the traditional firm.

By extending training opportunities, making employees more effective in their current firms but also more employable in other firms, and thereby easing the consequences of job loss, the stage can be set for more flexible and hence more productive employment systems. However, what appears to be crucial for the extension of work-life is for enterprises to extend training or retraining opportunities until the end of the career and not to reduce them from the age of 40 or 45 onwards. Greater psychological content has to be given to training if it is to help older workers to remain mobile, motivated and adaptable. This continuing training has now to be adapted to suit the older worker, whose learning and pedagogical needs are known to be different from those of younger cohorts. Training of older workers, then, must be designed to take full advantage of their experience and knowledge in introducing to them new ways of thinking, doing or being.

Moreover, early retirement policies have had negative consequences for firms because of the loss of experienced workers who have acquired enormous know-how and who in general have a lot to contribute to enterprise culture. Many firms in the EU have recognized these facts and, as we shall see later, have been reversing the trend. Older qualified workers also have an important role to play in the training of younger employees, whether it be in formal teaching courses or simply by working in teams. It is also becoming quite common to see qualified engineers, economists and insurance experts pursue a second career as teachers in their field of knowledge and work experience.

In their recent publication on the knowledge society, Orio Giarini and Mircea Malitza have explained the importance of interlocking training and education with work in an employee's lifelong career – what they call the 'double helix' (see Box 2.1).

Current practice

In the OECD, on average, 26% of employed persons participate in employer-sponsored continuous vocational training (CVT) each year. Each participant

Box 2.1 The double helix

The 'knowledge society', as everybody knows, requires an educated workforce, but how to develop such a workforce, when knowledge itself is becoming obsolete at an increasingly rapid rate, and educational systems are still concentrating most of their efforts and resources on children and young people of the traditional school and university age groups? In order to be employable, people now have to be educated and re-educated throughout their lives. And their lives are increasingly long-lasting, in the developed countries, well beyond the traditional age of retirement. Yet formal pension schemes assume – indeed force – qualified and capable workers to stop working, in the formal sense, at the still prime age of 60 or 65, when they might be at their peak of efficiency. At the same time, these pension schemes are strapped financially – the elderly are continuing to live off pension benefits 'beyond their time', and in many countries, there are fewer and fewer 'young' persons available to support them – not to mention the large numbers of young unemployed who are not contributing to any retirement schemes, their own or those of their elders. It would be better if older people could continue working – which most of them want to do anyway – but in that case, they would probably have to gain state-of-the-art knowledge in their respective fields. In fact, all workers need to do that – as is becoming increasingly apparent. And there are those who might want to pursue new educational objectives and different careers.

Taking the idea of the modularization of curricula and inspiration from the Double Helix genetic structure discovered by James Watson and Francis Crick exactly 50 years ago, Orio Giarini and Mircea Malitza, members of the Club of Rome, propose a vast modularization of curricula linked to a massive plotting of human knowledge and of employment possibilities, much as the Human Genome has been plotted. ...

With education, particularly higher education, that is modularized and available to those needing it throughout their lives, Giarini and Malitza postulate an interlocking system of learning and work, whereby workers in many, if not all, fields would alternate between education and work, earning credits for both, for a productive, active life extending at least to the age of 76. The myriad of advances that has occurred in the health science makes a 60-year-plus work life possible. Retirement schemes would have to be modified to allow for part-time work, if desired, in later years.

As the double-helix system matured, the distinction between work and education would blur, as credits for both would become increasingly interchangeable. Accomplishment in both areas would be evaluated and quantified. In addition to the usual degrees and diplomas, persons would earn 'stars' for continued academic accomplishment – with transferable credits from work. Over a lifetime of creative work and education, a typical person would accumulate credits – over a thousand of them for an academically ambitious person by the age of 76 – and a corresponding number of award stars. The aggregate outcome would be a tremendous boost to the development of human resources, the most important 'resource' for the knowledge society.

Jan Sadlak – Director of UNESCO-CEPES, in Giarini and Malitza (2003, pp. 9–10)

receives on average about 68 hours of training per year – that is slightly less than nine working days. This means that each employee receives on average an annual training volume of 18 hours. The country with the highest CVT volume and the highest participation rate is Denmark, where workers receive on average 36 hours per year of employer-sponsored CVT. This translates into about two working weeks per participant per year. However, in all OECD countries, the incidence of training tends to decline with age. In particular, the average training participation rate of workers aged 56–65 is about three-quarters that of workers aged 36–45. The inverse correlation between age and training is more clear-cut when measured in terms of training volume. On average, workers aged 56–65 receive 12 hours of CVT courses per year, against 18 hours for workers aged 36–45 years and 21 hours for workers aged 26–35 years (cf. OECD, 2003b, pp. 240–41).

Trainability of older workers

An important aspect of ageing and productivity is whether older workers have greater difficulty in learning new skills. Even if ageing typically does not reduce a worker's ability to perform familiar job tasks, a declining ability to adapt to changing skill requirements would tend to lower their productive contribution over time. 'Trainability' is not easy to measure, but the International Adult Literacy Survey (IALS) is an important source for evidence about the relationship between age, productivity and trainability. The IALS indicates that literacy skills improve with practice and deteriorate if not used. Therefore, workers employed in a learning environment appear much less susceptible to a decline in trainability. Evidence proves that the productive potential of older people does not appear to be substantially impaired by ageing *per se*. A decline in performance may be due to skill obsolescence or a burn-out phenomenon which may occur at any age and can be remedied through appropriate training practices or adaptation of working conditions.

Training and retraining are therefore important factors in enhancing the employability of older workers. They can be trained for specific vacancies or for the labour market in general. The International Labour Organization (ILO) argues that older workers should be allowed to participate on an equal footing with other trainees and should be given the same opportunities and treatment with respect to training. The conclusions concerning human resources development and training adopted at the June 2000 Session of the International Labour Conference highlighted that high-quality education and training are major instruments for improving overall socioeconomic conditions and for preventing and combating social exclusion and discrimination, particularly in employment.

Education and the retirement age

This position is also supported by the significant link between the level of education and the retirement age. According to the Danish report *Seniors and the Labour Market* published in January 2004, in Denmark, the employment rate among 60–66-year-olds with a university education is 52%, whereas a mere 16% of persons in this age category whose education stopped after primary school are working (Table 2.1). This gap increases with age. With more educated cohorts reaching 50 and 55, prospects for working later in life are therefore improving.

The European area for lifelong learning

But lifelong learning, as a long-term preventative strategy, is broader than just second-chance education for adults who did not receive education, qualifications

Table 2.1 Employment rate by educational level and age in Denmark (%)

	aged 55–59	aged 60–66	aged 67–74
Primary school level	58	16	4
High school level (10–12 years of education)	75	30	5
Short higher education (12–14 years of education)	81	37	13
Medium higher education (15–16 years of education)	86	39	10
Long higher education (17–18 years of education)	91	52	19
Total	**74**	**27**	**6**

Source: Statistics Denmark, Copenhagen 2004 (European Foundation for the Improvement of Living and Working Conditions, Online Newsletter, News update: Denmark).

or training earlier in life. Implicit in the concept of lifelong learning is the rejection of a society structured on the basis of age, and one in which education and training are one-off undertakings experienced only early in life. Instead, it embraces a learning society where everyone is motivated, able and actively encouraged to learn throughout life. Lifelong learning has to do with delivering job-relevant learning, and building the foundation for further learning.

There are three main reasons why lifelong learning is important. It can help to

- adjust workers' skills and competencies to labour market demand
- strengthen older peoples' links to the labour market and help them keep up with technological change
- overcome productivity declines after certain ages.

Lifelong learning is high on the agenda of the European Commission (Walker and Wigfield, 2003, pp. 24–5), which placed it from 1997 at the centre of an integrated approach to future policy action. Indeed, the theme of lifelong learning runs through many of the European Commission's recent initiatives: the *European Employment Strategy* features a horizontal objective on lifelong learning and specific guidelines that focus on employment and labour market-related aspects of lifelong learning; the *European Social Agenda* aims to reduce inequalities and promote social cohesion including through lifelong learning; the *Skills and Mobility Action Plan* aims to ensure that European labour markets are open and accessible to all by 2005; the *eLearning Initiative*, which is part of the eEurope Action Plan, seeks to promote the wide use of information and communication technologies in education and training. Together, these initiatives help to comprise the European area of lifelong learning (European Commission, 2001: Making a European Area of Lifelong Learning a Reality).

The position of the social partners

Governments also are increasingly encouraging social partners to engage in collective bargaining in relation to lifelong learning and training. The Swedish government, for example, has proposed that state investment in the information society should be focused on three priority areas: (i) confidence in information technology (IT);

(ii) competence in IT application, focusing on the provision of basic skills; and (iii) the accessibility of the information society's services. In France, already in 1994, a law introducing a 'time-saving account' for employees was adopted. This account has allowed workers to accumulate time credits over a number of years – using overtime hours or reduced working hours as part of the move towards the 35-hour week – and to decide whether to make use of this 'time capital' for early or gradual retirement, for taking up part-time work, or for training leave. So far, the use of the account for training has been limited. However, the social partners are currently studying how to stimulate the use of working-time accounts for training purposes, and new legislation was passed on this issue in early 2004 (see Chapter 8). In Germany, the government subsidises the training costs of workers aged over 50 and workers with no vocational qualification (or those with vocational qualifications but who have been in semi-skilled or unskilled occupations for more than four years). In May 2004, the Flemish government introduced an enactment which outlines the accreditation of prior learning: competences gained through formal or informal vocational training, but also through experience from previous employment, social or even everyday life can be officially accredited. This should enable people to obtain a certificate of competence for a given occupation without actually holding the relevant diploma. As Professor A. Walker sums it up: 'increasingly, it is being argued that lifelong learning is becoming as important an entitlement for today's employee as the right to a pension became in the past'.

Lifelong learning has also become the new employment security objective on the trade union agenda. In a project backed by the European Commission, Union Network International (UNI)-Europa is working with the European Federation of Direct Marketing Associations to develop common training standards and qualifications for people working in call centres. UNI-Europa has also made its own contribution to the EU's eEurope Action Plan in the area of employability and lifelong learning. Moreover, in some countries, trade unions have been influential in providing information and computer technology (ICT) support to older workers. For example, the Union Learning Fund in the UK was set up by government in 1998 to help trade unions use their influence with employers, employees and others to encourage more people to learn at work. It has benefited over 28,000 people in the workplace. The Graphical, Paper and Media Union (GPMU) in Greater London has run one of the most successful projects. Its aim was to increase the employment prospects of its union members by increasing skills, setting up learning centres, and encouraging online learning. Retired GPMU-members were invited to see if they were interested in getting involved and 2,000 members replied. There have since been at least six information technology courses for retired union members and the oldest person taking part was 87.

A new definition of old age

Behind the issues of employment and retirement after 60, lies the crucial question of exactly when the majority of us enter old age: when are we old? Research has shown that ageing is a long-drawn-out process and one which varies enormously between the sexes and from one region, occupation or individual to the next. Furthermore, the biological, social and physiological factors which applied at the turn of the twentieth century were far different from what they are today. For instance, our great grandparents – or even our grandparents – were lucky to be able to live to the age of 60 or 70. We live longer in much better health today than people did in 1900 or even in 1950.

This is why some people and institutions – the Geneva Association, which talks of 'a counter-ageing society' (see Box 2.2) among them – refuse to speak of population 'ageing' in the traditional sense. On the contrary, we regard the phenomenon of increased life expectancy as *the* major advance of the twentieth century. We feel that it is a mistake to describe 60- or 65-year-olds merely as 'elderly' or 'old', and that publications and statistics that apply these labels are simply out of touch with present-day social realities. Statistics do, however, serve a purpose, since it is at or around these ages that nowadays most workers end their labour force activities and paid work for good. What in fact is happening is that the *age of retirement* is becoming increasingly disassociated from the age at which people become *old*. Indeed, many workers leave their jobs not at the official or legal age for retirement but several years earlier either because they have taken 'early retirement' (voluntarily or otherwise), or because they have been laid off, or again, because they suffer from some form of 'incapacity'. This leads us to a conclusion: *the age at which people leave the workforce is usually neither the age of retirement nor old age.*

When does old age start, then? In a French report (Conseil Économique et Social, 2001), the authors define old age as 'the time when the population starts suffering from real incapacities' and argue that old age starts nowadays much later than in the past, even the recent past:

> Thus defined, the onset of old age can be observed to have been in constant retreat: from around 60 years for men and 65 for women in 1930, it had climbed by the beginning of the 1990s to 71 years for men and 77 for women. In light of this interpretation of things, the proportion of 'old persons' in the population appears to have fallen from 10% in 1980 to around 7% in the 90s. Taking this argument a step further, according to P. Bourdelais's calculation, stabilisation of the proportion of 'older persons' at its 1985 level would mean that the threshold of old age, estimated to be at 75 years in 1985, will have reached 82 years by 2040 – i.e. an annual gain of one and a half months. And if current trends continue, this is more than likely to occur.

This new definition of old age should be not only influencing the process of pension reform and informing any reassessment of employment prospects and policies but also moulding a new design and place for work within the life-cycle.

This new conception is cause for optimism not only as it relates to important macro welfare and work issues but also for each one of us by reason of the broadened, lengthened horizons it promises. Paradoxically, even in this post-modern world of ours, the life-style and life-cycle that await us could prove closer to those of the traditional farmer of times past – remaining active and socially integrated while, as strength diminishes, progressively reducing the number of tasks – but with a life expectancy our rural forebears could only dream of.

Box 2.2   An ageing society? No, a *counter-ageing* society!
Changing attitudes within organizations

The best indication of the success of the Industrial Revolution is the increased, and continually rising, life expectancy that obtains in almost all parts of the world.

This phenomenon is frequently described in traditional terms. It is, for example, said that *society is ageing*. If what is meant is merely that most people today achieve an older age than they expected to 50 years ago, then the statement is acceptable. But in itself, the expression 'ageing society' is both inappropriate and misleading. We must first recognize that there has been an increase in the length of the life-cycle which probably counts as one of the greatest achievements of the twentieth century. Second, it must be observed that what is really becoming *older* is the notion of age itself. We only need to read the European literature of the last century to learn how people felt at 40 years of age. It is also clear that the onset of physical and mental decline has been pushed back far later than was hitherto the case. In other words, at 50, 60 or 70 years of age, we are much younger today than we would have been at those ages in the not so distant past. Therefore *our societies are getting younger,* because we live longer and better. This phenomenon concerns the majority of countries around the world.

Failure to understand the situation in these terms can lead to serious mistakes: on one hand, we tend to marginalize far too early a growing part of the population (those over 60) while, on the other, we quickly run aground in the political debate about how far the younger generation should pay for the older. On both accounts, we find we have entered a dead-end street!

We need to turn the proposition on its head: the *older* are today *younger* and because the value of human beings is linked to their productive activities and endeavours, the key social and political challenge of the coming decades will be to what extent society succeeds in involving people from 18 to 78 years of age in the global venture of creating and sustaining the wealth of nations. There are already clear signs that things are beginning to move in this direction, although the global picture is as yet far from homogeneous.

It is important to welcome as good news the fact that we live in a counter-ageing society, since the change that is occurring in the structure of our planet's population constitutes one of the greatest achievements in human history. Our culture, our mind-sets and the structures of our societies must now adapt to this new and promising situation. For the inevitable significance of this new circumstance is that each of us has a potential for remaining an *active participant in society longer and more effectively* than has ever been the case hitherto. Achievement of that longer and more effective active participation must now become our goal and a key instrument of greater progress and justice for all.

The time has perhaps now come to launch a campaign similar to those promoted in the past for minorities and women. It would focus on those between on average the ages of 60 and 80 years or more, since up to that age at least 90% of people are, or should be, in good mental and physical health. Their capabilities will be enhanced even more by their remaining integrated in society longer. They will thus be able to exercise a *new right*, that of more mature people or seniors to contribute with their experience to our world.

▶

> Increasingly, educational programmes will help to provide those who are 60 and above with new skills and opportunities for embarking on a *new career* based essentially on part-time jobs and/or unremunerated activities.
>
> Any perception of our society as ageing and thereby in decay is unacceptable and constitutes the ugly face of a non-adaptive culture which, economically and socially, is simply unsustainable.
>
> *Orio Giarini – Secretary General of the Geneva Association from 1973 to 2000, Member of the Club of Rome, and Commission Member of the CSIS – Global Ageing Initiative, in Geneva Association, The Four Pillars Newsletter, No. 27 (August 2000, pp. 3–4)*

Active ageing

Reforming our pension systems, working or remaining active later on in life, living longer in good health – all involve changes that make a redesign of the principles and practice of retirement both possible and necessary. This 'new look and approach' is what some people have in mind when they use the expression 'active ageing'. For others, the redesign of retirement is part and parcel of the need to come to terms with the decline of the work-based structures and paid employment that have underpinned our societies. In any event, tomorrow the word 'retirement' will certainly mean something rather different from what it means today.

Ten or so years ago the Americans coined the term 'productive ageing' as a way of describing the trends that were emerging. The term, however, seems to us to be too narrow since it implies that older persons should continue to work in order to be able to go on producing goods and services. We ourselves prefer the term 'active ageing', a concept developed by the World Health Organization, because it highlights the very close links between activity and health. The idea that 'extra years have been added to life, hence we now need to breathe life into those additional years', conveys quite strongly the new thinking behind the concept of 'active ageing'. It suggests how important it is to enhance the quality of life into very old age by maintaining mental and physical well-being throughout the life-cycle.

For the time being, active ageing is both an aspiration and a social achievement. Many seniors are putting the principle into practice, for instance in their commitment to family, in voluntary work, in their association with the 'Universities of the Third Age', or with sporting and other leisure activities.

For 200 years the concept of life has to a very large extent centred around a base of paid employment and, initially at least, social protection also reflected this work-oriented structure. Today there are many whose vision of a future society includes activities other than paid employment, but activities that are essential to the quality of life, and these ideas are gaining acceptance and recognition. There are a number of countries that have replaced their social protection systems – based, as they were, on paid work – by systems based rather on residence and citizenship.

And since the expectation of life in good health continues to rise, our concern is not only to find solutions to the problem of financing our pension systems in

Box 2.3   Active ageing in Europe

Professor Alan Walker has summed up the current developments in Europe relative to active ageing in terms of the following seven key components:

1. Activity of all meaningful pursuits which contribute to the well-being of the individual concerned, his or her family, local community or society at large and is not concerned only with paid employment or production.
2. Active ageing should include all older people, even those who are, to some extent, frail and dependent.
3. It should be a preventative concept, which means involving all age groups in the process of ageing actively across the entire life course.
4. The maintenance of intergenerational solidarity is an important feature of any European approach to active ageing. This means fairness between generations as well as the opportunity to develop activities that span the generations. Active ageing is about *all* of our futures.
5. The concept should embody both rights and obligations. Thus the rights to social protection, lifelong education and training and so on, may be accompanied by obligations to take advantage of education and training opportunities and to remain active in other ways.
6. A European strategy on active ageing should be participative and empowering, giving citizens adequate opportunities to develop their own forms of activity.
7. Active ageing has to respect national and cultural diversity within the European Union, for example, in the ways that older people choose to participate.

The beauty of this strategy is that it is good for everyone: from citizens of all ages as ageing individuals, in terms of maximizing their potential and quality of life, through to society as a whole, by getting the best from human capital, extending community participation and solidarity, avoiding intergenerational conflicts and creating a fairer more inclusive society. Also, unusually, it is a strategy that makes sound economic sense, by responding to the economic challenges of ageing and extending employment, and, at the same time, it improves quality of life. Enhancing quality of life through an active ageing strategy, therefore, can further economic sustainability. There is a good economic case for doing the right thing in moral terms. Furthermore it shifts the focus of policy away from older people as a separate group who have aged, to all of us, who are ageing constantly. It also emphasizes the coincidence of interests between citizens, government and all major institutions, which is rare indeed.

Alan Walker – Professor of Social Policy, Department of Social Studies, University of Sheffield, in Walker (2002)

the future. We must also be thinking seriously about, and developing answers to, the new concept of retirement.

From the standpoint of the individual, any such new approach could include:

- being able to choose when and how to enter retirement
- remaining fit for as long as possible, by daily exercise
- ensuring that learning, cultural and creative pursuits continue for as long as possible

- maintaining involvement with and commitment to one's community and, where appropriate, continuing one's association with one's professional milieu
- keeping abreast of the needs of others and helping to meet such needs.

By offering people a wider range of life choices and by providing a decent income so that they can prepare themselves for an active old age in good health, we can all invest in a future society which will be marked by a sizeable proportion of 'older' persons.

From the sociological standpoint, people today must be made fully aware of the crucial role that older people can play in our societies and of the need to avoid any form of discrimination against them. *Age diversity* within institutions and organizations as well as *solidarity within and between generations* need to be encouraged in every possible way. The new life-cycle must be accompanied by social and economic policies which fully take into account the needs of the older population in our societies. We must look to *a society for all ages*.

As a conclusion, the famous WHO figure (Figure 2.4) illustrates our purpose that active ageing allows each person's resources to be realised more fully and that voluntary action at the individual as well as the collective level can prevent or delay diminishing functionality.

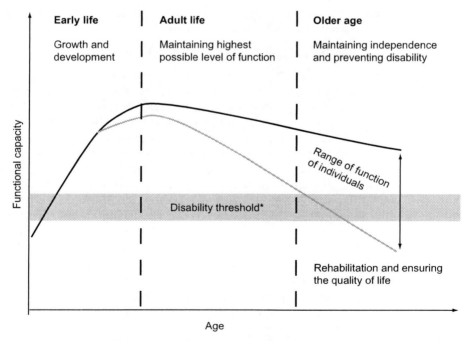

Figure 2.4   Maintaining functional capacity over the life course

Source: WHO (2002, p. 14).

The need for a transition between work and retirement

Historical background

Before the twentieth century, most workers, whether peasants or craftsmen, used to retire gradually, that is, in stages. With diminishing physical strength, they would work less and less. Gradual retirement of this kind was, as it were, a natural and progressive, sometimes imperceptible, downsizing of the workload, and even today many self-employed people – doctors, architects, lawyers, craftsmen and farmers – would, given the choice, not dream of retiring in any other way. However, with the Industrial Revolution, work conditions had to be regulated and progressively the idea of retiring people when they grow old and less useful became established. Retirement came to be fixed at a certain age; earlier, obviously, for miners and others doing physically demanding jobs than for clerks. Almost everywhere, however, retirement was soon viewed as 'overnight' and irrevocable – *la retraite couperet* or 'guillotine retirement', as the French were later to call it. Most people did not live for many years after retirement; a few years of rest, hopefully in good health, before death was all that could be expected. More recently, however, while the age of retirement has been lowered, life expectancy has been increasing rapidly, which means that, especially since the Second World War, retirement has ceased to be a residue and has progressively become a period of life in its own right, a new stage and fresh departure that can be planned and prepared for. And so, little by little, the idea of a transition between work and retirement has resurfaced, a transition suited to the needs of both the individual and the firm.

Negative effects of 'guillotine retirement'

Indeed, after working for 35 or 40 years, to go from full-time employment one day to full retirement/leisure the day after is a brutal change. Such sudden alteration in time allocation and life-style has well-known negative consequences on the worker, on his or her family and environment and on the firm for which the individual has often worked for long years. Medical studies (for example, He et al., 2003) have shown that workers retiring at once had very negative feelings of having lost their sense of purpose in life. They felt depressed, often developed illnesses and had great difficulties in falling back on their feet. People need transitions in life – from training to work, from work to family life, from work into retirement, and others. They have to get ready for stopping work and, because generally in good form, to prepare to rebalance their life and develop other interests and activities which will allow a new social integration. Having time to get ready for a new stage of one's life is a condition of a successful change of status. Most workers share their life with a spouse who also needs to reorganize his or her life within the couple once the other member of the couple stops working. Courses of preparation for retirement have had positive effects in the past when most workers were men and worked full time. Today, these courses have to adapt to new life-cycles and norms we described in order to keep helping participants to prepare for active ageing.

Companies have also been affected by the abrupt departure of skilled workers. Losing employees who had worked for them for long periods of time has not been easy. They have often lost the experience and savoir-faire of these employees but also, sometimes as important, their corporate culture. In some cases they had to call some highly skilled employees back into the workshops or factories so they could transmit their know-how to younger staff. Many industrial firms, such as Aérospatiale in France, went through that painful experience for companies and workers.

The need for transitions

The need for transitions affects not only the work sphere but also personal/family matters and of course income. Figure 2.5 describes well the difficult transitions that most persons have to go through in their 50s and 60s.

Personal transitions	Employment transitions	Income transitions	Family transitions	Care transitions	Leisure transitions
↓	↓	↓	↓	↓	↓
Midlife change	Career management; part-time work; self-employment; retirement	Pensions; benefits; salary/wage	Household change; children leaving home; divorce; living alone	Expanding/ changing care tasks	Expanding/ changing leisure activities

Figure 2.5 Transitions after 50

Source: Phillipson (2002, p. 10).

European surveys (Eurobarometer 2001) confirm that workers definitely need a transition between work and retirement. Employees of 15 EU countries were asked whether 'older workers should be allowed to retire gradually from work (for example, to combine a partial pension with reduced work)': almost three out of four persons agreed, 46% slightly and 28% strongly, while only 17% disagreed. Broken down by countries, the support was strongest in Denmark (69% strongly, 95% altogether), Sweden (61% and 88%, respectively), and the Netherlands (48% and 86%, respectively), as can be seen in Figure 2.6.

A decade of retirement

The need for a transition was very well expressed already in 1990 by the British concept of a 'decade of retirement' (Schuller and Walker, 1990), that is, the idea that when people reach 60 they should benefit from a number of years of transition between full-time work and complete retirement. Of course people nowadays remain active beyond 70. The proposal for a decade of retirement was intended as a transitional one, by focusing attention on the need for greater flexibility with the possibility, at some future date, of abandoning the upper age limit. It comprised a number of items, including:

1. The abolition of mandatory retirement before the age of 70 for both sexes. Certain occupations would be exempt from this rule, for example certain ranks

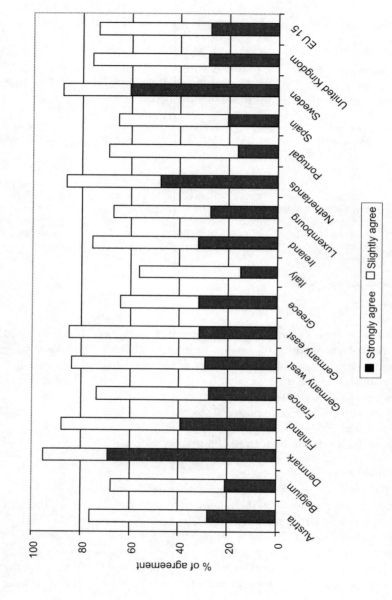

Figure 2.6 Older workers should be allowed to retire gradually from work

Source: Kohl (2002).

in the army and emergency services, but for the vast majority the retirement ceiling would be raised to 70.
2. The introduction of flexible retirement between the ages of 60 and 70 for both men and women.

Preparing for active retirement

Remaining active in the world outside the workplace is vital if there is to be a balanced and satisfactory existence in the new phase of life. This is the phase which precedes 'old age' and which is entered into at a time and in circumstances which obviously vary from one individual to another. Whilst a large number of those who retire still wish to pursue their hobbies or leisure-time activities, thus distancing themselves from their old place of work, an increasing number of them want to take up forms of voluntary work in the community or family and, in so doing, preserve their capabilities and remain socially very much a part of society. A recent study in the United States shows that 40% of those in retirement are active as voluntary workers. The personal benefit of remaining active during retirement has another dimension. In many countries, activity during retirement has become an important benefit for the community, the shortfall in social welfare budgets during the 1990s being offset by the help and commitment of a growing army of volunteer workers.

Everyone can find one or more enjoyable activities to undertake, and by doing so not only attain personal enrichment, but also help others and acquire new skills and knowledge. Voluntary workers, as is the case of those who are still active members of the labour force, are benefiting increasingly from continuing training, and particularly in the use of information technology.

Associations have been established to provide retired persons with information to help them not only to realize their potential, but also to find interests which reflect their backgrounds, qualifications, preferences and the needs of the communities in which they live.

In the United Kingdom, some firms offer those of their workers who are approaching retirement age the opportunity to undertake particular types of work such as transitional secondment or 'loan' to charitable organizations. Their task is to make their work skills available to the organization concerned and this may be for several hours a week, several days a month, or – in some cases – on a part-time basis for as long as one or even two years. The arrangements made by these firms are part of what they call their 'citizenship policies'; but they also give the workers a transition between work and active retirement, allow them to become acquainted with the work undertaken by charities and to rethink their post-working-life commitments. These schemes, such as those established by Barclays Bank, Marks & Spencer and by a large number of smaller firms, have proved to be both realistic and effective. Most of the time, they have constituted excellent transitions. Other companies, for instance British Telecom, Ford and SBC Warburg Dillon Read, have sponsored mentoring projects (GINA and the Geneva Association, 2002).

Not only is there a need for a transition, there is also the need for a choice. This desire of choosing one's working time and the expressed need of workers for transitions in their work-cycle has of course received strong support. Already 25 years ago, Jacques Delors, previously President of the European Commission and French Minister of the Economy and Finance, and his co-generation of humanist social thinkers, launched 'the revolution of chosen time'.

3
Economic Constraints and Welfare Reforms

New demographic trends will significantly affect economic growth, government expenditure and pension systems (both pay-as-you-go and funded). Over the last 15 years, numerous models, forecasts and reports prepared by international organizations, in particular by the OECD and the European Commission, have attempted to estimate the economic consequences of population 'ageing'.

According to OECD forecasts, 'ageing' populations could lower per capita GDP growth in Europe by around 0.4% per year over the period 2000–50. However, this is assuming that, for pensions as well as for labour markets, no stricter reforms than those passed in the 1990s are adopted and implemented. We believe with others (Mantel, 2001) that if Europe continues with its recent pension, social welfare and labour market reforms, the effects of population ageing could be largely offset.

This chapter will mention only briefly the macro effects of demographic change and concentrate rather on the future of pension systems, the early retirement trend and the main pension and social welfare reforms that have resulted.

General outlook

The main recognized macroeconomic effects of ageing populations are:

1. shrinking and ageing of the labour force
2. possible changes in productivity
3. increased public pension expenditure
4. possible changes in private savings behaviour.

The most immediate impact of demographic change is the effect it has on the size and age structure of the labour force. According to the findings of both OECD and EC models that support Jan Mantel's analysis, 'two-thirds of the potential negative impact on the economy originates from a sharply declining workforce relative to the non-working population' (Mantel, 2001). First, a slowdown in the growth, or even a decline, of the labour force can result in a slowdown in the growth of output, provided that demographic trends, labour force participation and unemployment stay unchanged. Furthermore, a rise in the dependency ratio will depress living standards since, unless productivity rises, the output of that labour force will have to be shared by a larger population.

The second effect of population ageing is on public finances through increases in pension and health care expenditure. This could be the other third of the potential negative impact of ageing populations on the economy. The pension budget is typically financed from a mixture of taxes and contributions. Both the latter will have to rise in all EU countries unless new legislation is brought in. The pension contribution rate for German workers, for example, was 19.5% of gross income in 2003. Were benefits to remain as generous as hitherto, it was projected at the end of the 1980s that that rate would exceed 40% of gross income by 2035 at the peak of population ageing. Moreover, since 1993, taxes used to subsidize the public pension system have increased dramatically, so that the overall financial burden per worker is already close to 30% of gross income. Taxes and social insurance contributions add up to more than 50% of total labour costs and make (west) German labour more expensive than that of any other EU country (Börsch-Supan, 2003).

Many economists regard high total labour costs as the main reason for the low demand for labour, and the resulting high unemployment and low economic growth. Reducing the pension burden is therefore not only important for the long-term stability and sustainability of the pension system itself, but also for economic performance in general. Both these factors need to be watched carefully since it is to economic growth as well that we will be looking for the future financing of pensions.

The third effect is on the savings ratio. If savings behaviour were to conform to the traditional life-cycle hypothesis, so-called ageing populations would lead to a substantial drop in the savings rate. According to some experts, however, the effect on the savings ratio would be limited.

When the benefits from public pensions are reduced, employees will have to pay more if the level of retirement income is to be maintained. According to Börsch-Supan (2003), in Germany, for example, for the younger generation born after about 1980, 4% could be sufficient to maintain retirement income at today's level or even improve it, but a saving rate of 8% would be required for the early baby-boomers born in the 1950s and early 1960s.

The fourth impact affects growth in productivity. Due to the conflicting empirical evidence, there has been much debate about the effect of population ageing on productivity growth. The OECD report concluded that productivity would decline by only a small percentage – 0.1% per year – over the next couple of decades (see Chapter 5). New technologies could in principle offset this effect, but we must remember that productivity increases in service economies are different from those in manufacturing in both volume and kind.

The OECD and the European Commission have both worked on reform scenarios and on the possible effects of labour market and budgetary reforms, and of more rapid productivity growth and increased savings. Some experts have pointed out that these scenarios are too conservative in the sense that unemployment and labour force participation could fundamentally change. As Mantel concluded:

> Ageing will make labour more scarce and we believe that this will lead to lower unemployment and, through the mechanism of higher wages, should also lead to higher participation rates in general. More specifically, it will lead to higher participation rates for women and for older people, attracted by good wages and stimulated by slightly lower pensions. An important message is that labour markets need to be as flexible as possible. (Mantel, 2001)

Forecasts of pension expenditure

In most countries the funding of pensions is currently from resources drawn from three pillars: (i) the first is the compulsory state pension, based on the pay-as-you-go principle; (ii) the second pillar is the supplementary occupational pension normally based on funding; and (iii) the third is made up of individual savings (personal pensions and investments as well as life insurance products). First pillar statutory schemes, by and large, are equal to the challenge of providing pensions for the great majority of workers, even atypical (part-time, temporary, self-employed workers) and mobile workers.

Second pillar occupational pensions have developed in a number of countries such as the Netherlands, Nordic countries, Switzerland and the UK. They often cover atypical workers less well.

Third pillar private pensions have been encouraged by fiscal incentives and have developed more in countries less well covered by occupational pensions or among high-income households.

First pillar public pensions

It is well known that social budgets count for around 30% of the GDP of continental European countries such as Germany, France and Italy and that broadly speaking expenditure on public pensions in Europe is around or above 10% of GDP. Austria and Italy are frontrunners with around 14% of GDP and in Germany, France and Spain, the current share is already 12%. Based on policies in place or legislated for at the end of 2000, projections by the Economic Policy Committee show that public spending on pensions is likely to rise, between 2000 and 2050, by between three and five percentage points of GDP in most EU member states (Figure 3.1). As a result the EU average would rise from 10.4% in 2000 to 13.3% by 2050, with wide variations from around 5% to over 20% (European Commission, 2003a).

Member states realise that, given the high financial burden of rapidly deteriorating dependency ratios, the generosity of public pension systems – in itself a great social achievement – will be threatened and fairness between generations at risk.

The main alternative options for stabilizing the balance between revenue and expenditure on public pension schemes have been:

Figure 3.1 Expenditures on pensions in the EU as a percentage of GDP, 2000 and 2040

Source: Börsch-Supan (2003).

44

- maintaining benefit levels by increasing contribution rates and/or taxes → places the burden of financial adjustment on the active labour force – something most countries are trying to avoid
- reducing benefit levels in order to maintain (or even cut) contributions → puts the burden on current and/or future pensioners; in some countries current benefit levels are high enough that the political cost of less generous pensions would be tolerable
- raising the statutory age of retirement → distributes costs and benefits more equally between generations; it is important, however, that whenever possible the effective age of exit from the labour market should be no sooner than 65 or later
- cutting expenditure in other policy areas and thus enabling governments to shift more funds to financing pensions
- increasing the labour force participation of the working-age population, especially that of older workers and of women; later chapters will deal with work beyond 60
- increasing the immigration of foreign workers in order to make up for the shrinking working-age population → this proposal did not win the approval of the majority of the EU population (Eurobarometer). If the gap between births and deaths were to be filled entirely with immigrants, their number would become intolerably large for such societies; however, in some countries a relative increase in the number of immigrants is still both possible and desirable.

Second pillar occupational pensions

In most member states, occupational pensions have developed considerably over the last two decades and this evolution should continue in the next ones. In several countries, their development is encouraged by tax incentives or rules that make membership mandatory. They play and will play an increasing role in ensuring adequate income protection in old age. The situation of member states is very varied. In some countries – Denmark, Ireland, the Netherlands – statutory provision consists mainly of flat rate pension benefits which are low and occupational pensions cover the great majority of workers and provide their main income during old age. In Sweden and Finland occupational pensions constitute also the main pension income. In other countries, such as Germany, Austria and Italy, where contributions to public pensions and their benefits are high, second pillar pensions are also developing, although less fast, since benefits from the first pillar will in the future not be quite as generous as in the past. France, on its part, has two mandatory pillars, but the second one is also financed on a pay-as-you-go basis.

An important way of preserving the adequacy of pensions, either first pillar or second pillar benefits, is to allow and encourage people to contribute longer to both systems, since replacement income will be needed for a longer period due to increased life expectancy. One interesting development has been the introduction of a life expectancy adjusting factor in some national schemes. In the reformed Swedish and Italian systems and in Finland (from 2009), rising life expectancy will lower the replacement rate unless people postpone their retirement. These schemes offer actuarial pension increments for those who contribute for a greater number of years (European Commission, 2003a). Such a fair system is to develop more in Europe, with certain adjustments made for categories of worker performing risky or difficult tasks.

Possible effects of extending working life

Given recent reforms in pension systems and other benefit schemes, it is instructive to update the assessment of their possible effects on the decisions of older workers to retire. Increasing the effective retirement age would alleviate the burden of future pensions. Assuming that those who retire later are in employment, delayed retirement raises the level of output, thereby increasing the resources available for consumption. This is the case even if older people, on average, have a slightly lower productivity than the young. People would also pay more taxes, including social security contributions, on income from work, thereby improving public finances. Some experts (cf. Kolikoff et al., 2001) argue, however, that with a shorter retirement period, people will save less as they need less wealth and lower savings will reduce the capital–labour ratio, productivity and real wages. Thus delaying retirement would increase the wage base on which social security contributions are assessed because of higher employment, but would reduce it because of the decline in the real wage rate. The net long-run impact of delayed retirement on the rise in payroll tax payments could therefore be not as high as believed at first sight.

As people draw their pensions later, they benefit from them over a shorter period of time. This could reduce pension expenditure, although this effect depends on the degree to which pension levels are linked to contributions. Currently, in the OECD, public old-age pension spending represents around 7.5% of GDP. Analysis indicates that if labour participation of older workers would increase by ten percentage points between 2000 and 2050, relative to the base-case scenario, total old-age pensions as a percentage of GDP could be reduced on average by 0.6% (Dang et al., 2001).

However, retiring later may also involve costs, as older workers may have to be retrained and jobs and workplaces may have to be adjusted to their needs and abilities. It is therefore important to set an appropriate framework for labour market and wage-setting policies.

The additional difficulty of 20 years of early retirement

In the late 1970s and 1980s, in the wake of rising unemployment (including youth unemployment) and restructuring of traditional industries it became common practice for enterprises to use early retirement schemes as a way of making labour force adjustments. Though life expectancy – and more particularly health expectancy – have continued to rise, and young people have been entering the labour market later, occupational life has shortened considerably.

Early retirement arrangements were thus often arrived at by consensus between, on the one hand, employers, who were faced with overmanning problems during the period of structural readjustment in the 1970s and 1980s, and, on the other, the trade unions, who had long been fighting for an earlier exit from the labour force. In some countries, such as France and Germany, these early exits were largely financed by the state in the hope that the vacancies left by departing older workers would be filled by the unemployed, and especially the young unemployed. Early retirement arrangements were thus part and parcel of employment policies in the 1970s and 1980s and, to a limited extent, in the 1990s also.

Box 3.1   Early exit from work in Germany

Since the average length of pension receipt was about 15 years in 1970, the increase in life expectancy represents an expansion of pension benefits by almost 50%. In fact, retirement age decreased since 1970, leading to dramatically low labour force participation among elderly workers. In particular, in Belgium, France, the Netherlands, Germany and Italy, very few people aged 60–64 are still in the labour force [see Figure 3.2]. This is quite different from the situation in the 1960s, in spite, at that time, of lower life expectancy and a higher prevalence of illness.

This decline is not a 'natural trend' tied to secular income growth. It did not occur, for example, in Japan and Sweden. Rather, there is convincing evidence that it has been largely 'engineered' by the incentive effects inherent in some public pension systems, in particular by an incomplete adjustment of benefits to retirement age. Germany is a striking example. The German public pension system with its 'flexible retirement' introduced in 1972 tilted retirement decisions heavily towards the earliest retirement age applicable because the annual benefit was essentially independent of that retirement age. Hence, retiring earlier gave a worker basically the same pension for a longer time. At the time, at the prevailing generous replacement rates, this was a pretty good deal.

The retirement behaviour of entrants into the German public retirement insurance system reflects these incentive effects quite clearly. Immediately after the introduction of 'flexible retirement' in 1972, the average retirement age declined dramatically by more than three years. We interpret this as a clear sign of a policy reaction. The most popular retirement age switched by five years from age 65 to age 60.

The 1992 reform, in force after 1997, has diminished this incentive effect, but pension benefits are still not actuarially neutral at conventional interest rates.

Professor Axel H. Börsch-Supan – Director of the Mannheim Research Institute for the Economics of Ageing, Mannheim, Germany, in Börsch-Supan (2003)

Enterprises in many countries, particularly in the Anglo-Saxon world, began to lay off workers in their 50s because of the need for economic restructuring. This sometimes affected very large numbers of workers who, in a number of instances, enjoyed little, if any, social protection. Where possible these workers sought employment elsewhere in what became known in the United States as *bridge jobs* – jobs which spanned the gap between traditional career employment and the official age of retirement. Normally they were lower-paid jobs, with reduced social coverage.

A number of countries, such as Sweden, Norway and Switzerland, had the good fortune to be able to maintain high rates of employment for older workers with the result that early retirement did not become an important issue in those countries until well into the 1990s. But when it did occur, Sweden, for example, was able to establish schemes to encourage older workers to move into other jobs,

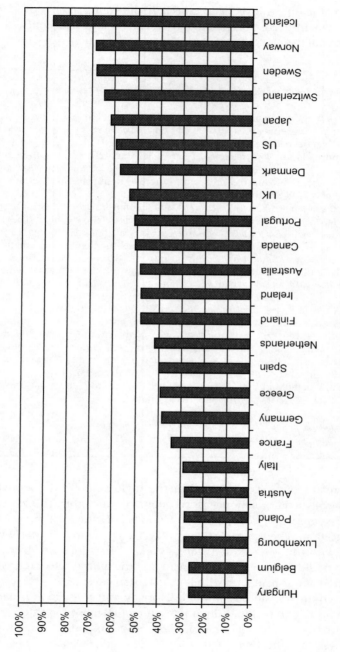

Figure 3.2 Employment rates of the population aged 55–64 in selected OECD countries, 2002

Source: OECD (2003b, pp. 304–7).

and particularly promoted part-time work arrangements. Other countries, such as Switzerland, had long enjoyed more favourable economic conditions and, more importantly, higher employment rates than their neighbours.

Towards the mid-1990s, European government authorities and also a number of enterprises began to take a closer look at the actual consequences of early retirement. These consequences were found to be serious, ranging from the exorbitant cost of early retirement arrangements, through to the loss of accumulated expertise and the disappearance of enterprise culture and solidarity with the departure of substantial numbers of valued workers. The practice proved, moreover, only modestly successful in recruiting unemployed persons to fill gaps in the enterprise workforce. Some firms were even forced to re-engage qualified ex-workers, often as consultants, in order to survive. More recently, the various economic players have begun to realise that with an ageing active population, priority must be given to the adaptation of work conditions to suit all personnel over a certain age, commonly 45 years.

At present, however, there are clearly conflicting views in many countries about early retirement arrangements. On the one hand, there are those who advocate raising the official age of retirement – even where the age is set at 65 years for both men and women – and, on the other hand, many companies still allow arrangements which both permit and encourage early retirement. Many experts point to a contradiction between the social policies of states (pension reform) and the employment policies of enterprises (early exits). Today, with the exception of one or two countries such as Switzerland which until recently have not made much use of early retirement arrangements, the trend is towards reducing early retirement and establishing new policies for extending occupational life at least up to official retirement age.

Recent pension reforms

For two main reasons – first, the need to ensure sustainable public finances in the EU, in particular the euro-zone, and second, the need to raise employment rates,

---

Box 3.2   Younger workers are not substitutes for older workers

In this connection, a number of points need to be made:

- Early retirement schemes have often been short-term answers to economic downturns and enterprise restructuring.
- There has been no evidence that older workers cannot fully participate in the employment growth of expanding sectors.
- There is no empirical evidence that younger and older workers can be substituted for each other. The fact that exits of older workers (55–64) and inflows of younger workers (15–24) do not occur in the same sectors suggests that this is not the case. In addition, experience in several member states demonstrates that growth in the employment rate of older workers goes hand-in-hand with growth in that of younger workers.

European Commission (2004, pp. 8, 22)

especially of older workers – over the last ten years significant reforms have been adopted by all member states. Some of the more significant reforms in several EU countries are described in Chapter 7. Here we shall merely indicate the adoption dates of the main reform initiatives: Austria (2003), Belgium (2002), Denmark (1999), Finland (2003), France (1993, 2003), Germany (1996, 2001), Ireland (2002), Italy (1995, 2004), Netherlands (1995, 1999), Portugal (2002), Spain (2002), Sweden (1994, 2001), United Kingdom (1988, 1999, 2002).

New member states, for example Hungary in 1998 and Poland in 1999, also adopted important reforms.

Regarding the budgetary impact of pension reforms (the level and the change in pension spending as a share of GDP), the most important measures are indicated below.

In the *conditions for public pensions*:

- a rise in the retirement age (or an increase in the number of contribution years)
- stricter linkage of the level of contributions and level of benefits
- greater flexibility in the age of retirement, and promotion of gradual retirement
- promotion of a lengthening of the contribution period and freedom to combine a pension with income from work
- a curtailing of early retirement (see below)
- a relative reduction in the benefit level, by indexing benefits to prices rather than to wages, and by taking as a reference for calculating the level of pensions a greater number of contribution years and
- complementary changes in the way retirement is funded.

These reforms – which have begun to make pensions less generous and to encourage longer working lives – have been drastic in some countries, such as Italy and Sweden and some Central/Eastern European countries, and have followed a more step-by-step approach in others. While national pension systems have been very diverse, it would appear that recent reforms have tended to be very similar, and all countries have experienced enormous political difficulties in getting the reforms passed.

Eventually, in relative terms, these reforms will diminish the size and importance of first pillar (public) pensions, which explains why governments have been encouraging the development of second and third pillar pension arrangements.

However, what these reforms mainly imply is that, as a general rule, people will need to contribute more years – in most cases 40 years at least – in order to get full benefits. Nowadays, because of longer education, most young people in Europe enter the labour market later, typically between the ages of 20 and 25, and often have to face periods of unemployment. As a consequence, the new pension rules will mean that they will need to work to a later age than today. Working beyond

60 until 65 and over will become not only a possibility and an option for some, but an obligation and a reality for most European workers.

In the development of *occupational pensions and private pensions* (second and third pillars): most countries have encouraged them by fiscal incentives. Second pillar or occupational pensions have been made compulsory in several cases (Switzerland, the Netherlands, Nordic countries, and so on) and will eventually cover much larger working populations. In most cases the methods for calculating benefits also encourage a longer working life and allow for more flexibility. Longer lives will also affect benefits from funded pensions since they have to be paid over more years.

Table 3.1 summarizes these important reforms and provides examples from the various countries adopting them.

Table 3.1 Examples of recent pension reforms

Higher statutory retirement age	• *Adapt female retirement age to male retirement age:* Austria, Belgium, Greece, Italy (from 2008), Portugal, UK, Switzerland (from 2009)
	• *Increase retirement age from 60 for men and 55 for women in new member states:* Czech Republic, Estonia, Hungary, Latvia, Lithuania, Malta, Poland, Slovenia For example, in *Hungary*, retirement age increased for men from 60 to 62 in 2002 and will increase for women from 55 to 62 by 2009 In the *Czech Republic*, the retirement age will reach 63 years for men and 59–63 years for women by 2013
	• *Increase retirement age for all in some EU member states:* Sweden (from 65 to 66), Germany (from 65 to 67, under consideration)
Longer contribution period	• *Increase the number of contribution years:* Austria, Finland, France, Italy, Portugal, Sweden, Slovenia For example, *France*: in 1993, the number of years for private sector employees increased to 40 years; in 2003, progressive increase to 40 years for civil servants; from 2008, increase to 41 years for both sectors
Flexibility of retirement age (that is, free choice of retirement age)	• All EU member states have added some flexibility, but some more than others: Austria, Belgium, Denmark (from 60 to 67), Finland (from 62 to 68), Italy (from 57 to 65), Netherlands (from 60 to 70), Sweden (from 61 to 70), Norway, Switzerland, Hungary For example, in *Finland*, from 1 January 2005, the retirement age will be made flexible between 62 and 68 years In *Switzerland*, payment of pension benefits can be postponed for five years after the official retirement age, that is, until the age of 70. This postponement is only possible for workers who remain with the same employer
Closer links between contributions and benefits	• *Increase of the period used to calculate pensions:* Austria, Finland, France, Netherlands, Portugal, Sweden, Hungary

Table 3.1   continued

	For example, in *Austria*, the contributory period will rise from the best 15 years to the best 40 years till 2028, with 12 months being added each year from 2004 onwards. *France*: from the best 10 to the best 25 years
	• *Bonus for years worked after retirement age:* Finland (from 2005), France, Greece, Italy, Netherlands, Portugal, Spain, Sweden, Norway, Switzerland, Hungary, Slovenia
	For example, in *Portugal*, there is an annual 10% pension bonus for workers between 65 and 70 who have paid contributions for 40 years and opt to remain in the workforce
	In *Spain*, 2001–02, retirement pensions for workers aged 65+ are increased by 2% for each year of contributions if the worker has contributed for 35 years or more
Pension indexation to prices and not to wages	• Most member states: Finland, France, Germany, Portugal, UK (already in 1989), Switzerland
	Some new member states: Czech Republic, Hungary ('Swiss model', that is, 50% to prices and 50% to net wages), Poland
Cumulation of earnings with pensions (after retirement)	• All member states: Austria, France, Italy, Netherlands, Portugal, Spain, Switzerland, UK
	For example, in *Italy*, old-age pensions for new and current retirees are no longer to be reduced if the person is receiving employment income
Occupational pension regulations	• *Employees should not pay occupational pension contributions according to their age:*
	For example, in the *UK*, changing tax rules allows people to continue work for their sponsoring employer whilst at the same time drawing their occupational pension
	In *Finland*, by 2007, the link between age and pension contributions will be abolished, that is, pension contributions will be the same for all employees, regardless of employee's age and size of firm

Source: Author's compilation from: Buck and Dworschak (2003); European Employment Observatory Newsletter No. 12–14, <www.eu-employment-observatory.net/en/newsletter>; Geneva Association, *Four Pillars Newsletter* No. 26–35, <www.genevaassociation.org/newsletters_menu.htm>; Maltby et al. (2004); OECD (2003b, pp. 164–5; 2004, pp. 7–20); Taylor (2002).

Recent reforms reducing the early exit from work

Since the mid-1990s the consensus and thinking on early retirement has altered radically – this is certainly the case in Finland, Denmark, the Netherlands and even in Germany, Austria, France and Italy. Governments became increasingly concerned about population ageing trends and enacted reforms deferring the official retirement age whilst, at the same time, discouraging public support for early retirement. In countries such as France and Germany the authorities established arrangements for *partial early retirement* – a form of gradual retirement – and provided firms with subsidies so that such continuing part-time work could be undertaken in lieu of full early retirement.

However, in many countries companies and workers facing restrictive measures on early retirement have turned towards other early exit roads, specifically disability and unemployment insurance. Thus within European welfare systems benefits continued to increase and public deficits to widen. It was not only early retirement that needed reforming but also disability and unemployment insurance.

Table 3.2 summarizes key measures taken in European countries to limit early exit from the labour force of workers before pension age.

Table 3.2 Reduction of early exit from work

Limited access to early retirement	• *Increasing the age of early exit:* Most EU member states, for example, Austria, Belgium, Denmark, Finland, France, Germany, Netherlands, Spain, Sweden, UK, Hungary, Latvia, Lithuania, Poland, Slovakia In *Austria*, for example, the eligibility age for early retirement was increased from 61.5 years for men and 56.5 years for women by 4 months in 2004, 6 months in 2005 and 8 months in 2006, 2007, 2008 and 2009. This means a gradual scrapping of the early retirement pension • *Early withdrawal of pension only with acceptance of penalty points, that is, less pension:* Germany, Netherlands, Spain, Hungary, Slovenia • *Penalizing firms by setting a price for early retirees:* Austria, France, Netherlands For example, in *France*, in 2003, pre-retirement schemes were limited to physically demanding jobs and restructuring firms In the *Netherlands*, the employer has to finance a proportion of the unemployment benefit for the older dismissed employees aged 57.5+
Restrictions on laying off older workers	• For example, in *Belgium*, since 2002, companies are required to fund job placement and search services for any workers laid off over 55
Limited access to disability benefit	• *Reducing access to early pension for occupational incapacity:* Denmark, Finland, Germany, Netherlands, Sweden, Norway, Switzerland For example, in *Denmark*, the reduction of state reimbursement subsidies for disability pension expenditure (the state now refunds only 35% of the local authorities' expenditure on newly granted disability pensions) has spurred the local authorities to reconsider granting disability pensions. In 1998–99, the number of disability pensions granted fell by 32% • *Obligation for disabled to look for new jobs, often part-time or 'soft' jobs:* Denmark, Finland, Netherlands, Sweden, Cyprus, Hungary, Latvia, Slovenia For example, in *Denmark*, the new policies use (i) 'flexi' jobs and (ii) 'soft' jobs to maintain people of reduced working capacity in employment by means of wage subsidies to public and private firms

Table 3.2   continued

Limited access to unemployment benefits	• *Reduction of the number of years covered by unemployment insurance:* Austria, Finland, Germany, UK, Switzerland, Slovenia For example, in *Germany*, by 2006, the period for drawing unemployment benefits will be reduced from 32 to 12 months • *Obligation to look for a job:* Austria, Belgium, France, Netherlands, UK, Switzerland, Slovenia For example, in the *Netherlands*, unemployed people reaching the age of 57.5 years after May 1999 are again to be obliged to register as jobseekers at the public employment office

Source: As Table 3.1.

Scenarios on the key importance of increasing employment participation

As a way of concluding this chapter on economic constraints and welfare reforms, it is interesting to follow the scenarios in Box 3.3, which explain in a simple way how crucially important the size of the labour force is, as well as the participation rate of older workers and other categories of worker for the coming decades. It shows that demographic pressures on social security systems could be manageable if accompanied by some economic growth and higher rates of labour market participation. This is not unrealistic when compared to past economic growth rates as well as the achievement of some European countries in relation to their labour market participation rates. Immigration could help to increase the size of the workforce, but should be considered only as one aspect of the solution.

Box 3.3   Increasing employment participation and sustaining pension schemes: optimistic scenarios

It can be shown that a dynamic economy – in particular a moderate economic growth (about 2% per annum, less than the average rate in industrial countries over the last 20 years) – would be sufficient to absorb the additional expenditure occasioned by a large ageing population. But such growth will only be achieved if there is both a continued rise in productivity and an increase in the size of the labour force. There is some justification for the view that there may well be a shortage of labour in a few years' time. What needs to be done now, without delay, is to find remedies for this situation. The size of the labour force can of course be increased, first, through greater participation in employment by women, and second, by encouraging 'older' workers, in particular prior to but also after the official age for retirement, to remain occupationally active. At the same time it could be made easier for persons with medium or minor disabilities to return to work. Finally, it may be possible, at least to a certain extent, to look to immigration as part of the solution. These steps should certainly help to reduce the economic dependency rates, that is, the ratio of retired persons to those in gainful employment. Also it should help to avoid the erosion of benefits or unmanageable increases in the cost of public pensions.

Two possible scenarios are set out below, using Switzerland, France and Germany as examples.

Scenario 1: Stable labour market
In this scenario, the labour market would remain stable – that is, the employment rate for the active population stays the same at 81% for Switzerland, 67% for France and 70% for Germany. Population ageing would indeed in this event lead to a significant rise in contribution rates because the ratio of retired persons to wage-earners increases:

- in Switzerland: from 10% (1995) to 15% (2020) and 24% in 2050
- in Germany, with its more generous pension arrangements: from 19% (1995) to 27% (2020) and 40% in 2050
- in France, where the retirement age is 60 years: from 20% (1995) to 27% (2020) and 35% in 2050.

Scenario 2: A labour market geared to 'maximizing' the active population
In this second, and more plausible, scenario, the female participation rate would reach the same level as for males by 2050. The participation rate of older workers remains the same as in 1980. Immigration is slightly higher than it was in the 1980s (for example, assuming an annual average immigration flow of 37,000 persons per year in Switzerland).

Population ageing leads to a modest increase in contributions:

- in Switzerland: from 10% (1995) to 12% in both 2020 and 2050
- in Germany: from 19% (1995) to 23% (2020) and 22% in 2050
- in France: from 20% (1995) to 23% (2020) and 21% in 2050.

This scenario also reflects the fact that unemployment should fall, through the shortage of labour, and that the cost of family allowances will drop due to the low fertility rate, with the resultant savings of social costs in these areas being transferred to help finance pensions.

The application of our two hypotheses to the three countries, Switzerland, Germany and France would seem to show that:

- Population ageing will remain a threat if no steps are taken to improve real activity rates (this book brings out the important steps which have already been taken).
- There is considerable potential for improvement in the level of activity in industrialised countries, many of which are still faced with high levels of unemployment, and for certain categories (particularly women and 'older' workers), where there remains a significant amount of underemployment. It is clear that in the medium term economic growth will be less than that recorded over the last 20 years if there is not an increase in the size of the active population.
- To maximize this, therefore, there would have to be an increase in immigration so as to achieve a labour force of the required strength. Immigration would, at the same time, help to offset the expected fall in the overall population figures in a number of European countries.

If sufficient priority is given to labour market issues, it would seem that the 'ageing crisis' could be softened a great deal, allowing governments to maintain the purchasing power of current pensions.

Roland Sigg, Head of Research, International Social Security Association, updated in 2004 from GINA and the Geneva Association (2002)

4
Employment Changes and Opportunities

General outlook

There is little doubt that some of the main employment trends observed over the last two decades constitute very favourable factors for work beyond 60. The development of services as a key factor of the modern economy has radically altered the existing work environment and in some respects created an entirely new one. Today four out of five workers are performing a 'service' job (Figure 4.1).

The very nature of service activities has brought into being a widening range of flexible job options. The rigidity that was so characteristic of the older manufacturing production chain contrasts starkly with the suppleness of the work patterns, flexible in both time and space, of our information age. A a result there has been an overall

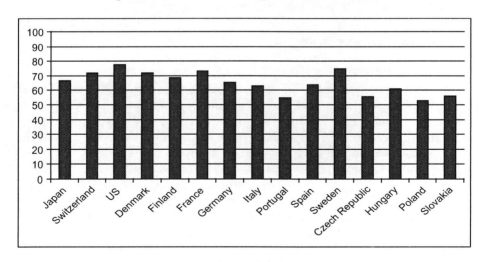

Figure 4.1 Civil employment in the service sector in selected OECD countries, 2003, as percentage of total employment

Source: OECD *Quarterly Labour Force Statistics*, Volume 2004/1.

growth in the amount of work performed in part-time jobs which, in some countries such as the Netherlands, the UK, Switzerland and Sweden, now constitute a third or almost a third of total jobs. Most part-time jobs are no longer of the old 'industrial' type (that is, related to lower and frequently unprotected employment profiles) but increasingly involve the deployment of qualified experience that, for various reasons, people cannot or will not exercise in a full-time job.

Flexible work, a category which includes also self and temporary employment, will become the new norm in the professions and even in management over the next ten or fifteen years. For instance, more and more people will be working from home at some time during the week, achieving a considerable improvement in productivity and a considerable reduction in office and transport costs.

In the EU countries where employment rates for workers over 55 are high (for example, Sweden, the UK) and in other countries, especially in the US and Japan, the frequency of part-time and self-employment increases with age. Moreover, self-employment often helps older individuals to remain economically active.

In addition, the employment rate of women has increased over the last two decades and an important proportion of them typically work part-time.

Last but not least, labour force ageing is going to be substantial in the coming years and decades: the median age of the workforce age slightly over 40 in 2000 in a country like Finland will rise to around 45 in 2020. The OECD average share of workers aged 45–59 will rise from 25% to 33% in 2030, while the proportion of workers aged 60 and older may rise from 5% to over 9%.

For all these reasons, employment changes that have occurred over the last two decades constitute real opportunities for increasing the employment participation of workers above 60, in particular on a part-time basis.

A changing labour market

Labour force participation in general

In the EU member states, as a general rule, the labour force participation rate of 69.8% of the 15–64 population in 2002 was lower than in some other OECD countries, such as the United States (76.4%). There has been only a slight improvement in Europe over the last decade (67.1% in 1990). There are strong differences between countries; for example, Sweden and Italy having respectively rates of 79% and 61.2%. This means that there is room for improvement since one can observe convergence in the economic and social norms and practice of various EU countries.

Of note also is the fact that in recent years the female participation rate has increased considerably, from 54.6% in 1990 to 61.0% in 2002. The overall increase in labour participation is actually due entirely to women working more frequently than before. A majority of women (82%) in the EU are employed in services with 33.5% in part-time employment (as compared to 6.6% for men). Important country differences exist and provide grounds for optimism about rising female labour participation over the coming years: in 2002, in Sweden, 77.1% of women were working as opposed to 47.9% in Italy.

Figure 4.2 shows that there is still scope for increasing participation of three categories of worker: the young could work more, in particular part-time, while continuing their education and training; women in middle age (25–49 years) look set to raise their participation, and there is scope for workers over 50 and even 65 to participate more in the labour market.

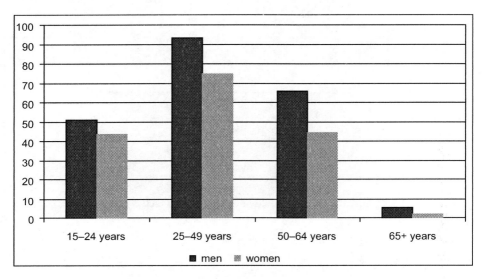

Figure 4.2   Economically active population aged 15 and over by age group and gender in the EU, 2002, as percentages of the male and female population in the given age groups

Source: EU *Labour Force Survey*, 2003.

The dominance of service employment

A decade ago, most studies suggested that, as the proportion of workers employed in service activities had risen to reach a 'plateau' of a kind, in future there could be only minor increases in some service branches. It is therefore interesting to look at the employment situation in the service sector in 2003. As can be seen from Figure 4.3, since 1995 the service sector has increased in most countries by more than 10%, and several developed economies saw a rise of around 15–20%. This means that, strictly speaking, in most countries employment in services should be in excess of 70%. Actually the number of jobs in the first and second economic sectors decreased in some countries, and services accounted for the entire increase in the number of jobs overall. For example, in Germany, compared to 1995, total jobs diminished by 0.5% for the period while in services there was a 7.9% increase. In Denmark, against an increase in total employment of 3.5% over the period, services increased by 11.1%. In France, total employment increased by 10.4% but by 16.8% in services (OECD *Quarterly Labour Force Statistics*, Volume 2004/1).

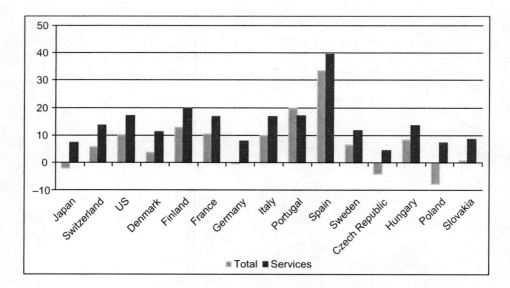

Figure 4.3   Development of civilian employment in selected OECD countries, 1995–2003 (1995 = 100%)

Source: OECD *Quarterly Labour Force Statistics*, Volume 2004/1.

However, if we consider not only tertiary sector service activities *per se* but also service functions in manufacturing and agriculture (such as research, planning, marketing, maintenance, storage, quality control, occupational safety and health, distribution), well over 80% of jobs in our economies are now in services, and this trend is set to continue in the years to come. Part-time employment is more developed in services, and most jobs in the service sector chiefly involve mental and social abilities. The latter hardly deteriorate over time and in some cases even improve with age (see Chapter 5).

Part-time and atypical employment

It should be noted that the labour participation increase over the last decade has been mainly the result of the increase in part-time employment. The rates here also vary considerably: from the Netherlands where over a third of jobs are currently part time, to Greece where the corresponding figure is only around 7%. Part-time work increased in most EU countries over the last decade, and substantially so in some countries: for example, in Austria, the number of part-time workers has increased by almost 50% over the last decade. In 1994 around 461,000 people worked fewer than 35 hours a week, compared to 668,000 today (that is, about 18.2% of those in employment).

It is common knowledge that women make up the vast majority of part-time workers, but in some countries, such as the Netherlands (21.5%) and the Nordic countries (11% in Denmark, Sweden and Norway), a higher proportion of men took up part-time employment.

If participation among workers over 55 and 60 is to rise, it is crucial that current part-time employment increases with age and that it become more common in service functions, as Figures 4.4 and 4.5 would seem to suggest.

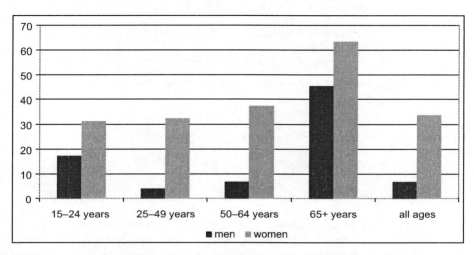

Figure 4.4 Part-time employment in the EU, 2002, as percentage of the total employment in each age group

Source: EU *Labour Force Survey*, 2003.

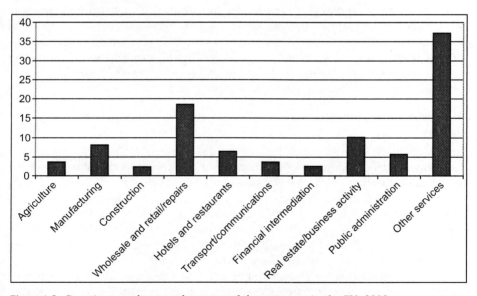

Figure 4.5 Part-time employment by sector of the economy in the EU, 2002, as percentage of total part-time employment

Source: EU *Labour Force Survey*, 2003.

Contrary to what is often asserted, only a minority of part-time employment is involuntary and this rate is especially low for workers aged 50 and over (Table 4.1). Involuntary part-time work was found to be more widespread, however, in Sweden, Denmark and Germany, and much less so in the UK and the Netherlands.

Table 4.1   Involuntary part-time employment in the EU, 2002, as percentage of total part-time employment by age group

Age group	Total	Men	Women
15–24 years	2.4	4.0	2.0
25–49 years	9.0	11.3	8.4
50–64 years	2.6	3.5	2.3
65+ years	0.0	0.0	0.0

Source: EU *Labour Force Survey*, 2003

A changing labour force: a more feminine and older workforce

With the prospect of rapid demographic change, labour markets need to be not only more dynamic but also, and this is crucial, more *inclusive*, if larger portions of the potential workforce are to contribute to economic growth, and not merely the best educated and most energetic. Not only have workforces become more feminine and older, but there still exist substantial untapped workforce reserves of women and older persons. These two categories of worker, moreover, who are frequently to be found in part-time service functions, declare themselves ready to work more. In the UK, for example, according to recent surveys (Mercer, 2004), as many as 93% of non-working people aged 55–64 would be ready to work if offered flexible work opportunities. Therefore policies which seek to help women and older workers reconcile work with family and health constraints will be making a very real contribution to meeting the challenge of 'ageing'.

A more feminine workforce

Current situation

Not only has the proportion of women in work increased overall during the last decade, but the share of women working part-time has also increased, from 28.8% in 1992 to 33.5% in 2002. Furthermore, more women work in temporary jobs than men: among temporary employees aged 30 and over the proportion of women exceeded that of men throughout the EU, and the gap was particularly large in Belgium, the Netherlands and the Nordic countries. As Figure 4.6 shows, women also work more in services than in agriculture and in manufacturing.

In OECD countries about one-quarter of female workers aged 25–54 are employed in part-time jobs. Countries where this share is high include the Netherlands (54%), Switzerland (52%) and the UK (almost 40%). The countries with the least women in part-time work are those in Eastern Europe, together with Finland and Portugal. Average proportions of part-time work declined in Nordic countries (women moved

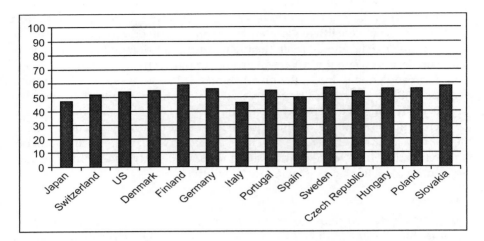

Figure 4.6   Share of women employed in the service sector, 2003, as percentage of total

Source: OECD *Quarterly Labour Force Statistics*, Volume 2004/1.

to full-time jobs) but increased in a number of other EU countries. In a large number of countries (for example, Germany, Austria, the UK, Switzerland, Belgium) a high percentage of women work part-time because of family responsibilities.

Reasons for women in atypical employment

Most women have to combine employment with family responsibilities and are therefore used to working flexibly, often part time, and to adapting to a range of work schedules which reflect their children's ages and/or parental needs, as well as their husband's or partner's career paths or health circumstances. In the Netherlands – the international champion of part-time work – in 2002, 73% of working women (aged 15–64) were part time while only 22% of working men were in part-time employment, a high rate for males, however, when compared to the European average (7%).

Thus the opportunities for finding part-time employment may be crucial to participation. The demand for part-time work is currently well above the effective level of part-time employment in some countries, notably in Ireland, Italy, Germany and the Netherlands, and to a lesser extent in Sweden, the UK, Austria and Belgium. In these countries, an increase in part-time opportunities would most likely raise female participation. Large discrepancies remain between actual and preferred employment patterns, indicating a potential for increased female labour participation. According to the European Labour Force Survey, in the EU as a whole the percentage of inactive women wishing to work is on average 12%.

There is a marked discrepancy between the northern EU member states, together with Portugal, where two-thirds or more of households are of the dual participant variety, and Spain, Greece, Ireland and Italy, where this proportion is under 50%. In both groups of countries, however, there was an increase in the incidence of dual participant households over the 1990s (Jaumotte, 2003).

The education attainment level of women seems to have a significant effect on their labour force participation, either on a full-time or a part-time basis: the higher women's educational level, the higher the proportion of dual participation households. Here again the *cohort effect* comes into play: the greater their access to education and good training, the more women will be in work, full or part-time, with a family or otherwise. There is a potential problem here in that increased female participation could reduce the birth rate – and the birth rate, of course, is a key determinant of future economic growth and hence of social protection systems. But Nordic countries and France are characterized by a relatively high number of children despite high female participation rates, while Italy and Spain have both low female participation rates and very low birth rates.

'Older' women

Not only are women more accustomed to part-time, flexible, temporary work patterns, but, because of their lower social contributions and more frequent career interruptions (for family/care reasons), their pension rights are often poor when compared with those of men with the same qualification level. In spite of the gradual adaptation of national pension systems across the EU, the Commission acknowledges that the 'significant coverage discrepancy in pension entitlements, particularly under second pillar schemes, of atypical women workers, will persist for a long time to come' (European Commission, 2003a). As a consequence, in the UK for example, a recent publication (Age Concern England, 2003) shows that one in four single women pensioners lives in poverty, and twice as many women as men rely on means-tested benefits in retirement. Fortunately, these rates are not as alarming in most other EU countries. However, the majority of women, in particular those ageing alone, either divorced, widows or single, will need to work beyond 60 and even beyond the pension age in order to improve their retirement income.

According to recent surveys in Switzerland (Widmer et al., 2001), women who would be prepared or need to work later than 63 (the current retirement age) would want to do so part time – a result not altogether surprising since the majority (68%) of older women (aged 55–64) already working do so part time. The same can be said of the UK: among working women, 47% aged between 50 and the state pension age, and 75% aged over the state pension age, work part time (Labour Force Survey, Autumn 2003, UK).

In the EU, since almost 60% of the over-65 population are women – they outnumber men significantly in all member states – measures encouraging the integration of a higher proportion of older women into the labour force will be of importance in the future.

An older workforce

Deciding exactly when a worker becomes an 'older' or senior worker depends very much on the sector and branch he or she is working in, on the job performed, on the education level attained and on the personal qualities of the individual concerned. Some athletes or dancers are considered 'old' by the time they reach 30 or 35. It is a well-established fact that workers leave the labour force earlier in industrial branches and blue-collar jobs than in services and white-collar jobs. In Scandinavian countries, the exit age of blue-collar workers is on average 59 years while white-collar employees on average leave their company at 64 (GIPMIS, 2004). In many service sectors, age is a relative factor: for a number of jobs, being older can be an advantage (see also Chapter 5).

Forecast of the ageing of the workforce

However, all forecasts show that there will be a much higher proportion of 'older' workers in 25 years from now (Table 4.2).

Table 4.2 Workers aged 45+ as percentage of the labour force

	1970	1995	2030*	2030**
Denmark	36.4	34.0	37.3	46.3
Finland	31.5	34.2	36.9	44.2
France	32.9	30.7	39.1	47.7
Germany	33.1	31.5	40.3	50.4
Italy	30.5	29.5	43.0	50.6
Netherlands	29.7	26.6	33.5	45.1
Spain	32.6	27.2	44.6	54.1
Sweden	39.3	38.6	40.7	45.7
UK	37.9	33.8	38.7	46.1
EU15	33.5	30.5	39.1	47.8
OECD	32.9	30.6	40.5	48.2
US	27.7	25.0	28.9	27.9

* low scenario; ** high scenario

Source: OECD (1998).

Labour force participation in the EU

For the time being, there are significant differences in labour force participation. The rates range from 20–29% to over 70%, and six categories can be distinguished (Table 4.3).

Table 4.3 Labour force participation rates of those aged 55–64, 2002

Labour force participation of the European population aged 55–64, 2002					
Labour force participation rates (both sexes)					
20–29%	*30–39%*	*40–49%*	*50–59%*	*60–69%*	*70%+*
Austria	France	Germany	Finland	Denmark	Sweden
Belgium	Italy	Greece	Portugal	Switzerland	
Luxembourg	Poland	Ireland	United Kingdom	Norway	
Hungary		Netherlands			
Slovak Republic		Spain			
		European Union			
		Czech Republic			

Source: OECD (2003b).

It is of course important to observe that thanks to recent policies a few countries have already been able to move from one category to another. For example, the Netherlands, which ten years ago had a participation rate of 29%, is now in the 40–49% group. This also applies to Finland which was in the previous category less than ten years ago. Table 4.3 says a lot about the need for policies for improving the labour participation of 'older' workers.

In deciding whether there will be a higher demand for older workers tomorrow, it is also important to look at where workers aged 50 and over are mostly to be found today. In France, for example, Figure 4.7 shows that the proportion of workers aged 50+ exceeded the average mainly in the finance (banks and insurance) and real estate sectors. They were less frequent in services such as retail, hotels/restaurants and information technology.

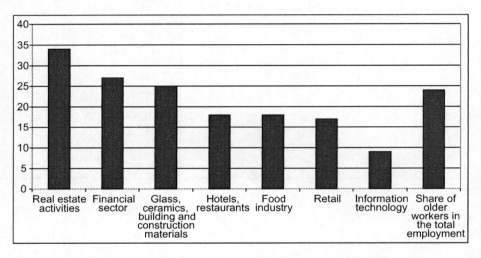

Figure 4.7   Branches that employ workers aged 50 and over in France, 2002, as a percentage of total employment

Source: *Le Monde*, 30 September 2003.

Employment of the over-65s

According to the EU Labour Force Survey, in 2002 some 5.5% of men aged 65–74 in the Union and 2.1% of women of the same age were still working. There are wide variations between countries, however, with over 26% of men in this age group and 14% of women in work in Portugal – much higher figures than anywhere else in the EU – as compared with around 2% of men and under 1% of women in Belgium, France, Luxembourg and Spain. In between these extremes, a relatively large proportion of men of 65 and over remained in work in Ireland (15%), Sweden (8%), Greece (8%) and the UK (6%), but in each case, the figure for women was only around 2–3%. Of course, studies mention that in reality this figure is much higher due to undeclared work.

Part time over 65 years

Around 45% of men and 63% of women in the Union in this age group (in 2002) who were in employment worked part time – under 30 hours a week – and of these, around 60% of women and just under half of men worked less than 15 hours a week. The importance of part-time work varied markedly between countries, with the great majority of both women and men in the Netherlands, Sweden, the UK and Denmark working part time (over 70% of women, 60% or more of men), most of them for less than 15 hours a week. Only a small minority were working part-time in Greece, Italy, Spain and Austria. Over a quarter of women and men aged 65 and over in employment in the EU worked in agriculture. Some 60% of the total number of men and 40% of the women in work were self-employed, while another 14% of women and 7% of men were unpaid family workers. Only around a third of men and under half of women in this age group who were still working were employees.

In looking at future employment prospects, it is crucial to have a better understanding of why in several countries half the workers in the age group 55–64 leave the labour force before reaching the official pension age. As Figure 4.8 shows, over a third of workers were made redundant or benefited from an early retirement scheme. But since early retirement policies have changed recently, there will certainly be substantial labour reserves for the future.

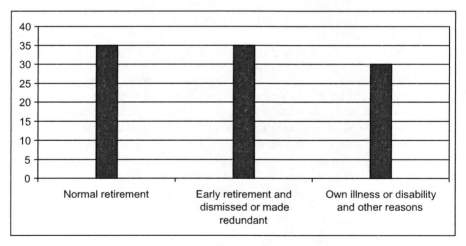

Figure 4.8 Main reasons for leaving last job or business for older workers aged 55–64 (%)

Source: European Commission (2004, p. 9).

A new work environment

The knowledge society has opened new perspectives for the quality of work: creating the conditions for change in existing jobs; generating new working methods and new ways of organising work; allowing greater flexibility in the workplace. Telework represents a specific case of ICT (Information and Computer Technology) driven flexibility, enabling new forms of work organisation and work-life balance, removing barriers to mobility and opening thus new job opportunities for people excluded so far from the labour market. (European Commission, 2003c)

Over the last 25 years, the work environment has changed significantly. The great majority of active persons now work in the service sector, and a number of jobs in industry have also been transformed. Educational levels and qualifications have considerably improved on the whole, and also the vast majority of workers are performing tasks in a better environment. These improvements help, and will help even more in the future, senior workers to stay active longer than today. The most important changes are the following:

- Work organization has been affected by the development of ICT which has resulted in a much greater autonomy of workers. In many service activities, such as banking and insurance, work has been transformed and employees both enjoy more freedom and take on more responsibilities. This improvement has also led to higher quality jobs and higher productivity which, however, in some cases creates stress and pressure from the management. According to a British firm's human resource director, 'We started introducing flexible working in 1992 and now almost 60% of our workforce take advantage of the opportunities. The corporate benefits are important. Our most common flexible workers are home workers and they are on average 20 percent more productive than office-based colleagues' (*Financial Times*, 5 April 2003).
- At the same time, team work is perhaps more important than it was in the past. Social qualifications are more in demand. A part of continuing training in firms has to do with communication, sharing problems and solutions between colleagues, and creating a positive atmosphere. The result might be higher productivity at the company level and personal development at the individual level.
- Social evolution has also led to more diversity in terms of qualifications, gender mix, age mix, origins of workers, and so on. The age diversity of teams is particularly important to match staff and customers, as in banks, insurance companies, hospitals, and so on.
- Work organization and work-life have also been transformed more in some branches and countries than in others by the new flexible methods and forms of work, including flexible working time. The previous sections illustrated this important trend.
- Telework is a specific developing form of flexible work which deserves more attention since it is projected to increase in the future. The last European Telework Survey (2000) shows a clear development of telework in Europe. In 2000, over 12 million workers used teleworking, which concerns around 10% of all workers. The countries with the highest proportion of teleworkers are Finland, the Netherlands and Sweden where this ratio is expected to

reach 25–30% of total employment by 2005. At the same time, these are the countries with the longest tradition of teleworking. On the other hand, the countries with the lowest rates of teleworkers are Spain and France where this development started only recently. In these countries the share of teleworkers will be around 5% in 2005. Teleworking is more common among men than women: three-quarters of teleworkers are men. Two-thirds of teleworkers are 30–49 years old. Teleworkers are often highly qualified workers (around 60%). Telework is much more widespread in large than in small companies: while two-thirds of companies employing more than 500 people have already used telework, only 12% of companies with at most ten workers do so. The branches with the highest share of teleworkers are business and information technology, software, financial services, manufacturing, and health care/pharmaceuticals. In these branches today, as many as 54% of total workers have used telework and as much as 80% of the workforce will have done so by 2005. According to the result of a survey of 1,200 AT&T managers, carried out in 2002–03, the main benefits of telework are as shown in Table 4.4.

Table 4.4 Major advantages of telework

Advantage	% saying major advantage
Improves productivity (e.g. by redirecting commuting time to work activities)	75
Balances work and family	74
Shows that the firm cares (a driver of job satisfaction)	69
Promotes trust	64
More personal time	63
Employee saves money (e.g. travelling cost to workplace)	63
Company saves money (e.g. reducing overhead costs such as real estate, and enhancing retention and recruitment)	61
Helps environment (e.g. eliminating the daily commute)	59
Retains best people	55
Reduces stress	47

Source: AT&T Telework White Paper, 2003, <www.att.com/news/item/0,1847,11947,00.html>

- In some sectors where mobility of workers is low, career planning has become very important so as to reassess at some stages one's qualifications and to be able to change job content in the same firm thanks to additional training followed in the company or outside. The new work environment is becoming very much a learning environment.
- A more and more widespread phenomenon is having not only one job but a portfolio of jobs, that is, a combination of either similar activities with different employers or completely different activities with different employers and/or in the framework of self-employment.
- On the other hand, more flexible organizations have also led to the subcontracting of a number of tasks and resulted in less stability and security in the individual's career. While it was common to have only one or two

employers in one's lifetime, employees now tend to have to move more often from one job to another. The one-job career is becoming a thing of the past. In this respect low-skilled workers have suffered much more, by being offered temporary or short-term contracts interspersed by frequent periods of unemployment. These workers without specific qualifications need to upgrade their skills by adult training, and in most countries such opportunities now exist.

Figure 4.9 summarizes the aspects mentioned here.

Worker's employability		Company's environment
	E	
• Qualifications	M	• Flexible work organization
Educational qualifications and actual	P	• Flexible working time
skills	L	• Fairness and equality (age, gender,
• Social qualifications	O	and diversity)
Ability to work in teams	Y	• Career planning, promotion
• Ability to work autonomously	M	• Continuing training
• Continuing training	E	• Health and safety at work
lifelong learning	N	• Social dialogue
• Flexibility and mobility	T	

Figure 4.9   Changing working environment

Source: Author's own compilation.

In order to improve work ability and employability, the quality of work has to be improved. The withdrawal from the labour market of older workers in low-quality jobs is up to four times higher than that of older workers in jobs of higher quality. Improvement of the quality of jobs means better educational qualifications, ensuring access to continuing vocational training, improvement of health and safety conditions at work, making work organization and working time more flexible, promoting diversity, making career progress possible. Job quality is also crucial to re-attract in the labour market older people and people with care responsibilities.

Box 4.1   Improving quality in work: a review of recent progress

Improving quality and productivity in work is one of the three overarching objectives in the EU Employment Guidelines for the period 2003–05, together with full employment and social cohesion.

In the 2001 Commission Communication, ten dimensions of job quality were identified. In the following we shall deal with the most important ones.

Intrinsic job quality
This dimension refers to the characteristics of a particular job, which make it satisfying for the worker and compatible with career prospects in terms of wages and status. The attractiveness of jobs is a condition for an increase of labour market participation. In

▶

the year 2000 in the EU as a whole, around 20% of all employees declared themselves dissatisfied with their job. Relatively high degrees of dissatisfaction in Greece, Italy, Spain and the UK contrast with very high shares (90% or more) of satisfied employees in Denmark, France, Ireland, the Netherlands and Austria. A positive trend can be noted in Greece and Portugal.

Skills, lifelong learning and career development
Since 1998 there has been a significant increase in adult participation in education and training in the EU. However, important differences exist between member states.

The latter have to implement policies to ensure in the EU by 2010 a level of participation in lifelong learning of at least 12.5% of the adult working-age population and to ensure that at least 85% of 22-year-olds should have completed upper secondary education. Ensuring basic ICT skills should become an integral part of enhancing employability. In some member states basic ICT literacy has already become mainstreamed in activation measures.

Gender equality
Although the differences in employment and unemployment rates between women and men have decreased in recent years, the gaps remain important. Member states' efforts to reduce gender employment and unemployment gaps include training (Ireland, Austria, the Netherlands, Luxembourg), review of tax, benefit and pension systems and incentives for enterprises (Belgium, Ireland, Sweden, the Netherlands, Spain, France), encouraging entrepreneurship (Greece, Sweden, Luxembourg) and better care services for children and other dependants (Ireland, Greece, Italy, the UK).

Health and safety at work
Work-related health problems and accidents at work generate a production loss estimated at 3–4% of GNP in the EU. Health expenditure and costs related to the loss of working days are estimated at €20 billion a year. Occupational diseases and work-related illnesses are among the most significant consequences of poor health and safety conditions at work. There is an increasing incidence of musculoskeletal disorders such as back pain and disorders caused by repetitive movements (52%), of stress, depression and anxiety (18%) as well as general tiredness, hearing disorders and cardiovascular diseases. Currently five member states (Denmark, Greece, France, Portugal and the UK) have set quantitative targets for the reduction of accidents at work and occupational diseases.

Flexibility and security
Flexibility with regard to work organization, working time, contractual arrangements and mobility is needed both on the part of firms and of workers. At the same time quality requires adequate security for workers to ensure sustainable integration and career progress. Thus, ensuring equal access to training, to health care and to social protection rights for employees under atypical forms of contract is particularly important to promote a good balance between flexibility and security.

Social dialogue and worker involvement
Collective agreements in particular are an important tool in the hands of the social partners to both shape industrial relations as well as improve quality in work. But other forms of worker involvement, notably information and consultation mechanisms, participation in works councils and other staff committees, such as those ensuring health and safety standards, should also be enhanced. In 2000, the European social partners signed collective agreements covering directly 70 million employees. The rate

▶

of coverage, that is, the number of employees covered by a collective agreement as a proportion of the number of employees, is around 80%.

Diversity and non-discrimination
Diversity management can be defined as meeting the needs of a culturally diverse workforce and of sensitizing workers and managers to differences associated with gender, race, age and nationality in an attempt to maximize the potential productivity of all employees. The Commission calls for efforts to implement effective disability mainstreaming in their employment policy in order to achieve a better integration of people with disabilities.

Overall work performance
The Lisbon strategy has defined a broad framework to increase long-run productivity growth using all the available instruments to stimulate technical progress, whilst at the same time encouraging labour-intensive growth in the medium term.

European Commission (2003c)

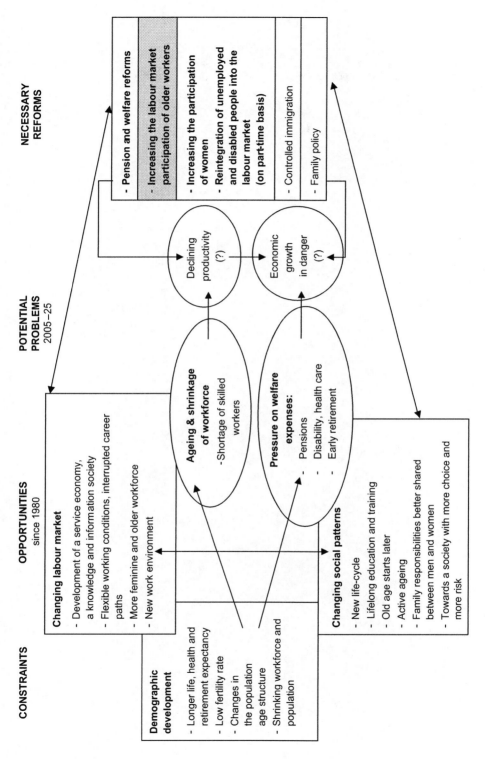

CONSTRAINTS   OPPORTUNITIES   POTENTIAL   NECESSARY
               since 1980   PROBLEMS   REFORMS
                                 2005–25

Changing labour market

- Development of a service economy, a knowledge and information society
- Flexible working conditions, interrupted career paths
- More feminine and older workforce
- New work environment

Demographic development

- Longer life, health and retirement expectancy
- Low fertility rate
- Changes in the population age structure
- Shrinking workforce and population

Changing social patterns

- New life-cycle
- Lifelong education and training
- Old age starts later
- Active ageing
- Family responsibilities better shared between men and women
- Towards a society with more choice and more risk

Ageing & shrinkage of workforce
- Shortage of skilled workers

Pressure on welfare expenses:
- Pensions
- Disability, health care
- Early retirement

Declining productivity (?)

Economic growth in danger (?)

- **Pension and welfare reforms**
- **Increasing the labour market participation of older workers**
- **Increasing the participation of women**
- **Reintegration of unemployed and disabled people into the labour market (on part-time basis)**
- Controlled immigration
- Family policy

Figure 4.10 Synthesis of Part I – Why working beyond 60? The global picture: new constraints and opportunities

Part II

Working Beyond 60 – How?

**The Reduction of Working Time and the
Promotion of Age Management**

5
The Part-Time Model for Working Beyond 60

A number of years ago, the Geneva Association proposed the addition of a fourth pension pillar to supplement the first three pillars. This fourth pillar would consist of resources from an income from part-time work for some years after reaching retirement age (or earlier in the case of earlier retirement). From the legal retirement age onwards, such fourth pillar income could be accompanied by a partial pension.

Figure 5.1 summarizes the trends towards a fourth pillar. On the left side we find the constraints, demographic and financial, we analysed in Chapters 1 and 3, and on the right side the changes and opportunities resulting from new social and

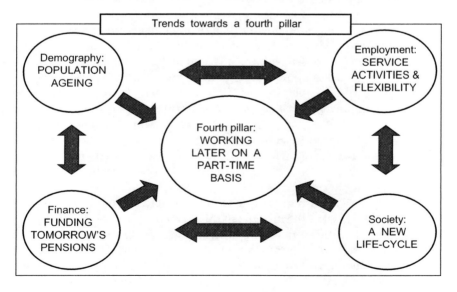

Figure 5.1   Trends towards a fourth pillar

Source: Reday-Mulvey and Giarini (1995)

employment patterns addressed in Chapters 2 and 4. Not only is a fourth pillar now more necessary than in the past, but the good news is that it has also become more possible than 20 or 30 years ago.

In this chapter, we shall study the proposed model for work-time reduction, the purpose of the latter being to facilitate and to encourage working beyond 60. Before the issue is tackled in substance, the first section examines the strengths and weaknesses of workers over 60. The second, with the example of one large industrial firm, takes a very brief look at the difficulties of maintaining seniors in employment without work-time adaptation. The third section deals with the main benefits of part-time work for employers, employees and the community at large. The fourth section describes the extension of work-life and at least some of the requirements for its successful operation in terms of the two phases into which it falls: (i) before the official retirement age of 65 when full early retirement is replaced by partial early retirement, and (ii) after the age of 65. The chapter concludes by showing how the fourth pillar can be made to dovetail with pension schemes through partial re-engineering of the latter.

Typical strengths and weaknesses of workers over 60

Currently in the labour market, workers over 60 frequently experience more long-term unemployment and tend to receive less training than younger people. There are a number of reasons for this: among other things, a negative attitude towards senior workers on the part of employers, workers' perception of themselves (for example, lack of confidence in learning and performing new tasks).

However, there is considerable sociological and scientific evidence that workers over 60 are no less effective or productive than their younger counterparts. What is striking is that differences between individuals of the same age, let us say at 45, are greater than differences between workers of 45 and of 25. Poorer health is stated as one of the main reasons of supposed lower productivity in older age. Even if the risk of poor health rises with age, increases in life expectancy have been accompanied by significant health improvements. Many studies confirm that as far as organizational behaviour is concerned, older workers demonstrate less absenteeism, lower turnover, fewer accidents, higher job satisfaction and more positive work values than younger workers. Workers at the end of their career, in general, also manifest greater loyalty to their employer, being less likely than younger workers to leave the organization in which they are employed.

The highly respected Finnish Institute of Occupational Health has done extensive research in this field. Most of the material in this chapter is based on the Institute's work, in particular on the work of one of the Institute's directors, J. Ilmarinen (Ilmarinen, 1999, 2001). As a general observation, Ilmarinen (2001) found that job demands correspond with the skills of 80% of workers, and that generally the response to skills-demand is better among workers over 45 than among younger workers in most EU countries.

In line with these results, an American study, conducted by the Society of Human Resource Management in conjunction with the American Association of Retired

Persons, confirmed that many stereotypical perceptions of senior workers are inaccurate (cf. Walker, 2003, p. 2). The study found that of almost 400 human resource professionals surveyed,

- 77% agreed that older workers have a higher level of commitment to their organizations than younger ones
- 68% concluded that training them costs less than or the same as training their younger counterparts
- 57% reported that age does not affect the amount of time required to train an employee.

The health status of older workers

In the EU, workers over 45 take marginally fewer short sick-leave periods (one to two days per year) but take slightly more long ones (three to eleven days per year) than those under 45.

According to studies made by the Finnish Institute, every other man and woman suffers from a diagnosed musculoskeletal disease during the last 15 years of his or her work career. Approximately one-quarter of women and one-third of men suffer from a circulatory disease. Approximately every fifth worker over 45 years of age feels that chronic disease hinders work. The prevalence of multiple illnesses also increases with age during the work-life. Of course these conditions rarely affect the performance of the older worker in the more mentally and socially based (as opposed to physically demanding) jobs of our service economies.

Ageing not only involves the gradual deterioration of health, but also changes in the way we evaluate health. Young people evaluate their health mainly in terms of symptoms and older people rather in terms of loss of functional capacity. According to a survey of work and health, as many as over half of the men and women in the 55–64 age range perceived their health to be fairly or very good. However, 54% of healthy people (no diagnosed disease) perceive their health as having deteriorated as of the age of 47.

The significant increase in the prevalence of disease during the last 15 years of work-life means that:

- the role of occupational health services will need to be thought of as a service system that both prevents and, more especially, treats diseases
- work methods and practices will have to change significantly to reduce the occupational disadvantages caused by illnesses and to prevent the aggravation of disease.

Physical functional capacity of ageing workers

Approximately 70% of people under 45 years of age have no functional disabilities, whereas the corresponding figures for 50-year-olds and 60-year-olds are approximately 60% and 40% respectively. Cardiorespiratory capacity weakens significantly between 52 and 62 years for both men and women, even though individual differences are great, as are the differences between muscle groups. The weakening of the musculoskeletal system affects both physical and mental work.

In terms of exposure to vibration, noise, heat, cold and impurities in the ambient air, it seems that physical work conditions do not change with age in the European Union. Any recorded differences reflect rather a reduction in exposure among older workers in comparison with younger workers.

Mental functional capacity of ageing workers

The most significant changes in mental functional capacity from the point of view of working life are the slowing of perception and performance. These changes can be well compensated for, however, by ergonomic arrangements in the work environment, a better organization of work (such as reduced work time) and personal aids.

Many characteristics of mental functional capacity can be strengthened with age. These opportunities of 'mental development' have to do, for example, with, among other cognitive functions, learning motivation, work commitment and life control. The distinctive signs of wisdom also become more manifest with age. For example, the ability to perceive, understand and evaluate what is essential in respect of different problems and the ability to give good advice and devise working solutions to these problems increases. Wisdom is crucial to problem solving, and should be a quality of increasing value in today's complex work environment. Moreover, a more creative use of work experience can significantly improve the ageing worker's ability to cope with work-life.

Mental load (using computers, working to tight schedules, performing complex tasks and new learning) seems to be lighter for older than for younger workers in the European Union. There are similar differences in kind and degree between the genders, except for complex tasks, which are more common for older than for younger men and less common for older than for younger women. There is a notable difference in mental load also between Finnish men and women. The differences between age groups are greatest in relation to the use of computers and the acquisition of new knowledge and skills, but this is changing with the arrival of new cohorts of workers.

Training ability of older workers

One of the crucial issues is of course whether workers after 45, 50 or 60 are as trainable as when the same workers were younger. Is the fact that continuing training decreases with age due to a lower ability, somewhat unadapted pedagogy, course contents, a lack of confidence or is it due to economic factors (such as a diminished return on investment)? The opinion of the social scientists is revealing (Box 5.1).

Social functional capacity of ageing people

There are at least two important aspects of social functional capacity from the standpoint of work-life: an individual's interpersonal relationships on the one hand and, on the other, the individual's active participation in different communities.

Box 5.1   Is ageing a cause for absenteeism in continuing training?

According to recent debates in political and social science, vocational training of older adults has become increasingly important. However, the percentage of adults participating in continuing vocational training seems to decrease with age.

It was therefore decided to examine whether there is a significant relationship between increasing age and decreasing participation in adult vocational training. Correlational findings seem to suggest that such a relationship exists, if age is interpreted monocausally. A new way of approaching this topic is to combine theoretical concepts of (non-)participation in continuing education with gerontological concepts of ageing. It is argued that approaches based on age according to the calendar should only be made within groups of younger and older people that are similar relative to other variables (for example, level of qualification, hours of gainful work per week) that also influence the participation in continuing education (relative age concept). Such analysis was undertaken on retrospective descriptive data collected for Germany. The subjects who were capable of gainful work were separated into five groups relative to their status of qualification and the conditions of their employment. Within these groups no statistically significant correlation was found between the amount of participation and age of the subjects.

The main conclusion is that a low rate of participation in vocational training is not a problem caused specifically by ageing but rather by the fact that such people find themselves in conditions that do not support participation in continuing education. Of course, many of these people happen to be older workers.

The general level of participation in vocational training is still low in Germany. Most probably too low to prepare the workforce for extended working lives. The implications of this study apply both to the practice of organizational as well as staff development. Organizational and staff development plays an important role in justifying educational efforts to the people concerned and to their organizations.

Wolfgang Gallenberger, BG Institute for Work and Health, Dresden, Germany, at a conference in October 2004 (Health and Ageing, the Geneva Association) and in Gallenberger (2002)

The new requirements of work-life emphasize the ability to function as part of a group or team, and as a consequence the need for social skills and an ability to work with different people on a daily basis has increased.

Social functional capacity can improve with age because over time an individual develops a keener sense of his or her own limitations and strengths and is able to use this knowledge of self to modify his or her behaviour accordingly. Moreover, ageing generally tends to enhance skills based on tolerance of others, self-knowledge and knowledge of human nature. With ageing also, the individual is able to develop interactive skills: for example, the social ability to transform one's 'own will' into 'the will of the group'.

Table 5.1 summarizes the results of an analysis of the characteristics of older workers and opportunities for integrating them in the labour market.

Work ability is the key to employability and re-employment. Employability can be improved with different support and service systems, with work and retirement legislation, through changes in values and attitudes, and of course through improved organization (flexible, part time, and so on) of work time.

Box 5.2   Synthesis on the work ability of senior workers

Work ability is the sum of individual and work-related factors. The different factors of work ability change dynamically with age. The work ability index developed by the Finnish Institute of Occupational Health has been used to determine the perceived work ability of ageing workers in both broad longitudinal studies of ageing workers (for example, in the municipal sector) and in cross-sectional studies of different occupations in Finland and other countries. Work ability can be classified as 'poor', 'moderate', 'good' and 'excellent'. The rating of 'poor' (7–27 points) strongly predicts work disability and retirement, while 'excellent' (44–49 points) predicts continued participation in work-life.

According to the longitudinal study of the municipal sector, the averages of the work ability index decrease notably between 51 and 62 years of age for both men and women regardless of the nature of their work (physical, mental, or combined physical and mental). Workers in mentally demanding jobs have higher work ability indices in general than workers in physically demanding jobs.

In the study of municipal employees, the work ability index showed a 29% decrease and a 10% increase in the work ability of employees who continued to work in the same place for eleven years. It did not change among almost 60% of the workers despite ageing. The decreases and increases in work ability did not depend on the nature of the work or the gender of the workers.

Again in the longitudinal study, 'poor' work ability increased with age similarly for both men and women, except in a few cases. It did not change notably between 47 and 51 years of age, but increased between 52 and 58 years of age. The increase was the greatest among physical workers in general. The work ability index was 'poor' for over 25% of the municipal workers after the age of 58 years in such occupations as supervision (kitchen), unskilled labour and domestic work among the women, and fitting, unskilled labour and transportation among the men. A large proportion of male teachers of 58 years of age also had 'poor' work ability (23%).

The examples of different occupations reveal differences in the proportions of 'good' and 'poor' work ability among workers of different ages. Two-thirds of construction workers in the 50–54 age group report at least 'good' work ability and approximately half continue to do so in the 55–59 year age range. Between the ages of 55 and 59 years only 14% of construction workers have 'poor' work ability, whereas the respective figure for municipal workers is almost twice as high. A four-year follow-up has indicated, however, that work ability weakens significantly with age. Nearly two-thirds of the workers reported 'moderate' or ' poor' work ability after the follow-up.

The results of work ability studies have specifically proven that individual differences increase strongly with age within an occupational group. Individual changes are more pronounced after the age of 55 years, and, at this age, the work ability of people in the same occupations and of the same age can vary from 'poor' to 'excellent' in physical, mental and combined physical and mental work. The findings underline the need for individual solutions to work with age, as well as for facilities for restoring, promoting and maintaining work ability.

Juhanni Ilmarinen – Department Director, Finnish Institute of Occupational Health, Helsinki, in Ilmarinen (2001, pp. 623–41)

In this context, early exit from the labour market is considered in some quarters a great waste of experience, valuable skills and human resources, particularly if employers have invested heavily in training. The benefits of retaining older

Table 5.1 Qualities of older workers and opportunities for integrating them in the labour market (SWOT analysis)

Strengths	Weaknesses
• Accumulated know-how, routine • Knowing one's own limitations and strengths • As creative and enterprising as younger workers • Soft skills, social capital • Wisdom in problem solving, clever handling of colleagues and clients • Quality and confident awareness • Greater loyalty to employer • Less absenteeism, lower turnover • Tutoring younger colleagues • Higher job satisfaction	• Increasing risk of morbidity • Decrease in physical functional capacity and slowing of perception and performance • Limited resistance to physical and mental burdens • High costs due to seniority wages (changing) • Relative lower education level compared with younger counterparts (changing) • Lesser flexibility compared with younger counterparts, for example, regarding technological change (changing)
Opportunities	Threats
• Growing life expectancy and rise in number of healthy years • Shortage of skilled workers • Adjusted and more flexible (part time) and safer work conditions • Increasing education level of up-coming cohorts • Lifelong learning • Career planning • Age diversity • Cooperation with colleagues of different ages	• Negative stereotypes about older workers' capabilities (for example, lack of energy, motivation, and diminished ability to learn new tasks/technology) • Desire for early exit • Discrimination

Source: Author's own compilation.

workers with a view to their training in turn their younger counterparts and the importance of age diversity within the workforce are also being recognized by more progressive employers.

On the demand side, the new cohorts of workers at the end of their career wish increasingly to remain in active employment beyond retirement age, especially if flexible or part-time conditions are available. Rather than invest their human capital even in voluntary activities, they would prefer to remain in the workplace as late as possible. 'Flexi-employability' is a new concept which well describes an occupational option that may prove beneficial to these workers and to the companies that employ them.

Research indicates that quality of life of those who work beyond pension age is higher than for others in the same age group. However, if this extension of work-life is to function satisfactorily, complementary measures are required, for example, improvements in work conditions in respect of health and safety, and support in helping older employees update their skills.

Figure 5.2 summarizes the interdependence between means and measures within the enterprise as also at the individual and community levels, enabling an ageing workforce to remain motivated, productive and active participants.

Maintaining full-time employment later

Understanding the real nature and rhythm of employment today is essential if we are properly to plan for employing the over-60s and over-65s in future and adapt work so that its pattern and practice remain beneficial for all concerned, workers and companies alike.

Working later full time is difficult for most workers for a number of reasons:

1. physical abilities decrease over time and as a result, beyond a certain age, some work demands may make longer recuperation times necessary
2. mental abilities do not necessarily decrease with age but stress certainly increases, and therefore recuperation time often needs to be longer; however, a number of jobs involving mental abilities – such as teaching – are in any case difficult to continue full time since social circumstances often make them more stressful today than they were in the past
3. absenteeism increases with age when work is done full time, but frequently decreases when the employee begins working part time
4. highly motivated workers, whether employees or self-employed, will always be able to continue working full time. They are, however, not representative of the average worker.

In a European Survey on Working Conditions (ESWC, cf. OECD, 2003b, pp. 45–7), which was carried out in the 15 EU countries in 1990, 1995 and 2000, workers were asked about various aspects of their work environment, including the nature of the tasks performed, health problems and the degree of job autonomy they enjoyed. The ESWC data provide a mixed picture of how health risks at work have evolved over the past decade. When asked directly, reported exposure to risk fell by about three percentage points between 1990 and 2000. However, workers' responses to separate and more detailed questions about specific hazardous conditions or health problems related to work suggested a worsening situation: 42% of workers considered their jobs to be non-sustainable, stating that they did not think they would be able or willing to do the same job by the time they reached 60 years of age.

In 2000, 31% of workers reported performing repetitive movements on a continuous basis, slightly lower than in 1995. In contrast, work intensity appears to have increased over the past decade. In 2000, 56% of respondents said that they worked at 'very high speed', up from 48% in 1990, and 60% said that they were working to 'tight deadlines', a rise of 10%. On a more positive note, workers also reported increased autonomy in their jobs.

While there has been a century-long trend towards a shorter working week, in recent decades this historic trend has slowed and appears to have stopped altogether in a number of countries. The most typical weekly schedule is around 38 hours, but

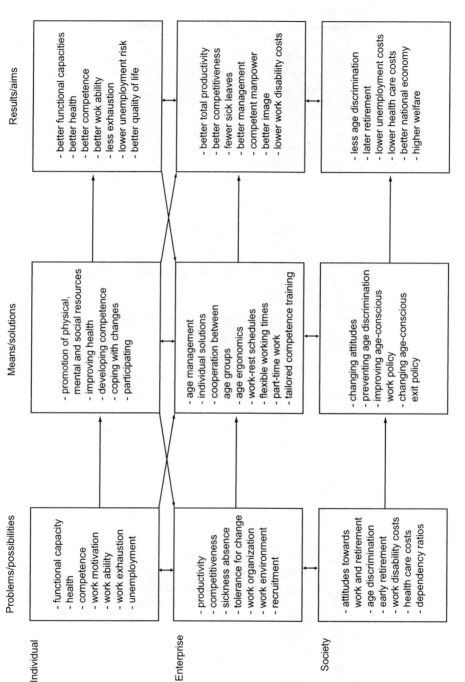

Individual

Problems/possibilities
- functional capacity
- health
- competence
- work motivation
- work ability
- work exhaustion
- unemployment

Means/solutions
- promotion of physical, mental and social resources
- improving health
- developing competence
- coping with changes
- participating

Results/aims
- better functional capacities
- better health
- better competence
- better wok ability
- less exhaustion
- lower unemployment risk
- better quality of life

Enterprise

- productivity
- competitiveness
- sickness absence
- tolerance for change
- work organization
- work environment
- recruitment

- age management
- individual solutions
- cooperation between age groups
- age ergonomics
- work-rest schedules
- flexible working times
- part-time work
- tailored competence training

- better total productivity
- better competitiveness
- fewer sick leaves
- better management
- competent manpower
- better image
- lower work disability costs

Society

- attitudes towards work and retirement
- age discrimination
- early retirement
- work disability costs
- health care costs
- dependency ratios

- changing attitudes
- preventing age discrimination
- improving age-conscious work policy
- changing age-conscious exit policy

- less age discrimination
- later retirement
- lower unemployment costs
- lower health care costs
- better national economy
- higher welfare

Figure 5.2 Finland – a new look at the relationships between ageing and work-life

Source: Ilmarinen (1999, p. 13).

85

the proportion of individuals working more than 45 hours per week is quite large, exceeding 40% of working men in Greece, Iceland and the UK. The share of men working very long hours appears to have increased over the past decade in most European countries. The largest increases in the share of men working 45 or more hours per week occurred in Iceland, Denmark, Finland and Belgium. Working very long hours is a little less frequent for women than for men. However, the share of women working very long hours also increased over the past decade in some countries including, notably, Denmark, Finland, Iceland and the UK.

Examples of firms able to lengthen work-life on a part-time rather than on a full-time basis abound in the industrial sector, and we cite here the example of Arcelor (Box 5.3). However, today in the service sector as well examples are more common and can be found in branches like care provision and hospitals, hotels and restaurants, supermarkets and teaching.

The benefits of part-time work for employers, employees and the community

Recently in the UK, Nordic countries and elsewhere, a growing number of employers have realized that it often makes good business sense to recruit, develop, motivate and retain older workers, and this for five main reasons (Walker, 1999): (i) return on investment, (ii) preventing skills shortages, (iii) maximizing recruitment potential, (iv) responding to demographic change, and (v) promoting diversity.

There is an extensive literature on part-time work and on the benefits or difficulties it engenders. The development of part-time work has been important over the last 25 years in almost every EU country, not only for women and young workers. It has been a crucial stepping stone to flexibility in many companies, and a key component of a healthy employment situation in countries such as the Netherlands, the UK, most Nordic countries and Switzerland. We here focus on part-time work for 'older' workers and the benefits it provides for companies, employees and the community.

Advantages for employers

The advantages for employers have been better recognized in recent years; chief among them are the following.

Reduction of costs and increased productivity

Part-time pay.   It is well known that per-hour productivity increases when a worker goes from full-time to part-time work, especially in jobs – numerous in service economies – where workers can organize their work and perform tasks independently of other colleagues or clients. This is not of course true of services like education, care provision or working with clients. In many jobs, workers can work intensively only for around six hours per day. However, while working four hours per day, many individuals can perform the tasks that they would otherwise perform in a five- or six-hour working day. Meeting and social time is clearly reduced for part-timers, and many state that they are trying to do an almost full-time job part time.

Box 5.3   Arcelor, a model firm in the industrial sector

Past trends:
- in the 1970s, major crisis in the steel industry worldwide
- in the 1980s, lower retirement age (around 50)
- in 1988 early retirement was found to be too expensive and was scheduled to end 31 December, 1990. Other solutions had to be found. Two basic schemes were set up to improve the employment situation: (1) pay for skills (no departures, skills improvement), and (2) manage employment (no lay-offs after 50 years)
- in 1994, after a long debate between unions and management, agreements were signed to organize employment after 50 on a part-time basis.

Keeping production workers in full-time jobs after 50 could have entailed several problems:

- safety
- productivity
- absenteeism
- motivation

Positive results of developing part-time employment after 50 for blue-collar workers:
In 1994, the objective of developing part-time work starts to be implemented: from around 200 workers to over 3,000 workers at the end of 1997, and with positive results as observed through a survey performed by occupational doctors on the sites:

- decrease in absenteeism
- decrease in the use of antidepressants, anti-high blood pressure medicines, sleeping pills
- shiftwork less tiring
- greater satisfaction at work
- transition between full career and full retirement at the age of 60, while the age of retirement went up from 50 to 60 and early retirement costs decreased substantially.

And the future?
Facing the challenge of *diversity* within the workforce:

- men and women
- old and young
- various countries of origin.

Daniel Atlan, Human Resources Development Management, Human Resources Corp, Arcelor, Luxembourg, October 2004

Companies are able to retain in-house invaluable experience and know-how while paying employees only part-pay, which often more than compensates for older workers' higher wages.

Reduction of work time is also an ideal way of helping the older worker to maintain vital energy reserves (Figure 5.3). Indeed, it is when these reserves fall beneath a certain level that the risk of falling sick increases.

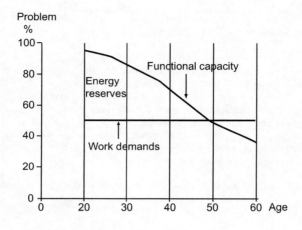

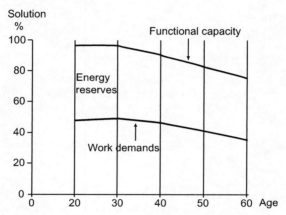

Figure 5.3   Basic problem and basic solution – the
relationship between human resources and work demands

Source: Ilmarinen (1999, p. 185).

High retention.   Senior workers working part time are observed to achieve high
retention rates, staying in their jobs longer. Thus, in many instances, employers
derive substantial benefit from this through reduced retirement costs.

Lower absenteeism.   It is also a fact that activities such as going to the doctor,
to the dentist or other necessary tasks are no longer done during work time but
during leisure time. Significant studies have found that when older workers reduce
their work time, absenteeism – often high at older ages (50+) – is reduced (for
example, in Sweden, France). The reason is that with age and changing abilities
absenteeism often increases when work is performed full time. Back problems,
for example, become more frequent, and stress is more difficult to cope with. As
a consequence, with diminishing energy reserves work demands lead to longer
recuperation time.

Company examples. In French firms participating in the partial early retirement programme (PRP, see Chapter 7), out of the ten companies surveyed in the Rhone-Alpes region, at least three observed improvements in the absenteeism of their employees (Direction régionale du travail, 1998). Recent surveys in Swedish and British firms tell the same story. According to a recent assessment of British companies,

> many organisations report an increase in productivity, morale, loyalty, recruitment, retention and a reduction in sickness rates when people are allowed to work flexibly, including working from home. Most flexible workers are homeworkers and they are on average 20% more productive than their office-based colleagues (*Financial Times*, 5 April 2004)

English firms retaining senior workers on a flexible and often part-time basis have also experienced savings on recruitment costs (four out of ten firms observed this (Age Positive, 2004)).

Improvement of age management and promotion of age diversity

Avoiding the rebound effect of early retirement. In French firms where drastic early retirement has been the norm for some time, the generation leaving for early retirement has had a negative effect upstream on the generation succeeding them. There has been contagion or a snowball effect on workers often aged no more than 45 or 50. These latter, almost all of whom are in good health, on seeing their older colleagues leave the company at a relatively early age, lose all motivation to take on more training or reappraise their career paths and opportunities – early retirement has had a 'rebound effect' (Guillemard, 2003) on the younger cohort of workers.

Better age management for all staff. Moreover, employers know that they must adapt management to an ageing workforce and that career planning, training until end of career and employment of older workers, that is, end-of-career management, are becoming priority issues. More generally, it is occupational life as a whole that is being re-examined so that its cycle be adapted to the abilities and needs of the lifelong worker.

Reducing the work time of the older worker also allows for better age management, younger colleagues being able to be given the promotion they expect and often deserve. Having teams of young and senior workers, of men and women, of various ethnic origins, that mix the abilities of older and younger workers and promote diversity within the firm, has become an important management strategy with benefits for team spirit and hence for productivity. The labour force within a firm is indivisible, and, for example, maintaining high motivation in a category of workers, like seniors, can have a positive effect on morale and motivation throughout the staff.

Company examples. French firms that develop part-time work at end of career have been able to rejuvenate their age pyramid and promote mobility (Direction générale, 1998) with positive effects. Another consideration is the firm's image as a 'good' employer. This has been important especially in countries like the UK and Finland where there has been a massive campaign of age awareness and an employers' code of conduct. Out of ten British firms surveyed, six mentioned this point (Age Positive, 2004).

Better match between customer needs and workers' age and experience

With the ageing of the population, it is important especially in the service sector to match customers and workers better. In a number of services, like banking, insurance and health care, customers are more often than not reassured when face to face with an experienced member of staff and a person who, consciously or not, shares the customer's values, norms and attitudes. Older employees in their contact with the client are often much more sensitive to, and familiar with, the latter's needs and preferences. It is not that younger employees are incapable of skills of this kind, but the older customer is often reassured by the presence of someone who has had something of the same experience of life. In France, for example, in beauty shops women under 40 years have difficulty in finding employment; it is important for the customer, most often over 45 years, to have tangible evidence of how quality aesthetic care and products can keep people in good shape.

Company examples.   Of ten companies surveyed in Britain, half mention the better match of workers and customers as very important (Age Positive, 2004). One firm concluded that

> from a business perspective, flexible retirement and the subsequent retention of older colleagues improves the employee age profile and helps gain commercial advantages associated with age diversity. These advantages include better communication and an understanding of the needs of customers of all ages. (Age Positive, 2004)

Tutoring younger colleagues

Improved end-of-career management also enables older workers to benefit from tutoring time with younger colleagues. Tutoring younger colleagues can of course also feature as one of the functions of workers at end of career on full time. But frequently a rethinking of the job content of part-time workers at end of career enables resource managers and staff personnel to free time for training duties. Training duty for older employees has thus proved to be an excellent end-of-career function, providing for a handing down of know-how, experience and corporate culture, and engendering good staff cohesion and team spirit.

Company examples.   In a survey of the Rhone-Alpes region in France, two out of ten firms stated that they had greatly benefited from this arrangement, while the same proportion obtained for a similar survey in the UK.

Advantages of part-time work or gradual retirement for employees

Employee demand for reduced work time after age 55 is usually very high, especially where financial conditions are favourable and if the workers are able to retain some of the social benefits of working full time (for example, pension rights). In the French scheme for early part-time retirement (PRP), it was found that many employees were ready to accept a drop in salary as a consequence of reduction of work time but were reluctant to go along with any decrease in social protection for the future. Much also depends of course on the nature of the job and whether it can be performed on a part-time basis without too great a loss of motivation and interest for the employee concerned. Frequently, posts with responsibilities are more difficult to perform part time. But, as we have seen, the nature of many service activities, as opposed to traditional manufacturing work, allows for more flexible work organization. Nowadays, many employees work autonomously, independent of their head of service, and working three or four days a week is no longer an obstacle to good productivity, to say nothing of the significant benefits to the employee of a reduced work rhythm and of more time to recuperate in activities outside the workplace.

Reduction of stress and improved health

Work has become in many ways more stressful mentally than it was ten or fifteen years ago (cf. Chapter 4). As mentioned above, it is now an established fact that, with age, stress is more difficult to handle. The reduction of work time, whether on a weekly, monthly or yearly basis, has now therefore become a key factor. Not only do part-time workers have more time to rest and to recuperate from tiredness, but they now know that they have more time to perform stressful tasks than before, and if working from home is part of their professional commitment, then they are able to fulfil their work programme in their own time. Stress is known to reduce the health status of older workers, creating a number of specific problems and generally reducing life expectancy. An older working population whose good health is not undermined by pressure in the workplace is therefore one burden less for the health care sector (Schumacher and Stiehr, 1996).

Enhanced job satisfaction and a transition between work and full retirement

Part-time work is an aspiration of a high proportion of workers in most countries, especially after the ages of 50, 55 and 60. Employees of all ages often have to accept full-time jobs because of financial constraints and commitments. With children leaving home and fewer material expenses, people in their late 50s can at last think of working less and of developing other commitments outside the workplace. Moreover, today people in their late 50s and early 60s often have elderly parents to look after – care of the elderly is now succeeding care of children. The part-time model offers people with ongoing care obligations a way of reconciling family with professional duties.

Surveys now show that workers aspire to a transition between full-time work and full retirement, and being able to continue in an interesting job by working part time provides the older worker with the best of both worlds. He or she continues to achieve job satisfaction, feels less tired, remains integrated socially, and still has income from work which in some cases can even improve pension rights for the future.

Box 5.4   Part-time work as a positive transition between work and retirement

At the Laboratoire Boiron (a well-known homeopathic medicine company), nobody speaks of 'older' workers or of 'senior' workers (above 50 or 55). They are normally integrated and have the same rights to continuing training and promotion as other members of the workforce. As early as 1976, the Director, Christian Boiron, adopted age management measures and the company has been a pioneer in this field. The management realized that most workers went through a very rough period when they quit the firm abruptly by retiring overnight. A scheme called 'Préparation Retraite' (Preparation for Retirement) has been in place for over 25 years now and is renegotiated with the social partners at specific dates.

On 31 December 2003, the firm had a staff of 2,222 employees, of whom 77% are women and a third on part-time. 150 workers are over 55 but this number will rise soon with the ageing of the baby-boom generation.

The scheme is optional and concerns all employees working full time and part time. About six years (usually around 54–55) before they end their career (depending upon the employee this might be at 60, 63 or 64), employees with at least five years' service in the company are invited to discuss their plans for end of career. If they wish, they can progressively reduce their work time in preparation for retirement. They benefit from a 'time-saving retirement preparation' of 100 hours (or 28 half-days) per year worked in the company, with a ceiling of 2,028 hours (580 half-days) to which can be added time saved over years. The resulting reduction of work time must be at least three hours per week the first year, and after six years employees work approximately from one-half to two-thirds of their previous work time. A diversity of end-of-career patterns is to be observed, and, of course, rates are pro rata for part-timers.

For a period of usually six years the scheme pays employees as if working full time. Within these six years, there are two main 'assessment points' during which workers discuss their plans with management and reduce work time both to suit their own needs and those of the department(s) for which they work.

This excellent transition between work and full retirement gives employees longer periods of rest and recuperation from work and a chance to reorganize their free time progressively in order to get perhaps more involved in voluntary, leisure or family activities.

As far as the company is concerned, the scheme allows for better management of skills and jobs; it also makes for a spontaneous system of 'tuition' between the senior worker and the younger employee who will be replacing the former, whereby knowledge and enterprise culture are transmitted from one occupational generation to the next in a natural, unhurried and customised fashion. The company insists on *age diversity* as one of the keys to a balanced and healthy team spirit within the firm.

The scheme so far has been mainly financed from productivity increases and has thus not altered other social benefits. The company has not received public subsidies. The scheme appears to have been satisfactory for both employees and management.

Renée Husson, Human Resources Manager, Laboratoire Boiron, Lyon, France, September 2004, and 'Depuis 1976, les salariés de Boiron préparent leur retraite en douceur', Le Monde, 15 January 2004

Improvement of social integration

Work is nowadays an important part of most peoples' social life. Since part-time work enables older workers to continue working much later in life than they would otherwise do, at the same time it enables them to continue to enjoy the social integration that the workplace affords.

However, when working full time, people have little time or opportunity to become socially integrated elsewhere – in their residential area, or in associative, family, sports and cultural activities outside their place of work. Part-time work, however, provides them with a period during which to adjust to greater spare time, to new interests and activities, and to make new contacts. It thereby eases, organizationally as well as psychologically, the transition from full-time work to full-time retirement.

Advantages for the community of part-time work or gradual retirement

On top of the benefits already mentioned in terms of the health, satisfaction and integration of older employees, there are three main advantages of part-time work for the community itself: greater social contribution receipts and taxes, the avoidance of black market employment and the development of voluntary activities.

More pension contribution receipts

Suffice to repeat here that part-time work allows for a reversal of early retirement and in the longer term a more widespread extension of work-life. It thus helps shift some of the financial load away from our pension insurance schemes and welfare systems. It is crucial that work-life be extended to match the continuous increase in life/health expectancy, if our welfare systems are not going to collapse.

Avoiding black market employment

Currently we observe a certain amount of undeclared work by workers over the pension age or performed by older persons who are officially unemployed or disabled. The reason is that employment is all too often overtaxed in European countries and that many workers, especially the self-employed or those in service professions, continue temporarily part-time, part-week or part-year work while drawing pension or alternative social benefits.

This situation is quite widespread in particular in the southern European countries – Italy, Spain, Portugal and France – where it is not unusual to see older craftsmen, farmers, nurses or consultants continue occasional work. For example, according to the OECD, there was an increase in black market employment in the 1990s, and in 2000–2001, black market employment was reckoned to be as high as 25% of GDP in Italy, around 15% in France, around 10% even in Austria and Switzerland (*Le Temps*, 17 January 2002).

This is one of the reasons why being able to combine part-time work with a partial pension is crucially important.

Promoting voluntary work

The phase of part-time employment at end of career offers the older worker an opportunity before full retirement to find or rediscover fields of interest for the future. In many cases the latter will include voluntary work and it can be assumed that such activities and the social participation they involve will continue during retirement. This adds not only to the quality of the individual's life but also to the general state of community life.

Implementation of the part-time model beyond 60

Gradual retirement

Our research work has focused on gradual retirement, whether before or after 65. Also known as phased, partial or part-time retirement, gradual retirement provides a transition between a full-time career and complete rest, and spans a period of between five and ten years. The worker, instead of working full time one day and fully retiring the next, can reduce work hours according to graduated schedules while drawing part-time pay, and in some cases either some form of partial pension (for example, in Finland) or a public subsidy which supplements income from work (for example, in Germany and France). The discussion on these countries in Chapter 7 will give some data showing the relative success of the practice.

In the past and for almost two decades in Sweden, part-time work was used to smooth the transition from work into full retirement for those aged between 60 and 65, and was successful. On top of part-time pay, workers were able to draw a partial pension. Depending upon the level of the partial pension (it changed over time), the take-up rate of the scheme would rise or fall. But whatever the result, part-time work was a way of shortening work-life which in Sweden traditionally was long.

Today, the situation has changed radically. There is now a need to reverse the trend towards early retirement and to extend working contribution years in order to ensure adequate pension financing in the future. Gradual retirement has been used to extend work-life beyond low exit ages. Although considered by some employees a 'second best' as compared to full early retirement, European gradual retirement schemes have proved positive for a number of reasons. First and perhaps most important, they have helped to change the prevailing mind set: workers have now come to accept that in future welfare systems will not be equal to financing retirement for 20 years or more. They also have provided a welcome transition between full activity and rest. Second, companies have had to develop more part-time opportunities, even for qualified workers. They have now experienced the positive side of part-time employment and are becoming more inclined to develop it further. Furthermore, gradual retirement has also gained the support of the majority of European citizens, as Box 5.5 indicates.

Gradual or partial retirement is distinct from the related concept of a flexible retirement age, where workers are given a range of ages at which they can retire but where the transition from work to retirement remains abrupt. Another transition pattern is intermittent full-time work at older ages. In this case, an older worker may leave a career job, be out of the labour force for a period, and then return for a period to a full-time job. Patterns of employment among older workers are of course gradually changing, as a significant minority of people – more women than men – now work part time before retirement (and even after). A minority of regular employees may move to self-employment, where hours are more flexible, or take

---

Box 5.5   The opinions and expectations of European citizens regarding work and retirement

As Figure 2.6 showed, the proposal that 'older workers should be allowed to retire gradually from work (for example, to combine a partial pension with reduced work)' gained broad support: almost three out of four persons agreed, 46% slightly and 28% strongly, while only 17% disagreed. Broken down by countries, support was strongest in Denmark (69% strongly, 95% altogether), Sweden (61% and 88%, respectively) and the Netherlands (48% and 86%, respectively). Since these are countries where partial pension schemes have been enacted in the past, it can be concluded that these experiences have been overwhelmingly positive.

The prospect of retiring gradually from work, according to one's own preferences and physical abilities, seems much more acceptable than extending work-life across the board by raising the statutory age of retirement. So this response can be taken as evidence that people are in favour of individual flexibilization of the transition from work to retirement.

Until recently, under the labour market conditions of high unemployment, a majority of citizens in the EU have supported the view that 'people in their late 50s should give up work to make way for younger and unemployed persons' (55%). Interestingly, there are strong cross-national variations in the response pattern to this question: the support for proposals to push older employees out of employment in favour of the young and the unemployed is strongest in Greece (91%), Portugal (78%) and Spain (73%), while in a number of other countries, a majority of the citizens is opposed to such demands: in Denmark (76%), in the UK (71%) and in Ireland (62%). This pattern of cross-national variations reflected differences in the labour market situation in the various countries, that is, the general level of unemployment and the unemployment rate among younger and older workers, in particular.

Jurgen Kohl, (2002) Institute of Sociology, University of Heidelberg

---

other jobs after leaving their career job. Some move from full-time to part-time jobs with their career employer. Taking a transition job sometimes requires finding a new employer. These transition jobs ('bridge jobs') often permit workers to reduce their hours by working part time for a period before taking full retirement.

The implementation of gradual retirement in several EU member states has provided a desirable opportunity as well as an efficient compromise in the conflict of interests between, on one hand, public social policy which is seeking to extend work-life for well-known demographic and financial reasons, and, on the other, company employment policies, most of which are still concerned to reduce the duration of work-life. Our research over the last few years has revealed that gradual retirement can be implemented on a wide scale and has considerable potential to facilitate an extension of work-life in European countries. By promoting work and age management at end of career, workers will be prepared to work later and continue to contribute to pension schemes, and enterprise will be able to reduce costs and benefit from increased flexibility. Gradual retirement can thus be seen to serve the several aims of worker, enterprise and public-policy maker alike, and to be a key factor for the extension of work-life without a necessary age limit. Working-beyond-60 policies have not been easy to implement. In most countries, and most of the time, they have had to be implemented in two stages:

- the first stage is in the short-term to provide a *bridge* between official (65) and effective ages of retirement (between 57 and 62)
- the second stage, in the medium to long term, is to flexibly extend working lives beyond retirement ages.

Part-time work as a bridge between effective exit and legal pension ages, sometimes called partial early retirement

People in general, and workers no less, naturally get used to advantages – leaving the firm earlier than pension age has generally been considered a social progress, although many workers suffered either from the lack of transition or from a sense of lost social utility – and, with the years, early retirement has been increasingly considered as a sort of 'new right' by the majority of employees in several countries. Therefore when social reforms and employment policies started to make people work later on a part-time basis, many employees put up some resistance since they were comparing their situation to that of many workers from earlier cohorts who had benefited in the same firm from full early retirement, more often than not with rather generous benefits.

This first stage is crucial also in the longer term since many policy makers in various countries, and more widely within the OECD, have advocated the need to increase the official retirement age by one or two years to reflect the rise in life expectancy. But of course increasing the retirement age makes no sense unless one is able to reverse the trend towards early exit.

Over the last decade, with the aim of reversing the early exit age and to provide for a transition, governments have adopted measures to encourage partial retirement before the age of 65, usually during the five years or so preceding the age at which they could receive full pension benefits. To facilitate this process, they have offered public subsidies to companies which set up measures of this kind and fill the freed work time with unemployed workers.

Schemes in Finland and France have been successful in both the public and private sectors. In France, by 1999 partial early retirement involved over 100,000 employees, of which over two-thirds benefited from state-subsidized schemes (over 15,000 were public sector employees). However, the number of workers concerned over recent years has decreased (see 'France' in Chapter 7). In Germany, by 1999 the gradual retirement scheme (Act on Part-Time in Old Age) concerned over 40,000 workers, and has developed further since. However, in this country, practice changed the spirit of the scheme. A car company, Volkswagen, started by making it possible to work part time for the last five career years condensed into two and a half years on full time with workers thereafter released altogether. This was called the 'block model' and further data showed that 90% of employees concerned in all firms opted for it (G. Naegele, in Jensen et al., 2002, p. 222).

Even with this development, we can conclude that partial early or gradual retirement schemes (before age 65) have been beneficial for workers and companies in starting to change early retirement culture and practice. Indeed, these schemes have usually obliged employers to reorganize work as well. When providing for partial retirement, they have needed to change other employment conditions besides hours of work, such as moving the employee to a job with less responsibility and sometimes lower pay. For some jobs involving teamwork, where the presence of the worker in the workplace enhances the productivity of other workers, a reduction of hours may be difficult. For example, it might be difficult for supervisors to take partial retirement while maintaining their supervisory position. Jobs differ as to the effects of reduced hours on worker productivity. One more obvious option would be to institute partial retirement in conjunction with job sharing, where two employees share a single job. And last but not least, partial retirement sometimes requires training older workers for new positions (cf. Latulippe and Turner, 2000).

Part-time work as an extension of work beyond 65

With the practice of partial retirement until 65 as well as the move away from the early exit culture, and the consequent changes in attitude and behaviour, more and more workers and companies will realize that work, in particular on a part-time basis, can be extended beyond 65 as well. Not only are shortages of qualified workers forecast for when the people born between 1946 and 1950/55 begin to retire, which is quite soon, but, in a few years from now, new regulations following pension reforms will be in effect and workers will begin realizing that they need to work longer in order to able to enjoy full pension benefits. Surveys have shown that many are already conscious of this future necessity.

Working beyond 65 had been normal in the traditional work environment. Farmers, craftsmen and other self-employed categories of worker continued to work in old age, but at a slower pace until finally they had to stop altogether. However, with social protection systems and industrial work these patterns have changed drastically. Today, according to the EU Labour Force Survey 2002, in the EU, some 5% of men and 2% of women aged 65 and over were still working. There are large variations between countries, however, with 26% of men and 14% of women in this age group in work in Portugal – much higher figures than anywhere else in the EU15 – as compared with around 2% of men and under 1% of women in Belgium, France, Luxembourg and Spain. In between these extremes, a relatively large proportion of men of 65 and over remained in work in Ireland (15%), Sweden (8%), Greece (8%) and the UK (8%) – the rate being over 10% in Switzerland, but in each case the figure for women was lower.

In the EU, around 45% of men and 63% of women aged 65 and over in employment work part time. The importance of part-time work varies markedly between countries, with the great majority of both women and men working part time in the Netherlands, Sweden and the UK (over 85% of women, 65% or more of men), but only a small minority working part time in Greece, Italy, Spain and Austria.

Practice in these countries is, for the time being, mainly driven by financial necessity. In Portugal the need to continue working for financial reasons is much greater than in most old member states and explains the high activity rate of people over 65. Pensions do not cover the entire retired population and benefits are often low and have not always kept up with prices.

In Switzerland, working beyond 65 is more common among the self-employed and qualified persons. The self-employed work on simply because more often than not they have no second pillar pension (not as yet compulsory for self-employed). Where workers do have a second pillar pension, the benefits can still be rather modest since second pillar pensions became compulsory for employees only in the 1980s and rights are still not fully established. Another reason for continuing in work is a second marriage and family, and having children that are not yet financially autonomous.

Women often need – and this will be increasingly the case in future – to improve their retirement income, and also need to draw the latter for a longer period. This is particularly the case with divorced women and widows. In most countries, women's pension benefits are much lower and poverty rates are higher than among men. As a consequence, they continue to look for opportunities to remain in work after pension age, at least part time. In the UK, for example, 20% of women who reach state pension age have no pension entitlements. State pensions are not very generous, the average weekly income for pensioners is around £200 for men, and only £150 for women. Only a third of women (two-thirds of men) today are covered by occupational pensions. This rate will of course increase with new cohorts reaching retirement, but the process will be slow.

In Switzerland, women who have worked part time are not well covered by second pillar pensions which are compulsory only above a certain wage level (see 'Switzerland' in Chapter 7). State pensions are more modest than in countries which have higher contribution rates, such as Germany.

In addition to economic reasons, a minority of women with interrupted careers continue working because they have discovered a social identity and financial autonomy late in their career.

Indeed, there are other reasons for continuing in work beyond 65: interest in the job, for example, or the desire to remain socially integrated, or a wish to continue to make one's contribution to a company or to society. The phenomenon of self-employed workers still active economically after 65 is also quite common in intellectual functions. For example, in international organizations in Geneva, interpreters, translators and revisers are among qualified freelance workers who often continue their profession well beyond 65, almost always on a part-time or part-year basis. The United Nations and its various specialized agencies have a long tradition of employing experienced consultants on a freelance basis, and many are over 60 or even 65 and work on temporary or short-term contracts.

Even in countries where the official rate of people working above 65 is very low, such as France or Italy, one observes a significant minority of people over that age working temporarily, mainly for economic reasons often in craft and retail jobs (pensions are lower than for employees), but this temporary work is widely undeclared.

In Norway, the retirement age is 67 and it is not rare to find companies with excellent senior worker policies. In Box 5.6, we give the example of a big Danish firm which has been able to keep a certain proportion of workers until the age of 67.

Box 5.6 Senior policy at Novo Nordisk

Novo Nordisk is an international medicinal company with over 15,000 employees, production facilities in around eight countries, affiliates or offices in over 60 countries. Approximately 65% of employees are located in Denmark.

Novo Nordisk has a special form of management, the so-called 'Novo Way of Management', according to which Novo Nordisk is committed to the concept of the 'triple bottom line'. This means that a company should be not only financially viable but also environmentally and socially responsible. As part this special form of management, Novo Nordisk also has a policy for senior workers.

The Novo Nordisk senior policy is a farsighted initiative, which has the goal of ensuring the firm a continued high qualification level and worker satisfaction among the absolutely and relatively growing proportion of senior employees. Hence Novo Nordisk wishes as much as possible to retain and make use of the experience and knowledge which the senior employees have acquired during many years in the firm, and Novo Nordisk attempts to create conditions which ensure that employees remain active until retirement age. The firm is thus quite ready to devote the necessary resources to education and to ensure that a flexible approach is employed in adapting the workplace to individual needs.

This seniors policy is designed to maintain and develop the qualifications, competencies, productivity, flexibility and satisfaction at work of the individual employee until he/she leaves Novo Nordisk in order to retire.

Efforts are made to ensure that this senior period is properly planned for whether it concerns maintenance and development of an existing job, job change or earlier/later withdrawal. As part of this planning process, an attempt is made by the firm to convince the employee to remain on the workforce until age 67. The planning is supposed to be the upshot of a transparent and mutually beneficial process between firm and employee.

Per Jensen – Comparative Welfare State Studies, Aalborg University, Denmark, 2003

The foregoing considerations suggest that work beyond 65 today is a by no means marginal trend that is set to become significant in the future. Often, following encouragement from the European Commission, member states in the 1990s passed legislation to allow people to combine pensions with income from work, and some new EU members have also adopted similar measures.

The fourth pillar and the redesign of pensions

Let us now take a look at how pension schemes need some redesign if policies for work beyond 60 are to be at all successful. Continuing work in partial retirement invariably requires adjustment of the current rules of pension schemes to allow for partial as well as total payment and for the benefits themselves to be so calculated that partial earnings at end of career have a positive impact on such benefits in future.

The legislation of most EU member states in the 1990s improved the conditions for combining pension benefits and income from work. For the most part these changes have been positive for workers wishing or needing to work beyond 65. For the time being in most member states they receive full pension benefits. But in a number of instances, benefits are not increased by paid activity above pension age (if the requisite number of contribution years has been achieved).

There are, however, proposals (and the Geneva Association is a strong supporter of them) to the effect that receipt of a partial pension until cessation of economic activity should be encouraged as being very much in line with the need to secure sufficient resources to ensure adequate pensions for a longer retirement period in future.

It is meantime absolutely essential that workers see the financial point of working later in life in terms of increased pension benefits, and the European Commission has insisted that adequate incentives to work longer be put in place. Nevertheless, in redesigning the pension rules, a choice will have to be made:

- either workers above 65 years draw a full pension and benefits increase by only a small amount
- or they could agree to draw a partial pension only (say 50–70% of pension benefits) but draw a bigger full pension when the time comes.

At all events, the calculation needs to be more generous than that which is actuarially fair.

Another issue is whether or not there needs to be an age limit for deferring retirement. In some member states, such as Germany, Spain, France, Italy, Austria, Finland and Sweden, pension reforms have set no upper age limit. In others, such as Denmark, Belgium, the Netherlands, Luxembourg, Portugal and the UK, the scope for postponing retirement is only three to five years (European Commission, 2003a, p. 52). The Geneva Association's preference is for the first of these solutions.

The issue of basing the pension calculation on average (the 10, 20 or 25 best years), as opposed to final, salary is of course crucial, as we shall see in Chapter 8.

To date, the fourth pillar has been having a substantial impact in countries where pensions are low for a sizeable proportion of retirees. These countries include Portugal, but also the UK and Ireland. Yet in the near future the fourth pillar will begin to gain ground in most, if not all, EU member states, and especially in the new members.

Figure 5.4 illustrates the relative place of the various pillars in retirement income over the next 15 years. The first pillar share could decrease from 55% to 40%, the second pillar's grow from its current 30% to around 35% at least, the third might remain largely unchanged, and the share of the fourth pillar could grow threefold from its current 5% to 15% by 2020. Because of its usefulness in lightening the growing burden of pension financing in future, the fourth pillar is emerging as one rather practical way of responding to the formidable challenge of ensuring adequate pension provision for retirees in the decades to come.

Share of income from the four pillars, as a percentage of the total pension income

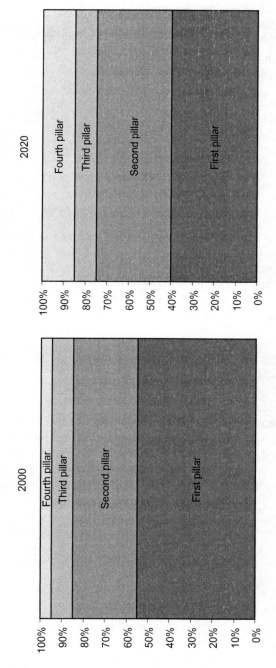

Figure 5.4 Trends of the fourth pillar model – a European example, 2000 and 2020

Source: Geneva Association (2002).

6
The Role of Supranational Organizations and Social Partners

International (OECD, ILO) and European organizations play an important role in disseminating information on various national approaches and promoting measures that can help member states in their efforts to improve their performance. In recent years the OECD and the European Union have adopted very similar objectives and recommendations for their members in the area of social and employment policies. In this chapter we shall focus on the European Union and summarize only briefly the OECD role, which has been referred to in other chapters (see Chapter 3).

Over the last five years the European Union has developed a number of common strategies and guidelines specific to the issue of employment after 60. These are parts of a wider framework to enable EU member states to better address the challenges of population ageing through closer collaboration on public budgets, employment and social protection reforms. In its development and promotion of policies for longer working lives and later retirement, the European Commission has used both the *best practice* approach and the *active ageing* concept. But it has also sought to underpin efforts of persuasion in the employment process and the open method of coordination on pensions by traditional legal instruments, such as a European directive outlawing discrimination in employment including on grounds of age.

There is a long tradition in Europe for developing and implementing economic and social policies in dialogue with the social partners, that is, with trade unions and employer organizations. In some countries, social partners have more influence than in others. In recent years, bipartite and tripartite dialogue at the national and European levels has resulted in significant agreements about *age diversity* in the workplace and better opportunities for ageing workers. Moreover, the active support of the social partners is seen as a precondition for changing well-ingrained practices of poor age management in workplaces and labour markets.

The role of the European Commission

As the executive arm of the European Union, the European Commission has provided member states with a wealth analysis which pinpointed the main areas of difficulty and explained how policies that raise the employment rate of all of working age, women and older workers in particular, are an important part of the key to sustainable pensions. The new working instrument, the so-called Open Method of Coordination, has freed member states to engage in close collaboration on sensitive issues of social policy while maintaining these as national policies and taking into account the diversity of national situations. Thus it has facilitated the adoption by member states of policies and action programmes within a more consistent and long-term framework. The main milestones in this process are summarized below.

As early as 1983 the Commission suggested guidelines on 'the principles of a European policy on retirement age'. But genuine possibilities for European policies only emerged after the Amsterdam Treaty and the final breakthrough came with the ambitious ten-year strategy for full employment and the transition to a competitive knowledge-based society launched at the March 2000 Lisbon Conference.

In 1998, member states adopted an Employment Strategy which *inter alia* committed them to increase the employment rate of workers aged between 55 and 65. The five-year 'Community Action Programme' against discrimination (including on grounds of age) and the European Directive on equal opportunities in employment were adopted in October 2000. Member states are to transpose the directive into national legislation countering discrimination by 2006 at the latest.

The report of the Employment Taskforce (*Jobs, Jobs, Jobs: Creating More Employment in Europe*, November 2003) chaired by former Dutch Premier Wim Kok, which prepared the road for raising active ageing to an absolute top priority for the EU, underlines the importance of 'a radical shift in policy measures, away from a culture of early retirement, towards comprehensive active ageing policies' along the following lines (so-called European Employment Guidelines):

- providing incentives for workers to retire later and in a more gradual way and for employers to hire and keep older workers by reforming the pension systems and ensuring that it pays to remain in the labour market
- promoting access to training and other active labour market policy measures for all regardless of age and developing lifelong learning strategies, in particular workplace training for older workers
- fostering working conditions conducive to job retention – such as recognizing the special importance of health and safety at work, and of innovative and flexible forms of work organization throughout the working life, including the provision of part-time work opportunities and career breaks.

As we saw in Chapter 3, EU member states are currently in the process of reforming early pension systems and labour market policies. However in many cases, the pace of reforms falls short of what is required to achieve the Stockholm and Barcelona targets for, respectively, the employment rate of older workers (50% by 2010, compared to 38.5% in mid-2004) and for an increase in the effective retirement age by five years by 2010.

The 2003 joint report by the Commission and the Council (*Adequate and Sustainable Pensions*) stresses that while there is no need to actually raise the statutory official

Box 6.1   Recent EU and EC initiatives for pension and employment reforms

March 2000, Lisbon: Adoption by the Council of the target of raising the overall employment rate to 70% by 2010; emphasis of the need to study the future evolution of social protection from a long-term point of view, that is, the sustainability of pensions systems in different time frameworks.

March 2001, Stockholm: Adoption of the 'three-pronged strategy' for financial sustainability (reduce public debt, maximize employment and reform pensions); new employment targets: 50% employment rate for older workers aged 55–64 by 2010; called for a report on how to increase labour force participation and promote active ageing.

June 2001, Göteborg: Definition of the three broad principles for modernizing pension systems: safeguarding the capacity of systems to meet their social objectives, maintaining their financial sustainability and meeting changing societal needs.

December 2001, Laeken: Adoption of the open method of coordination in the area of pensions: eleven Common Pension Objectives can be applied to all pension systems and will facilitate cooperation, mutual learning and some monitoring of national policies, under three pillars: *adequacy, sustainability, adaptability (modernization)*; recognition of the importance of reconciling social and financial sustainability.

The eleven common EU objectives:
Adequacy:
  1. prevent social exclusion in old age
  2. allow people to maintain their living standards
  3. promote solidarity between and within generations
Financial sustainability of pension systems:
  4. raise employment levels
  5. extend working lives
  6. ensure sustainable pensions in a context of sound public finances
  7. adjust benefits and contributions so as to share the financial consequences of ageing in a balanced way between the generations
  8. ensure that private pension provision is adequate and financially sound
Responding to changing needs:
  9. adapt to more flexible employment and career patterns
  10. meet the aspirations for greater equality of women and men
  11. make pension systems more transparent and demonstrate their ability to meet the challenges.

March 2002, Barcelona Summit: Decision to increase age at which people stop working (effective exit age) by five years by 2010; call for the reform of pension systems to be accelerated to ensure that they are both financially sustainable and meet their social objectives.

Policy response for increasing participation and active ageing in *Stockholm and Barcelona*:

  • life-cycle approach to ensure that present and future working generations remain in employment as they grow older
  • call for comprehensive policies in five crucial areas: (i) more jobs and better quality in work; (ii) making work pay; (iii) higher and adaptable skills at work; (iv) making work a real option for all; (v) partnership between government and social partners.

March 2004, Brussels Summit: Active ageing is highlighted as one of the three main conditions for delivering on the overall Lisbon strategy.

Author's summary, October 2004

retirement age, reviewing pension systems which often do not reward people who choose to postpone retirement might be necessary. Increasing employment rates of all is the key to better sustainability. However, higher employment rates will not of themselves be sufficient: even with the Lisbon targets achieved and sustained, a shrinking working-age population will cause economic dependency rates to rise. Increasing the effective retirement age should be at the centre of any reform efforts. Currently, most Europeans retire before reaching the statutory retirement age. If a one-year increase in the effective retirement age could be achieved without increasing pension entitlements, the expected rise in pension costs would be reduced by 0.6–1% of GDP in 2050. This means that a one-year increase in the effective retirement age would absorb about 20% of the average expected increase in pension expenditure in 2050.

The 2004 Commission Communication 'Increasing the Employment of Older Workers and Delaying the Exit from the Labour Market' (COM (2004) 146 final, Brussels 3 March 2004) states that although progress towards the Stockholm and Barcelona targets has been achieved, it is not sufficient; in particular, the employment rate of women aged 55–64 is around only 30%. Main recommendations are:

- member states must take drastic action. With the ageing and imminent shrinking of the working age population, older workers must be recognized for what they are: a *core* component of labour supply and a *key* factor for the sustainable development of the EU. Member states need to develop and implement comprehensive active ageing strategies and discourage early retirement, to make sure that work pays, develop good working conditions conducive to job retention, in particular flexible working arrangements
- the social partners have a major contribution to make in encouraging enterprises to take a forward-looking approach and in facilitating better and longer working lives. Active ageing is a *win–win* objective for employers and workers alike. Some of the key elements that social partners can support and encourage include reconsideration of the weight of seniority in determining pay, with a view to bringing pay more in line with productivity and performance; lifelong learning; removal of incentives for early retirement; and flexible retirement schemes, including gradual retirement.

The European Union supports *active ageing* through policy coordination in the area of pensions and employment strategies.

The role of the OECD

In the May 2004 OECD Ministerial Council Meeting in Mexico, but also in previous meetings and publications (cf. OECD, 2000, 2002, 2003a, 2003b), the OECD – while recognizing that population ageing is a good thing in that people are living longer and healthier lives – emphasized that policy adjustments are essential to sustain growth and healthy public budgets. Thus the OECD advocates policy changes with respect to early retirement and participation of older workers in the labour force.

Measures to cope with ageing populations should be taken particularly in two areas: (1) reducing the generosity of public pensions and, at the same time, enhancing the role of private pensions; (2) upgrading skills through lifelong learning.

The OECD reviewed early retirement incentives in OECD countries. A main finding is that ordinary public pension systems do not any more provide strong incentives to retire before the statutory age. To some extent this reflects the policy of strengthening the link between the number of years of pension contributions and eventual benefits so that pension systems become more actuarially neutral. However, there are other pathways to withdraw from the labour market at a relatively early age, in particular by using special early retirement schemes, unemployment-related transfer schemes, disability pensions and occupational pensions. While some of these schemes have also been tightened more recently, they still provide important fiscal incentives to retire before the statutory retirement age.

Labour market participation of older people differs widely across countries, and those with high participation rates also have high employment rates. This could suggest that supply factors are the driving force for employment. A number of specific issues need to be addressed to ensure that demand meets supply:

- wages have to be sufficiently flexible to adjust to productivity. If productivity declines at a higher age and wages are not adjusted accordingly, labour demand declines. However, where pensions are closely linked to wages just prior

---

Box 6.2   Recent OECD policy direction

In the OECD countries, policies are now moving in the direction of no longer discouraging employment of older workers (for example, replacement rate and the implicit tax rates have been calculated including recent reform measures). However, important incentives for an early withdrawal from the labour market are still in place, particularly in continental Europe:

- pension systems are not yet actuarially neutral
- implicit tax of all welfare programmes should be reviewed: (i) unemployment-related schemes interact with pension schemes and still provide incentives to retire early, (ii) disability pensions are still used as a pathway towards early retirement, (iii) occupational pensions also help to retire earlier (case of redundancies).

A broad policy approach can help to better adjust the effective retirement age to longer life expectancy and to alleviate the pressure from ageing populations on government budgets and on living standards of both younger and older generations. Therefore, the OECD suggests the following policies towards delaying retirement:

- distortions favouring leisure rather than work should be removed
- official retirement ages should be increased
- the implicit tax on continuing working should be reduced
- pension systems should be more neutral
- alternative pathways towards early retirement should be blocked.

OECD (2003b, pp. 147–53)

to retirement, there will be strong resistance to continue working for less, suggesting a need for reform of such pension systems
- if policy reforms manage to raise the retirement age, this is, in itself, likely to raise incentives for lifelong learning.

The role of European and national trade unions

Trade unions are heavily involved in the development and management both of the 'first pillar' statutory pension systems and of complementary schemes. This is particularly the case in France, Belgium, Italy, Germany, the Netherlands and Scandinavia. They have also been active in the debate and adoption of employment measures in favour of older workers.

European trade unions

The European Trade Union Confederation

The European Trade Union Confederation (ETUC) agrees with the main objectives of the European Union concerning active ageing and pensions. For the ETUC, a qualitative growth policy is a precondition to reach the targets set in Lisbon and Stockholm concerning employment in general and employment of older workers in particular. The sustainability of decent pensions – whatever be their design and type of financing – is dependent on the good performance of the European economy. Today economic growth in Europe is too low. Therefore the Confederation believes that the European Stability and Growth Pact needs urgent revision: it should ensure not only monetary stability but also economic growth.

The Union of Industrial and Employers' Confederations of Europe (UNICE)

Regarding the pension time bomb, the Union of Industrial and Employers Confederations of Europe (UNICE) identifies two priority areas:

1. Adopt appropriate labour market policies:

    Keep people longer in the labour force, by: discouraging early exit; reducing indirect labour tax; increasing the contribution period necessary to qualify for a full pension; making work pay through tax and benefit reforms; rewarding those remaining at work after the statutory retirement age; promoting gradual transition to retirement.

    Enhance employability of older workers by: adapting education and training systems to the requirements of lifelong learning; encouraging individuals to upgrade their skills; innovating in fiscal systems to encourage investment in training by individuals and companies.

2. Benefit from European social partners' contribution:

    framework agreement on part-time work (1997); framework of actions for lifelong development of competencies (2002); initiatives on employment guidelines; multiannual work programme of the social dialogue: initiatives on ageing workforce.

Box 6.3   The position of the European Trade Union Confederation

The employment status of the over-55 population is unsatisfactory; their employment figures falling short of the Stockholm goals. The gap between the average age of withdrawal from the labour market (the effective retirement age) and the statutory retirement age is significant and will require 7 million more jobs to close. Thus it becomes clear that the economy plays a major role in reaching the objective of higher employment beyond 60. Economic growth and the availability of jobs are preconditions to ensuring opportunities for people to work longer. Sustainable economic growth requires stable monetary relations between Europe and the US: in order to plan investments for the long term, the relation of the euro to the dollar must be known. We need to reinvent Bretton Woods!

The European Trade Union Confederation (ETUC) supports the Lisbon/Stockholm view that employment is too low and that the age of exit from the labour force should be higher. The dumping of older workers has led to a waste of human, social and economic resources. The ETUC favours an increase in the effective retirement age, but not an increase in the statutory retirement age. On the one hand, it does not accept the systematic exclusion of older workers from the labour market. On the other hand, it does not accept the European Commission's radical stance on generally discouraging early withdrawal. For the ETUC early retirement schemes should remain available as instruments to alleviate painful industrial restructurings if no other jobs are available and also as a normal exit route for workers performing particularly heavy or unhealthy jobs. Europe should devise policies that allow and motivate men and women to remain active until they reach the statutory retirement age.

Workers must be willing and able to work longer, and a carrot rather than a stick approach to public policy is preferable. Work should pay. If men and women work longer, that fact should be visible in higher pensions. Incentives should be sensible and substantial: for example, the reward for three additional years of work should be greater than the reward of one year. If people work longer, they should be given flexibility; working conditions should be adapted according to their needs and interests. Training should be considered a preventive measure and thus continuous; it should not start at 40 only. A proportion of productivity growth should go to training.

To speak of an increase from age 65 is a purely financially motivated proposal. Setting a fixed retirement age for all is not realistic. Neither is it a good idea. Workers should be allowed to decide when to retire. The main policies for moving forward include removing early retirement incentives and encouraging flexible retirement, legislation to counter age discrimination, awareness-raising campaigns to change employers' attitudes, guidance and training programmes targeting workers, and employment incentive schemes including active employment policies and special job offers for older workers. More attention should also be paid to often neglected policy issues, namely care infrastructures and services, if people, women as well as men, are to work longer.

Martin Hutsebaut – Administrative Manager, European Trade Union Institute, Brussels, 2004

UNICE globally shares the approach of the European Commission in its 'Strategy for Full Employment and Better Jobs for All', but advocates a sense of urgency not sufficiently reflected in the Commission Communication. Furthermore, it stresses that:

- member states should do more to encourage entrepreneurship and job creation, and should set targets for reducing the tax burden on labour. An improvement in the survival rate of new enterprises should also be targeted
- the countries that have made the strongest progress in terms of employment performance are those that have undertaken wide-ranging reforms. Therefore, emphasis should be put on a better articulation between the Employment Guidelines and the Broad Economic Policy Guidelines
- increasing 'activation' targets could perpetuate the predominantly quantitative implementation and undermine the objective of taking a more qualitative approach to this important issue
- increased investment by enterprises in the training of adults and for improved quality at work is imperative
- the autonomy of the social partners should be respected. Social partners have to be left the necessary space to develop their own agenda in this area. They have agreed on a common work programme for the period 2003–05, of which the main chapter is employment.

National trade unions – a few examples

Germany

German trade unions, and in particular the DGB (Deutsche Gewerkschafts Bund/ German Employees' Association), have played a crucial role in the debate and have stressed in particular:

- promotion of part-time work for senior workers and measures to fight age discrimination against part-timers
- organization of more flexible working schedules to meet older workers' needs
- continuing training for low-qualified workers.

The DGB president has advocated a more gradual transition between full-time work and full retirement, continuing training, part-time promotion and 'saving-time accounts', in order to increase employability of older workers.

The BDA (Bund Deutscher Arbeitsgeber/German Employers' Association) are quite far from the trade unions' policies, except on the item of saving-time accounts which according to them could well allow more continuing training.

In December 2000, they published a document summarizing their objectives:

- protection measures against the laying off of older workers should be suppressed. These measures play a negative role in hiring older workers
- pay must must be based on performance rather than seniority
- unemployed older workers should receive benefits for twelve months only, as for other workers; from 2002, indeed, a new regulation obliges unemployed older workers to continue looking for a job
- combination of income from work and pension from the age of 65.

Box 6.4   The European Employers Organization's Programme 'Proage'

Based on a number of seminars, the German, Danish, Dutch and Irish employers' organizations published at the end of 2003 a document, 'Proage', aimed at 'bringing about changes in the legal framework and collective agreement system to enhance the employment opportunities' (*Proage – Facing the Challenge of Demographic Change*).
    The main factors promoting an increase in the employment level of older workers are:

1. based on labour supply:
- guaranteeing actuarial neutrality at age 65+
- removing actuarial surcharges for retirement before 65
- incorporating the 'demographic factor' in statutory pension insurance
- reducing the level of compulsory contributions to statutory pension insurance
- limiting access to premature retirement schemes
- limiting access to alternative schemes
- making transfer payments less generous
- promoting age-specific continuing training.

2. based on labour demand:
- gearing age-pay profiles to productivity
- revising statutory age-specific protection provisions
- revising age-specific protection provisions in collective agreements
- providing tax incentives
- gearing transfer payments to employment criteria.

Proage – Confederation of German Employers' Associations (2003, pp. 47–8).

United Kingdom

In June 2004, the TUC (Trade Union Congress) held a national 'Pay Up for Pensions' demonstration in London, with the full support of the National Pensioners' Convention.
    The TUC is calling for:

- the basic state pension to be linked to earnings to provide a secure foundation on which everyone can build a pension
- a new occupational pension settlement based on compulsory contributions from employers and employees (with special arrangements for the low paid)
- urgent action to help women who face much lower pensions in retirement, including making it much easier for women who take career breaks to build up a full state pension
- more choice on retirement, not higher retirement ages.

This government has done many good things for pensions. There has been help for the poorest, and the new Pensions Protection Fund to protect those still in work. Yet politicians of all parties have yet to appreciate the depth of our pensions crisis and are avoiding the really radical action that is needed if large numbers of today's workers are not to face poverty in retirement. Fewer and fewer are members of good traditional occupational schemes, and pensions mis-selling, growing student debt and the high cost of housing have put people off making alternative arrangements. (Brendan Barber, TUC General Secretary)

7
Recent Public Policies and Best Practice in Selected European Countries

This chapter is divided in two sections: the first section analyses recent best practice of four countries (Finland, Denmark, the United Kingdom and the Netherlands) having adopted what one can call a global policy or an holistic approach with the aim of increasing participation of older workers in the labour market; the second section examines the case of five countries (Germany, France, Italy, Switzerland and Hungary) which have taken a number of specific steps towards the same objective but their policy is not yet global, and results have not yet been very conclusive. The case of Switzerland is different; it is one of the countries with the highest employment rate of workers beyond 60 but no official policy has been adopted so far. Each country is analysed in a similar manner so as to facilitate comparisons: first, general outlook; second, new public policies in the field of pensions, social welfare and employment; third, new practice with (when available) a number of results.

As an introduction to this chapter, Table 7.1 summarizes recent public measures taken to promote employment beyond 60 in European countries.

Table 7.1 Synthesis of employment measures taken to increase the participation of workers beyond 60

Employment measures

Information/education campaigns	• *Working conditions more suited to older employees:* Denmark, Finland, the Netherlands, Sweden, the UK For example, in *Finland*, following the National Programme for Older Workers (1998–2002), 60% of companies adopted a policy on managing older employees • *Voluntary action and ageing awareness campaign:* Austria, Belgium, Denmark, Finland, Germany, the UK For example, in the *UK*, in 1999, the government published a Code of Practice in conjunction with the social partners with a view to encouraging employers

to promote 'age diversity'. In December 2002, the British government released a Green Paper on pensions, 'Simplicity, Security and Choice: Working and Saving for Retirement', to help people to choose how they plan for retirement.

In *Austria*, a Job Coaching programme and a Come Back initiative have been implemented on the basis of the Social Partnership Pact for the Elderly of March 1999

- *Lifelong employment:*
  Denmark, Finland
  For example, in *Finland*, in 2002, a one-stop-shop was set up to underpin the labour market. Its purpose is to reduce long-term unemployment, ensure that people across all age categories maintain requisite employment skills and foster the reintegration of the unemployed

Incentive for continuing training

- *Subsidies for firms which continue training after 45 or 50:*
  Austria, Belgium, Denmark, Finland, France, Germany, Greece, the UK, Norway
  For example, in *Denmark*, employers in the public sector have developed senior-policy measures, targeting employees aged 45+, with the aim of strengthening an individual's qualifications and working capacities by means of 'lifelong learning'. Lifelong learning consists of theoretical and practical training, retraining and job rotation
  In *Norway*, since 1 January 2001, employees have had a general right to three years' unpaid leave for educational purposes

Subsidies for the employment of older workers

- *Employment subsidies:*
  Denmark, France, Greece, Sweden, the UK
  For example, in *Sweden*, since 2000, a subsidy corresponding to 75% of the salary is paid for two years to a company hiring someone unemployed over 57 for two years
- *Lower social security contributions for older workers:*
  Austria, Belgium, France, Italy, Spain
  For example, in *Italy*, since April 2001, workers and employers in the private sector are exempt from contributions to general mandatory insurance for old age, disability and survivor benefits once employees have fulfilled the minimum contributory requirements if they delay their retirement pension for at least 2 years
  In *Spain*, employers and employees are exempt from social security contributions for ordinary risks and for the unemployment of workers aged 65+ who have paid contributions for at least 35 years
- *Tax subsidies:*
  For example, in *Hungary*, a pensioner re-entering the labour market should pay taxes only on his/her wage and not the combined amount of his/her pension and earnings.

Reintegrate unemployed at age 50+

- Austria, Belgium, Denmark, Finland, France, Germany, Greece, Ireland, the Netherlands, Sweden, the UK, Slovenia

Table 7.1   continued

	For example, in *Greece*, a new law aiming at helping the most vulnerable groups of unemployed people, including women, the young (below 25 years of age) and older workers (55+), is under parliamentary discussion. The law will subsidize the amount paid by employers as social security contributions. Thus, for older workers the subsidy amounts to 50% of the sum to be paid for a period of 12 months.
Encourage part-time work age 55–65 and phased retirement	• Austria, Belgium, Denmark, Finland, France, Germany, Italy, the Netherlands, Spain, Sweden, Norway (between the ages of 67 and 70), Slovenia For example, in *Austria*, since 2000, partial early retirement benefit is available for women aged 50 or older and men aged 55 or older for a maximum of five years. Since 2003, it has been possible to opt for phased rather than early retirement, with a cut of at least 30% in working hours. In *Italy*, workers not more than 24 months younger than the age eligible for the old-age pension and with the necessary minimum contribution requirements, can combine pension and part-time work (for a period of no more than two years and until retirement age).
Anti-age discrimination legislation	• All member states of the European Union are obliged to adopt legislation by 2006 For example, in *France*, the 2002 law prohibiting age discrimination during recruitment bans any reference to age limits in job offers. In the *Netherlands*, the age discrimination law (in effect since 1 May 2004) has the following characteristics: (1) applicable to all ages: no minimum or maximum age; (2) prohibition of direct and indirect discrimination; (3) scope: employment, liberal profession, vocational guidance and training, membership of an organization of employees or employers; (4) half-open system of exceptions.

Sources: Author's compilation from various sources (see Table 3.1).

COUNTRIES WITH GLOBAL POLICIES

Finland – improving employment ability

General outlook

Contrary to other Nordic countries, Finland was marked by a pronounced early-retirement trend in the 1970s and 1980s. Early exit was possible chiefly through disability insurance. In 1994, the employment rate was very low for the 55–59 and 60–64 age groups. The general practice among the main economic actors was to permit early exit for workers over 50 or 55. As a result, there were low employment rates, a low educational level among workers at end of career, and discrimination and prejudice. Disability insurance was saddled with a huge deficit, and unemployment of older workers was high.

It should be mentioned also that, contrary to what obtained in other Nordic countries, part-time work was little developed in Finland.

Until 2020 Finland is expected to have the most rapidly ageing population of all EU countries. Already today, Finland has the highest proportion of 45–54-year-olds, which means that by 2010 it will have the highest proportion of the population in the 55–64 age bracket. In 2002, the employment rates of Finnish older men and women aged 55–64 were 48.5% and 47.2%, respectively, compared to the EU average of 50.1% for men and 30.5% for women. But over the four-year period 1998–2002, the employment rate of older workers in Finland increased by 10.1% for men and 13.1% for women, the increase being the highest of all EU states.

New public policies

The National Programme for Ageing Workers

Finland appears to be a very programme-oriented nation. Thanks to cooperation between several ministries (Social Affairs and Health, Labour, Education), trade unions, Employers' Associations and the famous Finnish Institute of Occupational Health (FIOH), a 'Programme for Ageing Workers' (FINPAW) was adopted in 1998 for a five-year period (1998–2003), with the theme *Experience is a national treasure.* Its purpose was to transform the ageing of the workforce into a national strength and to prevent early retirement and recourse to disability insurance. The programme was designed to provide positive results at a number of different levels: with the individual to enhance work ability, with business to put age management in place, within the workplace to develop a firm-specific community, culture and environment, and, in more general terms, with work-life and the labour market to build flexibility into working conditions and work schedules.

The programme covered three main areas:

1. *Employment*

   - subsidies to promote self-employment for workers from the age of 50 to 55
   - measures to stimulate development of part-time employment systems for older workers
   - flexible working practices
   - changes in regulations on pension schemes to diminish cost of ageing workers
   - development of gradual and partial retirement

2. *Training*

   - subsidies for continuing training of older workers until retirement and adaptation of training to mature experienced workers
   - encouragement of lifelong education strategies

- greater cooperation between social partners, training and research institutions to improve the work environment and adapt it to older persons (for example, information and awareness campaigns for human resource managers, line managers, different categories of worker, targeted training manuals, and so on).

3. *Information, awareness raising*, in particular:

- a broad-based media campaign designed to raise awareness of issues with the general public.

Some results and programme follow-up:

- the average age of exit increased from 58.8 in 1998 to 60.5 in 2002 and continues to rise (the target is 62–63 years)
- in 2000 over 20,000 workers were in some form of partial retirement instead of full early retirement
- employers and the general public are now considerably more aware of the problems surrounding older workers and of the need to implement the relevant policies.

Since 2000 an additional programme – Research and Development Programme for the Well-Being of Workers – has been launched to adapt corporate working conditions, especially continuing training and part-time work, to ageing workers at an earlier stage so as to have a preventive effect. The main goals of the programme are to:

- prepare employees mentally for change
- develop a community spirit within the workplace
- improve working conditions
- continue training and skills acquisition
- rationalize work schedules
- promote greater physical and mental well-being and a better work-life balance outside the workplace.

The provision of information about good practice as well as videos and handbooks should help with implementation within firms.

Finally, the Finnish Institute of Occupational Health has acquired a reputation in Europe and elsewhere for its numerous and authoritative surveys into the relation between age and work capacity. It has developed a number of tools for use in the firm and studied scientifically a wide range of variables affecting the worker. Chapter 5 lists some of these tools and Figure 5.2 clearly illustrates the interdependence of many of these variables.

Pension reform

The objective of lengthening the work-life by having older employees stay on at work longer was agreed to at the beginning of the 1990s, but it was only after the subsequent recession that the idea became a central policy goal. In 1999 this goal was incorporated into the Finnish government's programme, and in 2001 the Ministry of Social Affairs and Health identified it as one of the strategic focus areas for Finnish social protection policy over the ensuing decade.

Changes in early retirement legislation and regulation were introduced in 1998, and restrictions have continued ever since. There are three types of policy:

1. recommodification, that is, restricting any source of income which competes with gainful employment as well as increasing work incentives
2. cost containment, that is, limiting access to unemployment benefits, gradually raising the eligibility age for the early retirement pension, reducing pension provision, introducing a higher accrual rate for those who continue to work beyond the age of 60, and harmonizing employer social security (pension, disability) contributions
3. recalibration, that is, changes in the part-time pension programme and rehabilitation policy. For example, as the eligibility criteria for most early retirement programmes were tightened, the qualifying age for the part-time pension was gradually lowered from 60 to 56 years (but was raised to 58 years in 2003).

On 11 November 2001, a government bill dealing with a major reform of the statutory earnings related pension system was submitted to Parliament. This followed an agreement reached by the central labour market organizations. The proposals have now been debated by Parliament and, for the most part, legislation came into force on 1 January 2005.

The main goals of this latest reform have been to adjust the pension system to increased life expectancy, to postpone the average effective retirement age by two to three years, to minimize the need to raise the contribution level, to unify and simplify the pension system as a whole, and to support the ageing population's well-being at work.

Specifically, the main changes are:

- the retirement age has been made flexible between the ages of 62 and 68 years. Early retirement will be possible as of 62 years with a pension reduction of 0.6% per month (maximum 7.2%). The current early retirement rules have been abolished
- the pension will start to accrue as of 18 years and the pension accrual rate will amount to 1.5% per year between the ages 18–52, and to 1.9% per year between the ages 53–62. The accrued old-age pension will be paid at age 63 without reduction. If a person continues to work after 63 years, the pension accrual rate will be raised to 4.5% per year until the age of 68. In case of retirement after 68, an increment of 0.4% per month will be granted. Pension accrual will be extended to certain unpaid periods
- calculation of pensionable earnings will be changed
- indexation will be changed

- projected pension rights (in case of the invalidity pension) and their calculation will be changed
- right to rehabilitation will be granted
- a part-time pension will be granted after 58 years
- preparation for increased life expectancy through introduction of a lifetime coefficient: the purpose of the coefficient is that part of the increase in life expectancy should also be reflected in the number of years worked. This means that, as of 2010, the amount of a new old-age pension will depend on the development of life expectancy. If statistical life expectancy increases, the coefficient will decrease the amount of a pension starting in a given year. Irrespective of the pensionable age, the pension will be multiplied by a coefficient that corresponds to the coefficient determined during the year when the insured person turned 62. The coefficient is the same for men as for women.

New firm practice

According to the Finnish Labour Force Survey, most employees in Finland work full time. In 2001, only 13% of employees (9% of men and 18% of women) worked on a part-time basis. The analysis by age groups yields the following results: only 8% of the employees aged 25–54 were part-timers, while in the 55–59 and 60–64 age groups these figures were 16% and 31%, respectively, mainly as a consequence of the part-time pension.

According to a survey on part-time pensioners in the private sector (undertaken by the Central Pension Security Institute), almost all those drawing a part-time pension had the same job and worked in the same workplace as previously. Nine out of ten part-time pensioners felt they were part of the labour force. Only one in ten saw themselves as pensioners. The normal way of retiring was to shorten daily work hours, or to work two or three days a week. Part-time pensioners enjoyed as good health as those of the same age group who were working full time. Their self-perceived health was clearly better than the health of those having retired on a disability pension. This indicates that the part-time pension is seen primarily as an alternative to full-time work, not as a pension based on sickness. Experience of the part-time pension did not differ much between men and women, even though they were drawn from different types of occupation.

Chapters 5 and 8 include some aspects of age management developed and practised in Finland. Compared with average European firms, many Finnish firms today have a best practice concerning age management and good working conditions. The number of firms marked by a high rate of uptake of disability benefit is still important. However, concertation with the public and private insurance agencies led to a rise of the average age of exit into retirement or to applications for disability benefit for one or two years. These changes were possible thanks mainly to ergonomic improvements (adjustments to work stations and provision of breaks for rest and exercise) and to an enhancement of continuous training until end of career. In firms such as Ruoka-Saarioinen Oy (Reday-Mulvey, 2003), owing to that concertation, absenteeism fell dramatically and 'ageing' employees now enjoy higher levels of job satisfaction.

Denmark[1] – creating incentives

General outlook

Danish society is marked by a very strong work ethic, material or monetary benefits being far from the only reasons why Danes work. Indeed, high motivation in the workplace, as much as anything else, reveals the average Dane's concern to achieve self-realization through work, and identity through membership of the wage-earning community. It is therefore hardly surprising that the average age of exit among older workers (61.9 years for men and 59.8 years for women) as well as their employment rate between the ages 55 and 64 (65% for men and 50% for women) are relatively high compared to other European countries. Nevertheless, over the coming years, Denmark as well will be faced with a labour shortage, if unemployment, which has fallen dramatically since the mid-1990s, continues to fall. Thus, in Denmark, the combination of demographic ageing and labour shortage due to low levels of unemployment have made it imperative to maintain or increase the average age of exit among older workers. In addition, there is widespread interest in gradual retirement arrangements among Danes. For instance, recent data show that 54% of those employed desired to exit the labour market by way of part-time work or other types of flexible arrangement. However, the rules for flexible arrangements were often found to be complicated and/or knowledge of the existence of these arrangements was still too limited.

If older workers, therefore, are to remain in the labour market either full or part time, employment opportunities must improve. In Denmark, there is little expectation that anti-discrimination legislation will lead to any great change in employer practices or attitudes. Hence, efforts to encourage employers to change their recruitment practices have mainly taken the form of information campaigns highlighting the advantages of recruiting older workers. Various social actors – employers associations, trade unions and government agencies – have initiated this strategy. The employers' main concern has been the perceived labour-shortage problems in the near future. The public authorities for their part are more worried about the fiscal burden associated with early retirement and the potential risk that early retirement will lead to economic, social and political marginalization or contribute to the polarization of society.

New public policies

Information and campaigns for raising awareness

The employers' association in the *private sector* has for a number of years tried to persuade their member firms of the advantages of developing personnel planning

---

1. This section is based on an article written by Per H. Jensen (Comparative Welfare State Studies, Aalborg University, Denmark) in the Geneva Association, International Association for the Study of Insurance Economics, *Etudes et Dossiers* No. 268, April 2003, pp. 77–86.

which targets older workers and uses informational measures such as (i) information about the consequences of demographic ageing; (ii) the benefits of keeping older personnel at work (in terms of their greater experience and job stability compared to younger workers); and (iii) outlining a code of good practice towards older workers – all initiatives that were followed up during the collective bargaining negotiations.

Following the 1995 negotiations, most labour agreements now include 'social clauses' allowing the local creation of new types of job in terms of wages and working conditions for people with reduced working capacity. The 'social clauses' include older workers as one of several target groups, others being disabled people, and so on. The new policies use two types of measure to maintain people of reduced working capacity in employment by means of wage subsidies to public and private firms. The two types of measure are: (i) 'flexi' jobs, and (ii) 'soft' jobs.

Simultaneously, employers in the *public sector* have developed a broad variety of senior-policy measures, the goal being to promote and strengthen individuals' qualifications and working capacities by means of 'lifelong learning'. 'Lifelong learning' consists of 'job enrichment', theoretical and practical training, retraining and job rotation in order to broaden employee qualifications. Senior measures are targeted at employees over 45 years of age. Management is committed to continuously assessing whether there is a mismatch between the employee's qualifications and the job requirements. And management and employee are obliged to enter into a constructive dialogue regarding which measures (inter alia flexible and part-time work) can best help the individual employee enhance his or her prospects on the labour market.

Active labour policies

In 1998 and 1999, the National Labour Market Board discussed how to strengthen senior policy efforts. It recommended that activation efforts be enhanced in order to counteract long-term unemployment among workers aged 50–59. At the local level, these recommendations have led the Regional Labour Market Boards, which implement the active labour-market policy, to initiate a broad variety of activities including:

- informational measures targeted at firms to raise awareness
- persuading firms to retain their older employees and to recruit new workers from among the senior segments of the workforce
- advising on the possibilities for supplementary training for older unemployed
- increasing the activation opportunities available to older workers.

Changes in social security systems

The 1999 early retirement scheme offers the older worker considerable financial incentives to postpone early retirement. The government expects that the new early retirement scheme will increase labour force participation by about 2% among people aged 60–64 within the next three to five years, and by 4–5% within the next ten years.

During the 1990s, a new strategy emerged with a focus on reducing exclusion from the labour market and ensuring that people who have not totally lost their employability remain in the labour market. The goal of including rather than excluding disabled and older workers from the labour market was to be achieved by a multiplicity of instruments. Indeed, the system of financing disability pensions has been changed. Previously, the state fully reimbursed the municipalities for their disability pension expenditures. The state now refunds only 35% of local authority expenditure on newly granted disability pensions. The reduction of state reimbursement subsidies has functioned as an incentive to the local authorities to reconsider granting disability pensions. In 1998–99, the number of new disability pensions granted fell from 19,696 in 1998 to 13,435 in 1999, a decline of 32%.

As of 2003, these instruments were supplemented by a totally new approach in the treatment of disabled persons. The old criterion, that is, 'loss of employability', is being replaced by *'working capacity'* in approaching the problems of older and disabled persons. Attention is directed towards the disabled individual's resources and development potential rather than their problems and limitations.

Employer new practice

In Denmark, various methods have been used to analyse the extent and character of senior policy instruments utilized by firms. In 1997, for example, Jørgensen published a study of 914 enterprises with more than ten employees. The study showed that 68% of all enterprises had an active senior policy, though it is significant that senior policies existed in 85% of public sector entities and in 60% of private firms. Although this survey is a little old, it appears that the results remain representative of the situation in 2004 (Table 7.2).

Table 7.2   Share of enterprises (with more than ten employees) using senior-policy instruments

	Public sector	Private firms
Part-time work as an exit opportunity	84	53
Bridge jobs	43	38
Appraisal interview	54	27
In-service training	23	14
Courses on how to cope with early retirement	12	4
Senior Club	14	3
None of the above policies	15	40

Source: Jørgensen (1997).

Concluding words

The Danish labour market is marked by high degrees of 'numerical' flexibility (the average tenure of employees is short, and personnel turnover is high). Numerically flexible firms are thus subject to age-conditioned exclusion mechanisms. Nevertheless, Denmark maintains a high average age of exit from the labour market.

Box 7.1   Carl Bro

Carl Bro is an international consulting firm with 3,150 employees, sales of DKK 2,000 million, and 80 offices worldwide. It offers consulting services in environmental, industrial and marine, IT and telecommunications project management, building and construction, energy and agriculture.

In Denmark, the number of organized trade unions is relatively high. However, the workers at Carl Bro are not unionized, nor are they covered by collective bargaining agreements. According to the informant at the firm, this has functioned as a prerequisite for bringing about a very flexible senior policy. The purpose of the senior policy is to create motivation and possibilities for senior employees, so that employment can continue as long as possible with a content that is beneficial to both firm and employee, and equally to ensure that the transition from an active work-life into retirement becomes a positive experience.

The senior policy, which covers all firms based in Denmark, operates in the following way. In the year they reach 50, employees together with their spouse are invited to a briefing where they are given information about private and public pension options and about prevailing work arrangements for seniors. On reaching 55 years of age, the senior is once again invited with his or her spouse to a seniors' course. The senior is offered an opportunity to discuss and devise an individual career plan covering the following areas: (a) future job/career possibilities; (b) knowledge and experience transfer, (c) relevant educational and training needs, (d) work reduction options, (e) timing of exit from labour markets. The key features of the policy for seniors are thus gradual withdrawal (the feature most widely employed) and/or lifelong learning. Career planning for seniors should as far as possible meet individual employee needs while serving the firm's overall strategies and should be put in place sufficiently in time to avoid unplanned withdrawals.

At Carl Bro, a Seniors Club, not part of management, has been set up with as one of its functions the supervision and monitoring of implementation of senior policies within the firm. The Club brings together pensioners who have left the firm and seniors still within it – employees when they reach 55 are invited to become members. The Club is represented on the firm's InfoCenter, provides support for its members and promotes relations between the firm and its retirees.

Per Jensen – Comparative Welfare State Studies, Aalborg University, Denmark, 2003

Employment of older workers has increased in spite of early retirement arrangements still relatively generous in terms of provision and entitlements. Older workers are free to take early retirement between the ages of 60 and 67, and disability pensions may be granted on social grounds for people between the ages of 50 and 67. The Danish experience confirms that it is possible to combine extensive and generous welfare policies with late exit and employment of older workers.

In a report published in July 2004, the Danish National Institute of Social Research (Pedersen and Tranaes, 2004) presented its main findings following its studies of the labour market:

- on-the-job training in private firms seems to be the most effective measure to regain employment

- persons experiencing a high level of job satisfaction will retire from work later, while women especially will retire earlier if they are exposed to new technology or forced to take part in further training
- economic incentives will influence retirement plans; thus persons with favourable pension schemes will retire earlier.

The positive functioning of the Danish employment system has attracted the attention of the OECD (OECD 2003b, 2004). Denmark is described as an interesting combination of high labour market dynamism and relatively high social protection – the so-called *flexicurity* approach – a combination of flexibility, social security and active labour market programmes.

The United Kingdom[2] – convincing employers

General outlook

In the UK, in 2002, the employment rate of workers aged between 55 and 64 was 62.6% for men and 44.7% for women. This is considerably above the EU average (50.1% for men, 30.5% for women). Also, older workers in the UK have lower employment and higher inactivity rates than those of the 15–64-year-old population as a whole.

According to data produced by the Third Age Employment Network, nine out of ten who start job hunting aged over 50 give up within twelve months. Eight out of ten who are made redundant at 50+ never work again on a regular basis. The reverse is true of those under 50. Those who do get back to work at age 50+ have to settle for an average drop in pay of 27% (cf. *Journal of the Pre-Retirement Association*, Vol. 3, Issue 3, March 2004, p. 7).

To reverse these trends, over the last decade, UK policy makers have begun to implement policies designed to promote employment of older workers. In fact, a new policy emphasis on inclusion of older workers had already begun to emerge at the end of the 1980s. But there was little evidence that the policies that were introduced – wage subsidies, education campaigns for employers, removal of age barriers to government training programmes and changes to state pension rules – had much impact on the labour force participation rates of older workers.

The recent programmes have included: 'Age Positive', 'New Deal 50 Plus', 'Workforce Development and Success for All', a new pilot scheme 'Pathways to Work' to help 50+ on incapacity benefits to return to work, and a further 50 pilot schemes to test ways of reaching the economically inactive. A merger of the Department of Social Security and the Employment Department has since 2001 given rise to the Department for Work and Pensions (DWP), with specific responsibility for a policy for people aged 50 and over.

2. This section is based on an article written by Dr. P. Taylor (Cambridge Interdisciplinary Research Centre on Ageing, University of Cambridge) in the Geneva Association, International Association for the Study of Insurance Economics, *The Four Pillars*, Newsletter No. 32, February 2003, Geneva, pp. 4–7.

One important battleground in the debate on older workers in the UK over the last decade has been that of legislation versus voluntary codes and education in overcoming workplace age barriers. Throughout the 1990s the government firmly ruled out legislation, despite lobbying from among other groups representing older people. However, the EU Directive for Equal Treatment in Employment now obliges governments to legislate to prohibit age discrimination by 2006. As a first step, the government has been consulting widely about the issues the directive raises. It has set up an advisory group made up of members of employers' organizations, trade unions and groups representative of older and retired persons. The Department of Trade and Industry has responsibility for drafting the legislation.

New public policies

A code of practice on age diversity

Following consultation, the Government's *Code of Practice on Age Diversity* was launched in the spring of 1999 and accompanied by a media campaign. To date, 68,000 copies have been issued. The code sets out the principles of non-age-biased employment practices. Included is guidance on the application of the principles and examples of best practice. However, research indicates that the code has had a limited impact. Although half of the employers surveyed were aware of the code, only 9% were using it. More representatives of larger companies had seen a copy of the code – one in five larger employers compared to one in twelve smaller employers. A very small number of companies stated that they had changed policies as a result of the code.

In addition to publishing its code of practice on age diversity the government has banned upper age limits in recruitment advertisements in official job centres. In 1998 it also committed itself to publish annual Key Indicators showing the position of older workers in the labour market. Since 2000 the government has run *Age Diversity in Recruitment Awards of Excellence* and has aimed to raise awareness of the issue in specific sectors via the placement of articles in trade publications and more broadly via articles in the general business and regional press.

New Deal 50 Plus

In April 2000 it also implemented a new programme for non-working older people – *New Deal 50 Plus* – which aims to provide them with the practical assistance and support needed to compete effectively in the labour market. It offers employment advice to non-employed older people who have been claiming benefits for at least six months or more and who wish to return to work. The programme is voluntary and is open to people inactive on benefits as well as those who are registered unemployed. A wide range of practical help from a personal adviser is available: help with job-search skills, costs for travelling to interviews, work-based learning for adults and work trials. There is also a range of help specifically for people with disabilities. It pays an Employment Credit – an extra £60 a week, tax free, on top of a person's wage if they take a full-time job – £40 for a part-time job. This top-up money is paid directly to the employee, not the employer. *New Deal 50 Plus* guarantees a take home wage of at least £180 a week (over £9,300 a year) for the first year of work in the case of full-time employment. The Employment Credit can also be used to help set up a small business. An in-work Training Grant of up to £750 is also available.

There has been a steady increase in the take up of *New Deal 50 Plus* since April 2000. In 2002, the total was of 50,000 workers, two-thirds of clients being men. Two-thirds move into full-time employment but almost one-third move into part-time employment. The main element of the programme was felt to be the Employment Credit, about which views were positive. Clients felt that it was an incentive to take low-paid work both in terms of level and reliability of income. While the level of the credit was considered acceptable there were concerns that it only lasted for one year. Few had heard of or were interested in the training grant element of the programme. The main factors influencing whether or not a client had entered work were that they were aged 55 or younger, female, that they had not had a long spell of previous unemployment, and that the availability of the Employment Credit was a decisive factor in persuading them to take a job with a lower wage. Regarding what they thought they would do after the credit ended, 40% of clients felt they would probably remain in the job, 11% felt that they would return to benefits, while the rest had plans to remain in work and increase their earnings.

Age Positive initiative

The *Age Positive* website (<www.agepositive.gov.uk>) was launched in 2001 and comprises a variety of informative and interactive features including: employer case studies (see below), a discussion forum, advice and guidance, updates on the government's *Age Positive* campaign and progress towards legislation. The *Second Chance* website (<www.dfee.gov.uk/secondchances>) provides advice and guidance to older workers wishing to undertake learning activities.

Social security policies

The UK is gradually raising the state pension age for women to that for men (65), although it is not clear what effect such a move will have on the employment patterns of women aged 60 and over. In addition, to reduce public expenditure on health and welfare associated with an ageing population the government allows income from work and pensions to be obtained simultaneously. The 'earnings rule' which restricted the amount those beyond pension age could earn before their National Insurance pension was reduced was abolished in 1989.

The *1998 Better Government for Older People* programme established 28 pilot projects designed to pilot integrated interagency schemes tackling a range of issues including employment and lifelong learning for mature-age workers. The programme brought together central and local government, the voluntary sector, academia and older people. The programme's aims were to improve public services for older people by better meeting their needs, listening to their views and recognizing their contribution. This work has provided the basis for the recommendations contained in a report – *All Our Futures* – published in 2000. Its main recommendations for action relate to the need to combat age discrimination, engage better with older people, improve decision making, meet older people's needs better, and promote a strategic and joined-up approach to an ageing population. Although the programme has now come to an end, the BGOP (Better Government for Older People) Network, a forum for local authorities, other service providers and older people and their organizations, continues. It offers access to best practice and advice and support in developing effective solutions to the challenges presented by an ageing population. Recognizing that age discrimination impacts on many areas of policy, the government has also created a *Ministerial Group on Older People* to coordinate work across government departments.

A recent report commissioned by the government and prepared by the Cabinet Office's Performance and Innovation Unit sets out a number of key recommendations:

- develop a strategy for setting out its vision of the role and value of older people in society
- increase contact with and job-search assistance for people on sickness and disability benefits
- provide careers information and advice for older displaced workers
- raise the minimum age at which an immediate pension is payable
- increase the transparency of occupational pension schemes by showing the cost of early retirement in company accounts
- promote the advantages of diversity and flexibility in working practices through a group of 'champion' employers.

Each civil service department has to review the case for increasing its retirement age to 65.

The report recommends that responsibility for implementing its conclusions should rest with the *Ministerial Group for Older People*. The group is taking forward various strands of work under the banner *Life Begins at 50*.

Employer new practice

A survey by Reed Consulting of 3,000 jobseekers over age 50 found that 50% of them intended to work past retirement age. This is way above the findings in DWP Research which showed 23% of men and women reckoning to work beyond age 65. But in both cases this is well above the current post-65 employment rate which is just short of 10% (cf. *Third Age Employment Network Newsletter*, Spring 2004, p. 3). Research shows that the expectation of extending working life increases with age. In the 55–60 age bracket, for example, 75% of men and women stated their wish to work beyond state pension age. They wanted to continue working for fulfilment and for money. The companies that attract larger numbers of over-45s in the workforce are those offering flexible terms and conditions.

The chances of extending work-life are significantly affected by qualification. Those who extend their work-lives beyond state pension age in the UK represent 28% of men and 14% of women with degrees. They represent only 6% of people with no qualifications. Returning for 'push' reasons versus 'pull' was about 50:50

for people with incomes greater than £6,000. For incomes over £26,000 the ratio was 80:20.

Case studies of UK firms with policies of age management are available at the Age Positive website. Each case study outlines the company policies and identifies the business benefits of age management. In Chapter 8, we shall select a number of companies having set up age management measures, in particular flexible retirement.

A number of independent organizations have been active in the field of employment beyond 60 with positive effect. We shall mention here just two of the most significant examples. First, an independent employer forum, the Employer Forum on Age (EFA), which has over 160 member companies (employing more than 14% of the UK workforce), has a positive influence on the development of more flexible forms of employment for workers beyond 55 or 60. The Forum has widely disseminated the business benefits gained from employing an age diverse workforce and implementing end-of-career management policies. It has also made proposals to the government for improving measures or setting up new measures or incentives to help extend working life. And, second, the Third Age Employment Network (TAEN) is an association of independent regional and local organizations and companies committed to combating age discrimination and championing the contribution that age diversity makes to business and a healthy society. It campaigns for better opportunities for mature people to continue learning, working and earning. Its regular publications, in particular its Briefings, are important in disseminating knowledge, guidance and new public and company policies and incentives. TAEN also make proposals to government as well as supporting the existing programme.

Moreover, professional organizations, such as *The Tomorrow Project*, the *Pre-Retirement Association (PRA)* and the *Chartered Institute of Personnel and Development*, have also performed useful research and counselling in this area, in particular regarding the management and development of mature workers and people.

The current debate

An important debate in the UK at present concerns the implications of the provisions of the European Employment Directive on Equal Treatment. The government was pressed to legislate against age discrimination in the provision of goods and services as well as employment and legislation was passed in January 2005. Some groups are also arguing for the legislation to outlaw discrimination at all ages.

Pension reform is high on the policy agenda. Advocacy organizations are calling for changes to current pension regulations to enhance flexibility and allow gradual retirement. In addition, the Labour Party's General Election manifesto committed it to investigate options for encouraging flexible retirement. In contrast to other European countries where government schemes have been introduced in an attempt to encourage gradual retirement, this is rare in the UK. Occupational pension scheme rules and tax laws have discouraged this, although the government recently published a consultation document which may be the first step towards encouraging much greater flexibility in retirement. In its manifesto the Labour Party stated that: 'To help bridge the gap between work and retirement, we will examine ways to ensure that people will be able to draw on their occupational pension and continue to work part-time for the same employer, phasing their retirement without compromising their pension.' However, in March 2004 the government announced a delay from April 2005 to April 2006 of the long-promised changes to Inland Revenue rules that will allow simultaneous earning from part-time work and draw-down of pension income from the same employer. Each year approximately 1 million people are denied the possibility of changing flexibly from work to retirement.

The debate on pension provision is also raising considerable controversy in the UK where income security on retirement remains more vulnerable than in most other EU15 member states. It has been pointed out that a combination of rising longevity, poor stock market performance, tax changes and clearer accounting rules has contributed to a decline in employer provision precisely at the time when greater savings are needed. In December 2004, the Taskforce on Pension Provision urged employers to reverse this decline with adequate employer-led pension provision and to increase savings from both employers and employees through the voluntary framework designed to restore some of the risk-sharing to employers. The Association of British Insurers has been calling for a new incentive for smaller employers to provide occupational pensions.

The Netherlands – encouraging atypical work

General outlook

The current ageing process and prospects in the Netherlands are not as drastic as the European average. In 2002, only 14% of the Dutch population belonged to the age group of 65 and over compared to 17% in the EU as a whole. However, it is expected that after 2010 the Netherlands will be confronted with a fast increase of the 65+ age group, faster than the other countries within the EU.

The Dutch recent experience of employment for older workers differs significantly from that of other continental countries. Summarized, over the last seven or eight years, like Finland, the Netherlands have been able to start reversing the early retirement trend and improve employment at the end of career.

Between 1970 and 1990, the employment rate for 55–64-year-old men decreased from 65% to 46%. The employment rate for 55–64-year-old women remained stable but at a low level (14% against the EU average of 26%). Concerning both sexes, less than one person out of three in this age group was active in 1990, the lowest rate in the EU. This low performance was the result of a number of generous institutional regulations, namely those for disability insurance, unemployment insurance, and early retirement, all of which have been drastically modified since the mid-1990s.

Major reforms were initiated around 1995 and accelerated under the second government of Prime Minister Kok (1998–2002). The decision was taken to aim at an annual rise of at least 0.75% in the net participation rate of people aged 55–64 from 1999 onwards so as to reach the EC objective of a 50% employment rate of this group by 2010. One important government publication was the 'Integral

Programme of Action Policy of the Elderly 1995–1998', which boldly proclaimed that 'age discrimination must be combated'. Since 1999, the prohibition includes 'recruitment, selection, work-related training, education and promotion'. The most recent legislation, which came into force in May 2004, is even more inclusive. In 2000 the government set up a Taskforce on 'Older People and Employment' with the main aim of keeping people of over 55 in the workforce. It was mandated to (i) bridge the gap between policy and practice; (ii) promote changes in attitudes; (iii) promote good practices. The Taskforce started work in June 2001 and presented a final report with recommendations for policy in December 2003.

The second reason for change is the risk of future shortage of qualified workers, already existing in some areas (for example, in the health sector); and for very qualified workers, the shortage might mean a risk of increasing wages and therefore a long-term risk of job losses because of competition. As elsewhere, the general political context is also not favourable to more immigration.

The recent change has also been the result of economic growth, the so called 'Dutch miracle', which led to a high rate of employment growth. As labour supply did not keep up with labour demand, older workers were no longer seen as a threat for upwardly mobile youngsters, and Dutch employers were also less inclined to use exit routes for older workers (van Dalen and Henkens, 2002).

The last element of the Dutch development has been the promotion of part-time work for all workers at all ages. According the EU Labour Force Survey, in 2002, part-time work concerned 43% of 50–64 year old-workers, against 28% in the UK, 22% in Sweden and 19% in the EU. Among older Dutch workers, part-time work is more extensive among women (79%) than men (21%).

As a consequence, the Dutch employment rate of 55–64-year-olds increased from 30% in 1995 to 42% in 2002 (for men from 41% to 55%, for women from 18% to 29%), and the average age of exit from work increased from around 60 in 1995 to 62 in 2002.

Surveys (for example, Delsen, 2002) also demonstrate the cultural evolution concerning life-cycle and exit age in the Netherlands. In 1995, more than half of those persons surveyed hoped to retire before the age of 60. In 2000, this proportion was only one-quarter. Even if over half of workers hope to retire before 65 (27% before 60, 38% between 60 and 65), over a third believe that they will need to work beyond 65 (29% until 68 and 6% after 70). That means, however, that as in other countries, there is still a gap between the expected and preferred retirement age, that is, between awareness and willingness.

New public policies

Changes in disability insurance

In 1990, 14% of the active population was considered as disabled in the Netherlands. In 1992, the country spent 7.5% of GDP on disability pensions as compared to the EU average of 2.5%. In 1997, 8.6% of the active population was disabled compared to 5% in Germany, 5.4% in Denmark and 6.2% in the UK. The disability scheme has been a popular way for firms to offer older workers an early exit. The use of this scheme – not for strictly medical reasons, but also for labour market motives – was 'legitimated' by the social partners and government.

With recent reforms, the ability to work has been redefined without referring to the previous occupation, and a 'direct and objective relation' has been established between a decrease in capacity and sickness or handicap. Contrary to the past, partly disabled workers over 55 who cannot find a job cannot get full disability benefits. Active measures oblige those who can still work part time or in another job to go back and accept the proposed job. Other changes which have been introduced are a differentiation of disability insurance premiums and the introduction of 'private risk' for both employers and workers in case of sickness and disability.

Changes in unemployment insurance

Unemployment has also constituted a door for the early exit of workers, in particular for the 60–64 age group, and in a way even more so since the changes in disability insurance mentioned above. According to Delsen (2002), 30% of older inactive workers are unemployed. In 1999, 100,000 of over-55s were unemployed, while there were 170,000 disabled workers in the same age-bracket.

Because of reforms, one out of two older unemployed persons went back to work in 2000 against one out of seven in 1995.

Since January 2004, unemployed persons reaching the age of 57.5 years have been again obliged to register as jobseekers at public employment offices. This new regulation applies to older people receiving unemployment insurance as well as to those receiving a social minimum benefit. They have to accept suitable employment if such is offered to them by employment offices.

New legislation in 2002 sets up financial penalties for companies laying off workers over the age of 57.5. The maximum penalty can be as high as 30% of unemployment benefits calculated until the age of 65.

Changes in the early retirement scheme towards a flexible retirement system

Started in 1995, the reform of the VUT early retirement scheme (abbreviation for 'Voluntary early retirement') – previously very generous for wage earners and costly for the state – was done through collective bargaining, with the aim of making it financed by individual funding. This is a deep reform substituting private responsibility for solidarity principles (pay-as-you-go financing).

Although there are numerous schemes depending upon branches, one general rule is that the withdrawal of full pension is possible from the age of 60 with a contributory period of at least 35 years. The new formula's replacement rate is around 70% of previous wage (against 80% with the old VUT). In addition, the favourable tax treatment for early retirement schemes has been phased out from 2003. On the whole, the transition from pay-as-you-go early retirement schemes to funded pension and pre-pension schemes discourages early exit and encourages employment until 65 years (legal retirement age for both men and women) and over. Those working until the age of 70 can benefit from 100% of the latest gross wage.

In 2002, 95% of workers benefited from this new flexible funded system. The Dutch example shows that such changes, although difficult, can be made.

Pension regulations

It is well-known that one of the obstacles to later employment in the Netherlands was pension regulations, which meant that most often the pension was based on the last year's or years' salary. In most collective agreements, a reform took place whereby pension benefits are now based on average wages during the career contributions. In 2002, almost 60% of wage earners had already passed to a system based on pensions calculated on the entire career. According to Ruud Fux of the FNV Confederation, this new method of calculation means that it is no longer a disadvantage to go from full to part time at end of career.

Another improvement is that the transferability of rights from one firm to another has been increased.

Policy measures to encourage employment of older workers

To supplement measures reducing early exit, a number of measures have been recently taken to promote later employment. The most important ones are:

1. *2003 legislation against age discrimination*
   The 2003 law banning age discrimination at work (implementation of the EU Directive), in effect since 1 May 2004, has a much wider scope than the previous legislation. Its main characteristics are:

   - applicable to all ages – no minimum or maximum age
   - direct and indirect discrimination
   - wide scope: employment, vocational guidance and training, membership of an organization of employees and employers
   - 'half-open' system of exceptions.

   This means that the Equal Treatment in Employment Bill makes it illegal to distinguish according to age in employment: recruitment and selection, appointment, job-finding, vocational training and promotion. Age discrimination is permitted only in cases in which setting an age limit is objectively justified.

2. *2001 legislation on part-time work*
   To supplement the 1996 Equal Treatment Working Hours Act ('part-time law'), which gives equal rights to part-time workers and other workers on flexible contracts as well as the 1999 Flexibility and Security Act, which includes measures making it easier for employers to manage their companies flexibly while providing employees with job and income security, new legislation was introduced in 2000 on part-time work (Adjustment of Hours Act). According to this law, after having worked in an organization for one year, employees have the right to change their contract and work longer or shorter hours per week, unless the employer can prove this to be a problem for the business.

3. *Tax measures to promote senior employment*
   In 2001, a new measure was introduced to reduce social contributions for long-term unemployed persons over 50 (previously reductions did not come into effect before the age of 57.5).

Under the 2002 tax plans, an additional employment incentive was introduced for older employees under the statutory retirement age, and employers receive a discount on the disability insurance (WAO) premium for employees aged 58 and over to make it more attractive for them to retain or take on older people.

A number of measures exist also for workers aged over 65 who accept temporary work; temporary work agencies do not have to pay any social contributions for this category of employees and there are fiscal advantages for workers who combine pensions and work.

4. *New fiscal system for early and pre-pension schemes in Tax Plan 2004*
It is planned to abolish tax relief for early retirement and pre-pension schemes. The social partners also agreed that wages should be frozen in 2004 and 2005.

Collective agreements and position of employers and trade unions: reduction of working time and adaptation of working conditions for older workers

Since 1997 and even more very recently, the Dutch government has encouraged the social partners to debate various formulas to reduce working time and introduce a transition between full-time work and full retirement. One of the formulas allows workers over 55 to benefit from a partial early pension with part-time income.

In some sectors suffering from shortage of workers, such as education and health, workers in retirement recently came back to work with their level of benefits not being reduced. In the health sector, for example, 25,000 workers were called back over two years (2001–02).

In around a quarter of collective agreements signed in 2001 (compared to 8% in 2000), career planning of older workers was an important clause. From the age of 55 (45 in the retail sector), measures have been taken to adapt jobs to the changing abilities of workers. It is becoming more common to change jobs, to be assigned less demanding tasks or a less demanding (and paid) job. Often, there are particular regulations for employees to compensate the loss of earnings by keeping the same benefits in their pensions.

Moreover, a number of collective agreements include regulations to adapt working conditions to older workers. Many companies are now conscious of the importance of preventative measures, such as design of functions and ergonomics.

Other surveys also show that continuing training has become an important issue, not only for workers over 55. Thus the percentage of those aged 50 and over with a job involved in training in the Netherlands is above EU average. The metallurgy industry, for example, recently created a special fund for continuing training of workers aged over 50.

Since 1998, fiscal advantage has been given to firms who devote substantial funds to continuing training, especially for employees aged over 40, and this advantage has been especially important for small and medium-sized firms. In 1999, this type of advantage was made available for the public sector in the form of higher social contributions. Individual training plans are also becoming more frequent in many industries (Table 7.3).

Box 7.2   Managing an ageing workforce and a tight labour market: the views of Dutch employers

In Dutch firms, the most widely implemented measures to improve the employability of older workers are those aimed at accommodating older staff. Ergonomic measures are implemented by no fewer than 65% of employers. Additional leave/increased holiday entitlement for older staff is also common (62%), as are measures such as part-time early retirement or part-time pre-pension (51%) and flexible working hours (47%). Measures such as introducing age limits for irregular work and/or shift work, exemption from working overtime for older workers, and reducing the workload for older staff are slightly less common, but are nevertheless implemented by between one-third and 40% of employers. Prolonged career interruptions and training programmes for older workers are less common (12% and 21%, respectively). However employers said they were considering implementing in the near future training programmes for older workers (top of the list at 46%), followed by a workload reduction for older workers (44%). Reducing older workers to a lower rank with a loss of salary, commonly known as demotion, was found among no more than 7% of respondents.

Whilst 8% of Dutch firms (involved in this survey) did not implement any of these age-conscious policy measures, employers were found to implement an average of four of the measures mentioned.

K. Henkens, C. Remery, J. Schippers and P. Ekamper, in Henkens et al. (2003)

Table 7.3   Participation of employed people in training courses in the Netherlands, by age, 1992–2002

Age	1992–94	1994–96	1996–98	1998–2000	2000–02
16–24	29.0	43.6	29.9	33.3	33.6
25–34	34.8	41.2	43.6	41.2	44.7
35–44	26.3	33.8	41.2	38.0	43.1
45–54	18.4	28.0	35.9	33.6	38.0
55–64	5.0	20.7	23.7	23.8	29.1

Source: Fouarge et al. (2004).

Since incentives have been introduced to reduce early exit, it is considered crucial to reduce working time at end of career, even in the public sector. Trade unions have had an active role for teachers aged over 55. Surveys for employees from the age of 45 show that it is more popular to work less than not to work at all.

Trade unions have also promoted the role of older workers as tutors, since this measure has several positive effects: training of younger staff, improvement of staff morale and team spirit, and so on. Guidance on age management measures is becoming also available through the social partners.

A number of large employers have set up innovative age management measures (for example, Shell, DSM, Unilever, Siemens NL); smaller firms have also improved their age management policies (for example, the IT firm PinkRokkade).

Current debate

In the autumn of 2004, Dutch employees went on strike to express their dissatisfaction with government policy and the trade unions jointly managed to organize the second largest post-war demonstration in the Netherlands (in Amsterdam alone, some 200,000 demonstrators gathered on 2 October). On 5 November the government and the social partners finally managed to reach an agreement, called 'the Social Accord', of which the main items are summarized below:

1. *Early retirement and 'life-course arrangement'*. The government's decision to abolish the fiscal advantages of early retirement and pre-pension arrangements as of 1 January 2006 remains unchanged (excluding persons aged 55 years or more from 1 January 2005). The 'life-course arrangement' will serve as an alternative, which means that employees can save up to three years of leave at 70% of their wages. Thus employees who can make full use of the life-course arrangement can retire at the age of 62. Moreover, employees who have contributed to a pension fund for over 40 years will have the possibility of lowering their age of retirement to 63.
2. *Disability benefit scheme*. The Disability Benefits Act (WAO) will still be replaced on 1 January 2006 by the Act on Work and Income by Work Capacity (WIA: Wet werk en inkomen naar arbeidsvermogen). The new agreement provides full income security to people totally unable to work as well as to people who have minor chances of recovery. The latter group will have to undergo an annual re-examination in the first five years after commencement of a disability benefit. The age limit for the re-examination of current disability benefit recipients will be lowered from 55 to 50.

COUNTRIES WITH PARTIAL POLICIES

Germany – more awareness than willingness

General outlook

In the field of employment of older workers, Germany occupies a middle place. In 2002 the employment rate for men aged 55–64 was 47.1% (the EU15 average was 50.1%), and 30.1% for women (the EU average being 30.5%). Until the mid-1990s, as in other European countries, early retirement was governed by legal regulations. From 1996 when the first pension reform was put in place, measures were gradually introduced to extend work-life. The reform stipulates that, until 2012, the earlier pension pathways can still be used, but progressively deductions from the normal pension operate when the old-age pension is drawn before retirement age of 65. Various measures have been backed by financial incentives. The second pension reform of 2001, called the 'Riester' reform, generally provides for a reduction of full pay-as-you-go benefits together with a complement to the first pillar in the form of a second funded pillar. The whole question must of course be viewed in the broader context of the reunification of the two Germanys and of the drastic financial adjustments to which the latter process gave rise.

As elsewhere, the employment rates of older workers decreased in West Germany between the 1970s and the mid-1990s. After reunification and until the mid-1990s, early retirement with good benefits was common practice in both parts of the country. Unemployment for older workers was high. The reasons for this situation were mainly unemployment among the young and the financial shock of reunification (since 1 January 1992, the earlier West German pension law has also applied in East Germany).

Early retirement plans were the result of a social consensus arrived at through collective negotiations. Here are some of the main features of these plans:

- persons with invalidity insurance benefited from a full pension from the age of 60
- women who had worked 10 years over the last 20 years were able to retire with full benefits at the age of 60
- workers of both sexes could retire at the age of 63 if they had made pension contributions for 35 years
- unemployed male workers from the age of 60 could retire (if they had made pension contributions for eight of the last ten years); and from the age of 58 unemployed workers were not obliged to look for another job (the so-called '59er regulation').

However, there were also measures to help senior workers to keep working: for example, subsidies to companies helped them recruit workers after the age of 50 (for example, by financing 70% of their wage) on the principle that 'it was less expensive to finance employment than unemployment'. All in all, these measures were in competition with generous regulations and had only limited success.

From 1995 the employment situation improved in Germany as elsewhere, in particular until 2001. A number of steps were taken to promote employment of older workers, but, as just indicated, the pension reform itself was not introduced until 2001. However, unemployment rates for older workers remained high: for example, in May 2003 the unemployment rate for those aged 55–59 amounted to 11% in the western part of the country, and 27% in the eastern part. At the same time, the unemployment rate of workers aged 60–64 was 8% in West Germany and 23% in East Germany.

In 2000, only a third of workers leaving the labour market were of pension age. Because of restrictive measures for unemployed workers, there were 180,000 unemployed persons dispensed from looking for a job (from 300,000 by 1995). A fair number of workers also had left at the age of 63 after 35 years of contributory service.

New employment measures were taken in an industrial context where more often than not older workers were well protected against lay-off:

- the Integration Contract (or 'Social Plan') for categories of worker having particular difficulties getting back to work – among them older workers, with financial subsidies from the state

- in 1998, 1999, 2000, the social partners devised a Strategy for Employment (called 'The Alliance for Jobs'), Training and Competition: this coordinated, government-sponsored initiative, included measures for promoting part-time work and continuing training for older workers.

At the end of the 1990s, 30,000 out of some 500,000 unemployed workers had benefited from these programmes.

New public policies

Part-time early retirement (1996)

In 1996, the Old-age Part-time Act was passed whereby full early retirement was replaced by partial early retirement for workers between the ages of 60 and 65; and from 1998 this measure applied to workers from the age of 55 to 65. This measure was encouraged by subsidies from unemployment insurance (20%): workers who agreed to work part time (50%) could receive around 70% of their previous full-time net wage and their pension contributions could continue on a 90% basis. A company qualified for subsidies if it hired unemployed persons.

Collective agreements of, for example, VW, DB, Lufthansa, Preussen Elektra, have improved upon statutory requirements. In these companies employees get 85% of their last salary for working half time. They have been common in a number of branches – the chemical industry, the power plant sector and insurance. At the end of 2000, over 40,000 workers were on some form of gradual retirement and accompanying measures had been taken to encourage its development.

However, some collective agreements, including public sector employment, were later signed with what was called the 'block' option. This meant that rather than benefiting from part-time work for five or more years and thus having a transition between full-time work and full retirement, there was the possibility of working, for example, for two and a half years full-time and then retiring totally. A well-known example of an agreement of this kind was that signed by VW which unfortunately received too much publicity, compared, that is, to other agreements of the same type which were much more in the spirit of the 1996 legislation.

The main reasons for the relatively small implementation of partial early retirement have been:

- the difficult labour market situation which led firms and social partners to give priority to hiring younger rather than older workers
- the cost of the scheme for the companies
- the fact that most companies were not accustomed to developing part-time work for senior workers or, indeed, for most workers.

2001 Global 'Riester' pension reform

The German pension system has been based on a very substantial first pillar pay-as-you-go pension. In 2000, state subsidies to balance the system were estimated at almost €50 billion, that is, over 20% of the federal budget. The main aims of the reform were to:

- reduce the weight of future government expenses to balance the first pillar system, in the expectation that thereby this subsidy would not exceed 20% of wages in 2020 and 22% in 2030. To achieve this objective, public pensions are to be kept less rigorously in line with prices; compared with the current system, there will be a total reduction of 6% in 2030. The replacement rate will be at least 67% for 45 contribution years (compared to 70% previously)
- introduce and promote voluntary occupational (second pillar) funded pensions through financial incentives: workers have the right to have a certain percentage of their wage paid into such schemes (up to 4% in 2008) and this sum is not taxed
- give greater weight to child-raising periods in pension provision. Individual cover for women was to be expanded.

This reform was criticized by the trade unions since the legislation provided for no employer contribution. This is why several collective agreements were passed in the chemical industry, in metallurgy, and in other sectors with employers contributing 1% or 2% of wages to pension funds. The debate is currently continuing on the need for further reforms, such as raising the retirement age to 67 (Rürup Commission).

Besides introducing the principle of private and company pension plans, the 2001 reform also adjusted the retirement age for women to the retirement age for men, that is, since 2004 the retirement age is 65 years for both sexes. Moreover, the reform abolished early retirement resulting from a long period of insurance and early retirement resulting from long-term unemployment and set penalties for retirement prior to the full pensionable age. The reduction amounts to 0.3% of the pension for each month during which the pension is claimed earlier.

2004 legislation

The latest legislation, the so-called Hartz laws, will further reduce public pensions. Today, workers with a contributory period of 45 years can draw a pension corresponding to 70% of their last net wage. This replacement rate will decrease to 50% by 2050. Concerning older workers, the new law, which came into force on 1 January 2005, will change, for example, the former legislation against dismissal by employers, according to which older workers were protected by collective labour agreements. That meant that older workers were normally the last to be dismissed because younger workers were expected to find a new job more easily. In addition, it makes possible the employment of older workers on the basis of contracts with limited duration. The Hartz law also reduces the period of drawing unemployment benefits and the amount of these benefits.

New public and firm practices

The Transfer Project: demographic change initiative

Since 1999 and until end of 2003, the Federal Ministry of Education and Research (BMBF) studied important projects in coordination with companies. A total of 127 companies were funded to find solutions for ageing-appropriate personnel policies. The main topics studied were:

- the impact of demographic change on the world of work
- balanced age structures and innovative ability of companies
- ageing-appropriate work and personnel policy
- employment and new fields of occupation for older employees.

The main target groups of the transfer network were companies, the labour force, employers' and trade union organizations, employment services, social insurance institutions, politicians and the media.

Preventive measures for the employment of senior workers

Overall, the employment strategy has had positive results within the regions and in companies since the concepts of ageing and employment were integrated into the debate. Modernization and improvement of job design were also important items. Since 2001, there has been an increasing focus on continuing training.

Programmes of age awareness have been set up in order to disseminate good practice to small and medium-sized firms. Regional agencies have been created to promote second careers and self-employment. In 2000, the Federal Agency for Employment launched a campaign '50 Plus – They are able to do it' which is still running.

Social actors' attitudes and objectives

Chapter 6 has already defined the significant role of German trade unions (for example, DGB) and employers' organizations (for example, BDA).

Recently, the trade unions' association (DGB) has called for significant changes in the work environment and the adjustment of working conditions to abilities of older workers. In its most recent publication (DGB, 2004), the DGB stresses that over 40% of firms in Germany do not employ workers aged 50 years or over and that the employment rate of 55–64-year-old workers is relatively low (39%). In the DGB's opinion, an important reason for these facts is that recently working practice and organization in most of the companies do not match older workers' abilities. Older workers are very often psychically overloaded at the workplace and become disabled. In order to remedy this unfavourable situation, DGB advocates changes both in companies' human resource management and in the state's legislation in this field.

According to a recent public publication (DGB, 2004), companies should

- have a health promotion strategy to prevent diminishment of health conditions and so to keep workers in the labour market healthy until reaching retirement age or even after

- promote lifelong learning and ensure access to training for older workers
- adjust work organization and working time to needs of older workers, for example, part-time work, time accounts
- give workers more autonomy regarding the organization of work.

For its part, the state should

- punish companies who inflict costs on social security systems by abusing early exit schemes
- make higher contributions to the prevention of unemployment, for example, by supporting the training of older workers in medium-sized enterprises
- change the law on gradual retirement and forbid the use of the 'block model'
- create and finance employment programmes for the long-term unemployed
- support and enforce lifelong learning by law.

Box 7.3 Munich Transport and Tariff Association (MVV), Public Transport, Germany

Since 1993, MVV in Munich has had a so-called Human Resources Development and Workplace Health Promotion Programme, which aims at reduction of psychical load and stress among older underground drivers. In this way MVV wants (i) to reduce absenteeism among older workers, (ii) to make it possible for drivers to continue their profession until reaching retirement age, and (iii) to reduce or avoid conflicts with passengers caused partly by overloaded drivers. As a norm, after reaching the age of 49, drivers were usually employed in indoor service but this work was for the employees neither challenging nor financially advantageous.

The programme consists of 20 working days per year. Employees aged around 50 are invited to participate and are compensated with full salary. The drivers take part in six groups of 16 employees guided by a professional psychologist. The aim of the programme is to improve drivers' physical condition through gymnastics on the one hand and to teach them how to cope with stress by means of relaxation exercises on the other. Exchange of experience plays also an important role.

Since 2003, not only drivers but also other employees have been involved in the programme. The programme still consists of 20 days per year but only 75% of time spent in training is counted as working time.

In the last four years, 400 employees participated in the programme. On the basis of their experience, the programme was evaluated as follows:

- health condition of drivers was significantly improved
- there was a reduction in complaints about stress at work, back and heart problems
- older drivers took less sick leave
- team spirit and company atmosphere were improved
- drivers had few complaints about problems with customers.

Initiative Neue Qualität der Arbeit & Bundesanstalt für Arbeitsschutz und Arbeitsmedizin (2004)

Best practice companies

A company in the automotive industry, Brose (one of the best employers in Europe) – supplying products for more than 30 vehicle brands, developing and producing electro-mechanical components and systems for automobile doors with 7,500 employees and 30 locations worldwide – would like to take advantage of the ageing of its workforce by using skilled and experienced older workers aged 50, 55 or even 60+. Indeed, during the 1990s, the average age of employees was continuously decreasing and older workers could not help settle and train younger colleagues; traditional working methods became neglected resulting in a drop in efficiency. The new age-management strategy is not intended to be a response to the demographic challenge but rather to make use of the experience and knowledge of older workers.

Recent research and work on age management of 'ageing' workers has resulted in a number of publications which provide examples of best practice firms, for example, the Neue Qualität der Arbeit & Bundesanstalt für Arbeitsschutz und Arbeitsmedizin, *Mit Erfahrung die Zukunft meistern! Altern und Ältere in der Arbeitswelt* (New Quality of Work and the Federal Office for Occupational Safety and Health, *With Experience You Can Manage Your Future! Ageing and Older Workers in the Workplace*).

As an example, we summarize the practice of a firm based in Munich in Box 7.3.

France – starting to reverse the trend

General outlook

France is a typical example of a country marked by a very early exit culture. Young people often enter the labour market only in their 20s and the majority leave work before age 60, creating a greater paradox than elsewhere given that life expectancy is among the best in the EU (for women the highest).

In 2000, only 32% of active persons over 55 were in employment, which places France very low among European countries. The EU average is 41%, with 68% in Sweden, 53% in the UK, 29% in Italy and 26% in Belgium.

As elsewhere, the situation is also marked by rapid ageing of the workforce: the proportion of workers aged 50–59 in firms increased from 16% in 1995 to 21% in 2001. From 2005, the number of persons aged 60 will rise from 500,000 to 800,000 per year.

However, important measures taken over the last decade have led to a change in direction. In 1993, pension reform started with an increase in the number of contribution years to 40 for private sector employees and changes in the way benefits are calculated. In 1996, partial early retirement was brought in to replace full early retirement, and the scheme has had some success. Companies and employers organizations have been debating the adoption of age management measures, and some companies have already made considerable progress in this direction. Continuing training for older workers has also improved.

In November 2001 legislation was passed against age discrimination but, in contrast to what occurs on other EU countries, age discrimination is rarely the focus of public debate in France. There is growing concern for age diversity but integration of young workers is still a social priority nationally.

In 2003 a second important pension reform was passed, not without political difficulties. Conditions for full benefits for civil servants have been adapted to those of private sector employees and a number of measures taken to make the future of the pay-as-you-go system more viable financially. Later and more flexible retirement is to be promoted.

In 2004 a new law encouraging promotion of continuing training in particular at older ages was passed. We shall be looking at this below.

Although these measures have been important, one is bound to conclude that a global strategy for increasing the employment of older workers is still lacking. It is as if workers in France are perfectly well aware that work beyond 60 is needed both for pensions and economic growth, but at the same time wish to put off as long as possible the nettle of accepting later exit from the workforce. For the time being, the main thrust of public policy is to maintain older workers in employment until 60 or later, in many cases, that is, until they can benefit from a full pension.

New public policies

Recent pension reform

The law of 23 August 2003 on pension reform is intended to reverse the early retirement trend. Not only will the number of contribution years be 40 from 2008 (and 41 years from 2012) for all workers, civil servants as well as private sector employees, but the law which took effect on 1 January 2004 also changes a number of other pension conditions and as a result the terms of employment of older workers.

To promote work after 60, workers extending their work-life after their 40 contribution years will see their pension benefits increase by 3% per year. Furthermore, the mandatory age has been raised from 60 to 65 even for those with 40 contributory years. However, this mandatory age can be decreased through branch agreements, and such agreements have already been passed in the metallurgy, textile, chemical and pharmaceutical industries.

From 2005, there is no further public authorization of early retirement and the older worker lay-off tax will increase by 23.5%. However, over 200,000 workers who had started work at the age of 14, 15 or 16 will be able to retire before the age of 60. Employment of senior workers is one of the priorities of the current French government. The Ministry of Employment is supposed to provide companies with some of the means whereby they may more easily retain the older members of their workforce. The ANACT (Agence Nationale pour l'Amélioration des Conditions de Travail) with its regional agencies is working on age-management measures suited in particular to small and medium-sized companies.

Early retirement

Since the mid-1990s, public funds for full early retirement have progressively dried up; there has been as a result a marked decrease in full-time early exit schemes. In 2001, for example, there were less than 7,000 new beneficiaries with public support.

'Early retirement' currently tends to occur only in firms in economically-depressed regions and, more importantly, principally to two kinds of worker:

- workers who entered the labour force very young, through a public fund (ARPE – allocation de remplacement pour l'emploi). This scheme created in 1995 is now being wound up
- workers who have experienced hard working conditions and started work-life young can exit through the CATS (Cessations anticipées d'activité). In 2003, the number of beneficiaries of CATS (or CASA for the automobile sector) increased from 21,873 at the end of 2002 to 36,180 at the end of 2003. Up until March 2005, when the measure is to be abandoned, around another 32,000 salaried employees could be concerned.

However, on 19 December 2003, the UIMM (Union des Industries Métallurgiques et Minières) signed an agreement with four trade unions (CFDT, FO, CFTC and CGC) on the CASA, extending it until 31 December 2006. Thus a further few thousand workers could be concerned.

Of course, as in other countries, there are several large companies with their own early retirement schemes financed exclusively from private funds.

Part-time early retirement

Since the mid-1990s, partial early retirement (PRP – préretraite progressive) has tended to replace full early retirement. By providing subsidies and incentives to companies, partial early retirement for workers aged 55–65 has developed well in recent years. The principle behind PRP in France is broadly the same as in Germany.

The employee earns a wage paid by the employer for the part time he or she has worked, and until retirement receives for the unworked half-time a supplement equal to about 30% of the daily reference wage (up to a ceiling). This supplement is provided by the state under the condition that the firm fills the vacated time with new employees. The income is evenly spread over the entire period even in cases where the half-time is worked on a pluri-annual basis. This scheme had the approval of both employer representatives and the unions. Enterprise leaders view the scheme as an opportunity for offloading certain categories of employee, for rejuvenating the age profile of their workforce, for developing part time throughout their staff structure and for improved management of workforce skills. Trade unions and workers have seen it as a way of reducing work hours on favourable financial and occupational terms for flagging employees approaching end of career. Even so, gradual retirement is still frequently perceived as 'second best' by comparison with full early retirement which certain firms have continued to finance.

Gradual retirement also facilitates skills transfer and the supervision of newcomers who have joined the workforce to fill the work hours vacated by part-time gradual retirees – 'traineeship schemes' is the name given to such supervised apprenticeship arrangements, most frequently encountered in industry and construction.

Unemployment

The greater proportion of older persons outside the labour market consists of the older unemployed. Some 7.5% of active 50+ are unemployed (the average was 9.9% at end 2003), that is 366,500 persons, of whom two-thirds were registered at the ANPE (Agence Nationale pour l'Emploi) for more than a year. However, around 380,000 unemployed over-55s were until recently dispensed from looking for a job.

In December 2002, the renewed agreement between the social partners on unemployment insurance has for the first time lowered the cover for older workers:

- the duration of cover for the 50–55-year-olds is now 23 months, 36 under specific conditions, as against 45 previously
- the age at which one can benefit from non-decreasing unemployment compensation till retirement has been raised from 55 to 57.

The justification for these measures is that they oblige firms to abandon the practice of using unemployment insurance as a way of funding early exits.

Sickness absenteeism

Over the five-year period 1997–2002, the number of days that workers missed due to illness increased by 46% (*Le Monde*, 8 June 2004). The length of absence has also risen. According to an official study, the main reason for this increase appears to be the ageing of the workforce. One specific reason mentioned is that work rhythms among older workers are often the same as for younger cohorts. In the past, careers lasted longer but there was a tradition of giving easier jobs to older workers. In many companies this has ceased to be the case. This trend shows that ageing workers will need to find alternative exits from work if no adequate age management measures are taken to adapt to workers with changing abilities. According to the authors of a special issue of *Santé et Travail* (Revue de la Mutualité française), of April 2004, 'the frequency of long-term illness among the 55–59 year-olds shows that workers have to resort to sick-leave since early retirement schemes are more difficult to find'.

Firm practices

Part-time work at end of career

In 2000, over 42,000 (in 1998 the number was around 100,000) salaried workers from the private sector were on *pré-retraite progressive* (partial early retirement) plus around 20,000 civil servants. Over 60,000 workers were therefore benefiting from public subsidies. One should of course add to this number salaried workers in firms not benefiting from public subsidies but which had taken similar measures – no statistics have been found but these latter appear to be at least as numerous as the first category.

Firms in all sectors and of all sizes (building, manufacturing, services, hospitals, banking and insurance) have been involved. Examples of firms having adopted 'gradual retirement' schemes in the 1990s were: in the manufacturing sector, Arcelor (see Box 5.3, p. 87), Rhône-Poulenc, Aérospatiale, Total, Framatome, Elf Atochem, Péchiney Emballage Alimentaire, Péchiney Rhénalu, IBM, Hewlett-Packard; in services, banks such as Crédit Agricole, Caisses d'Epargne, supermarkets such as Casino, insurance companies, and other types of enterprise, such as hospitals and hotels/restaurants.

The Caisses d'Epargne et de Prévoyance, a group with over 40,000 employees, have replaced early retirement by part-time early retirement. Negotiated in 1999, this scheme has two main objectives: to set up new age-management and management of end of careers, and to provide solutions to a lop-sided age pyramid with too many employees in the 35–55 age bracket.

The ESSA (Emploi des salariés selon l'âge – Employment along with age) survey conducted by the Ministry of Employment in 2002 gives some insights into firm practice towards ageing workers. While 23% of establishments employ more than a quarter of over-50s, only 13% have a global approach to the ageing issue. This is the case mainly in large firms (200 employees and over) and in some sectors (namely banking, insurance and housing activities). More than a third of establishments having used early exit schemes say they are now looking at ways of keeping older workers in employment.

The new CATS scheme seems to favour greater awareness in firms and a transition to a new policy regarding older workers. In fact, currently firms have to prepare for when this scheme ends (it is transitory and will last for a maximum of five years), and manpower planning is mandatory if firms want to qualify for partial public support from the Ministry of Employment and Social Affairs. Two quite distinct examples are:

1. *PSA Peugeot Citroën*. This firm is a large car manufacturer. In 2001 it signed a collective agreement on improvement of working conditions (CASA). The aim is to reduce by half the number of hard jobs over the next five years. This concern is built into every stage of a car development process, from the design of a new model onwards. The CASA agreement includes new working conditions for older workers, mainly continuing training and flexible work time. The company signed another collective agreement in September 2004 on 'the key importance of diversity and social cohesion and of fighting all forms of discrimination'. This involves creating and maintaining a good work spirit between young and senior workers, men and women, qualified and less qualified employees, French and foreigners. 'Variety which is both balanced and comprehensive is an asset for innovation, performance and competitiveness' (*La Croix*, 15 September 2004).
2. *Thalès*. This is a high-technology firm. In 2001 it concluded a collective agreement on valuing experience and end-of-career management. This agreement creates an individual training credit of 100 hours and a double wage-scale (a new scale is aimed at encouraging horizontal mobility in a context of limited managerial positions). There also exists in Thalès a small unit, Thalès Missions et Conseil, which provides older workers with an opportunity to start a new career, by becoming temporary consultants. In December 2002, fresh negotiations focused

on better reflecting the experience of workers aged 50 and over who account for 30% of some 33,000 staff on the firm's payroll in France. This 'recognition of experience' comprised a number of measures: skills assessment; continuing training plans for over-45s; part-time work for over-55s and time for tutoring and for volunteer activities; gradual retirement as of age 60; promotion of internal mobility and an opening up of work functions.

Continuing training and lifelong education

The new Law on Lifelong Training and the Individual Training Entitlement of 4 May 2004 provides for the right to 20 hours training per year for all employees who have worked at least one year in the company. Employees having worked for two years in the same company will be able to benefit from a professional interview during which they will have an opportunity to talk about their training needs and desires. All continuing training courses and experience will be written up in a 'training passport' which will accompany all employees throughout professional life.

Companies of over ten employees will have to devote 1.6% (instead of 1.5% until 2004) to continuing training. This percentage is reduced to 0.4% in 2004 and 0.55% in 2005 for firms with less than ten employees.

Chapter 8, in particular Box 8.4, provides details on this new legislation and more widely on continuing training in French companies.

Entreprise et Progres report, 'The employment of seniors: the right to remain active throughout the lifecycle'

Entreprise et Progres, a think tank of important firms – industries, banks, insurance companies (including *Groupama*), and others – held regular meetings in 2003 to discuss the important issues of the ageing workforce and the need for new measures to better manage senior employment and diversity at end of career. The report published in June 2004 evinces a solid understanding of the new issues and identifies solutions to be taken in the near future.

The think tank's main proposals for encouraging employment until retirement age are as follows.

1. At all ages, to smooth out entries into and exits from the labour market (recruitment, negotiated exit, dismissal and lay-off).
2. Above and beyond pension reform, to develop and promote customized work-time arrangements for workers. Such arrangements also encourage the planning and realization of a second career.
3. Encourage those responsible for collective bargaining to ensure that greater resources are devoted to the older worker and to enhancing the employability of workers of all ages.
4. Bring the fiscal arrangements governing retirement pay into line with the conditions governing severance pay so as to remove any incentive to early retirement.
5. Move occupational medicine in the direction of the 'health' of workers, by promoting the prevention and detection of disease as of the worker's entry into

the workforce. Improve monitoring of the worker's general health and life-style, not merely of the latter's occupational aptitudes.

The think tank also makes proposals for promoting the worker's right to remain active throughout the life-cycle:

1. Allow all workers to combine income from work with a pension by permitting an unconditional return to, or continuation of, work after retirement age.
2. Reward retirees who remain active and continue paying their old-age contributions. Abolish the contributions of those not wishing to avail themselves of a retirement bonus.
3. Exonerate working retirees from unemployment and pension contributions.
4. Set a ceiling on sickness contributions (at the level reached for the wage average for the last three years preceding removal of pension rights).

Recent surveys of firms

According to a thorough CEGOS Study of 23 March 2004 (*Le Monde*, 31 March 2004), the number of French firms having already set up measures to face the *'papy-boom'* (the baby-boomers becoming grandparents) was still low, at around 9%.

The percentage of human resource directors who consider the impact of workforce ageing to be important in the short term was 57% as opposed to 48% in 2003. In particular, in big firms, 40% thought this impact was important in 2004 compared to 18% in 2003. An increasing number of human resource managers see the coming situation as a risk rather than an opportunity (2003: 22%). Concerning the future

---

Box 7.4   CEGOS survey of companies and end of career management

The recent CEGOS study shows that only one firm out of five (22%) is ready to recruit a person aged 50 or more, as against one out of three in 2003. However, small and medium-sized enterprises are more open to this opportunity (30%) as compared to 7% among big firms. Only 27% of firms are ready to modify their recruitment policy as compared to 39% in 2003.

However, there were some more positive results in the study: the need to set up a specific personnel policy to extend senior employment is better recognized; 11% of firms have already set up such a policy and 37% are planning it, which is almost half the firms, as compared to 30% in all in 2003.

The measures set up or that will be set up to motivate older workers and to allow them to remain in employment in the firm are mainly:

*   specific training programmes (53%)
*   work time reduction/organization (53%)
*   development of programmes supplementing retirement income (46%)
*   possibility to contribute more years to get full pension (21%).

'Le "papy-boom" apparaît de moins en moins comme un appel d'air pour l'emploi', Le Monde, *31 March 2004.*

departure to retirement of older workers (the baby-boom generation), they believe that this departure will be compensated by internal mobility (91% of surveyed persons, while only 20% mentioned recruitment). In the public sector, opinion was different since 87% believed that they would need new recruits.

Another less representative survey, a Gallup poll on 11 March 2004 (*La Croix*, 29 March 2004), included the question 'To encourage workers of 50 and over to extend their working life, do you think that it would make sense to: (i) modify/reduce working times, (ii) promote tutoring of younger workers by older employees, (iii) set up new training courses in new technologies?' Responses showed that 80% are in favour of (i), 77% in favour of (ii), 69% in favour of (iii).

Debate and experience: the example of a large insurance company

To conclude this section on France, the example of a large insurance company, CNP Assurances, well illustrates the current state of the debate in France and recent policies adopted or envisaged for the near future.

Box 7.5 Managing the senior worker, CNP Assurances

Although the age pyramid in CNP Insurance shows an average age lower than in most insurance companies, the social policy pursued by CNP gives considerable attention to the problems of extending work. Indeed, CNP, following a negotiated agreement within the firm, has put in place for the period 2003–2005 a pre-retirement scheme enabling employees over 55 under specified conditions to quit the firm.

This agreement contains a section on motivation of employees over 50 years. Moreover, a survey of staff between 45 and 55 years was made in 2003 in order to get a clearer picture of the aspirations, plans and any occupational difficulties faced by workers in this age group. Following these initiatives a plan of action was drawn up:

1. In 2003, a two-year agreement was concluded with an outside specialist organization which would assist employees as of age 45 to calculate out their pension benefits so as to get a clear idea of their situation. A survey showed that the significance of raising the age of departure into retirement was still not very clearly understood by employees, many of whom had great difficulty in conceiving of an exit later than those they had seen occurring around them in recent years. A study of individual situations shares the conclusion that awareness raising is necessary if workers are to be able to envisage the possibility of an occupational activity after 55.
2. In 2004, attention was focused on workers over 50 in connection with a campaign for individual advancement. Follow-up on activities for the over-50s is provided by the HR department: by mid-year, 15% of employees over 50 had received a counselling session on career mobility, and for 6% in-house transfers and career assessment with a view to occupational retraining or 'coaching' had taken place.
3. In 2005, two initiatives are planned:

   - a study of working conditions, especially of stress, since this issue appears to be of concern to senior workers. What is required is identification of the causes and levels of stress before proposing remedial measures to improve work conditions. The issue is clearly broader than that of keeping seniors in the workplace

▶

- for the lower qualified employee, the issue of recognition of skills and expertise acquired over occupational life was clearly a major concern in that it was this experiential capital that would make workplace adaptation easier and enable the individual to remain in work until end of career. The feasibility of setting up some kind of system for the validation of this experiential capital will be studied as part of the drive to improve occupational training in general.

A branch agreement is in the process of negotiation. It is designed to provide employees aged 45 or over with information about available company and branch training facilities. Moreover, employees of 45 and over will be able to benefit from a period of 'professionalization' – comprising a series of training initiatives designed to maintain and enhance their employability. These new initiatives will complement such measures as CNP has had in place for many years to turn the know-how of seniors to full advantage:

- tutoring of young recruits by experienced staff;
- participation of expert employees in the content design of training courses and help with instruction during the latter.

Direction des Ressources Humaines, CNP Assurances, October 2004

Italy[3] – first pensions, then employment

General outlook

Compared to other EU countries, Italy is characterized by huge spending on pensions (14% of GDP) with less resources invested in other areas of social protection, since pensions represent over 70% of social expenditure. There are still substantial 'passive' social protection benefits to employees (such as early retirement), especially in strong occupational sectors in medium- and large-sized industries and in public services.

The employment rate of workers aged 55–64 is one of the lowest in the EU, around 30% in 2003 as compared to the average of 38.5%, and it has not increased over recent years. There are two principal modes of exit from the labour force before the legal retirement age: through early exit mechanisms, that is, the so-called 'social support schemes' for workers in crisis areas, and through retirement after long service. Thus older workers are often well protected in terms of social security. However, there exist at present few measures (such as training, and even less redesigning of the organization of workplaces, career planning) enabling them to remain in employment.

Reform of the so-called 'social support schemes' has been on the political agenda since the end of the 1990s. The debate about pension systems is centred on their sustainability, equality criteria, efficiency and effectiveness. The most important changes focus on increasing the retirement age as of 2008 and fostering the development of second pillar pensions.

3. This section was prepared with the assistance of Mara Tagliabue, Macros Research, Milan.

Pension reform

Although there have been two other pension reforms, the most significant set of measures for lengthening active life are those contained in Law no. 335/95, which is concerned with welfare rather than the labour market. This law provided for the following:

- postponement of the retirement age to 65 years for both men and women (the change comes into force in 2008)
- increasing the minimum retirement age to 57 years. In 2008, it will become compulsory to have reached the age of 57 and to have a minimum of 40 years of paid contributions. Currently, eligibility for seniority pensions also includes a mixed criterion which combines contribution years with age (as of 2004, 57 years of age and 35 years' contributions for most workers). As of 2008, eligibility criteria to qualify for such a pension will be tighter (with a few exceptions) and 40 contribution years will normally be required. It will still be possible experimentally until 2015 to retire with a minimum of 35 contribution years and 57 years of age, but in this case workers will face a penalty
- part-time early flexible retirement in the two years before reaching normal retirement age which means that workers not more than 24 months younger than the age eligible for the old-age pension and with the necessary minimum contribution requirements could combine pension and part-time work (for a period of no more than two years and until retirement age)
- gradual retirement and tax reductions for the accumulation of pension and work incomes
- the possibility of continuing part-time work after reaching retirement age (ministerial decree no. 331/97). Between 2004 and the end of 2007, the government also grants a tax-free incentive to private sector workers who fulfil the current requirements for seniority pensions, but decide to postpone retirement for at least two years.

Treasury officials estimate that the tightening of pension eligibility criteria, by increasing the effective retirement age by three to four years on average, will reduce the ratio of pension expenditure to GDP by around 0.7% of GDP between 2010 and 2040, compared to the present system. Expenditure for pensions would peak in 2029 at around 15% of GDP, instead of 15.8% (cf. European Commission, 2003b, p. 11).

Every new attempt the government makes to bring about more reforms (for example, shortening the implementation period of the pension reform) is met with strong opposition from the unions. The majority of Italians still view early retirement as a social support mechanism not only for older workers but also for those among younger ones experiencing unemployment, even in the rich northern provinces.

In July 2004, however, the government made further changes. By 2008, to be able to draw a pension one will need to be 60 years of age and to have contributed for at least 35 years or be younger with 40 contribution years. By 2010, the minimum retirement age will be 61 (62 for self-employed) and by 2013 this age will have climbed to 62. Over the period 2004–07, private sector employees are free to continue work beyond that age, without paying pension contributions (currently very high in Italy at 32.7% of the payroll).

As far as the development of funded pension schemes is concerned, government action has focused on harmonizing legislation on collective and individual pension funds, to eliminate distortion, increase competition among them, and in general promote second pillar pensions.

Employment practice

The reasons for the low official employment rate for those aged 55–64 are many. We would in particular mention:

- pension benefits are too generous, making it more convenient to retire than to continue working. Currently, Italy provides the highest incentives to early retirement among the OECD countries and Italian companies have long encouraged a human resource policy of 'young in, and old out', that is, older workers being replaced by young workers who are considered to be cheaper, more flexible and more productive. Companies commonly consider older workers more expensive than younger workers, because of the higher wages, fringe benefits and social contributions the former incur
- the relatively low level of qualification of older workers. However, this is about to change
- after retirement many workers continue to work illegally, contributing to the growth of the informal sector (it is estimated that 1,200,000 pensioners work illegally). It is an urgent requirement that incentives be put in place to enable large numbers of these pensioners to emerge from the shadow economy
- part-time work, an ideal form of work for senior workers, is still low compared to other EU countries and as yet does not attract enough interest (9% compared with the European average of 18%, and with high rates of 42% and 25% for Holland and the UK).

Active policies for older workers

The concept of ' active ageing' is a recent one in Italy. Until now the focus of attention has been to improve older people's social integration rather than to increase their employability through active labour market policies. A recent report on occupational policies issued by the Ministry of Labour points out that employment policies for workers over 45 constitute only 6% of active labour market policies overall, though this cohort represents 13.6% of the people seeking employment.

However, the recent reform of the labour market, the so-called 'Biagi Law' (Legislative Decree no. 276 of 2003), has brought some, albeit limited, change. The main goal is to build more flexibility into the labour market and to introduce financial incentives for older people trying to re-enter the labour market (the 'reinsertion contracts'). The employment fiscal bonus for people with no permanent employment over the previous two years, introduced in 2000 and extended to 2006, has seen the recent introduction of an age differentiation, with a bonus supplement in the case of older workers.

The so-called 'Lavori Socialmente Utili' is a kind of Job Allowance Scheme in the areas of the environment and social assistance. Its aim is to help unemployed people, and it has a relevant role for older workers because 25.8% of all jobs provided are performed by people over 45.

A survey of Isfol (Institute for the Development of Workers' Training) in 2001 points out that although active labour market policies for older workers are an urgent question, there were very few service-oriented schemes for people over 50. The survey covered 99 Employment Bureaux (Centri per l'impiego) but only three of them offered special services for older workers. These services were the following: individual plans for outplacement; individual lifelong learning; promotion of some types of atypical job; and plans for self-employment.

Over the next years these employment centres plan to develop two special areas of employment: one for young people with low education levels and another for older workers. The employment bureaux are expected to build up skills, counselling, and develop links to a range of activities and services. At present, it is for the most part local municipal authorities that pursue active policies for older workers.

There exist certain underlying conditions that have so far hindered wide application of recent initiatives. Measures in specific areas have been lacking – for example, in the organizational redesign of enterprises, work quality and health at work at older ages, continuous vocational training and lifelong learning, and regulations to combat age discrimination. Thus, for the time being, economic conditions have not encouraged many people to combine (at least officially) work and pensions.

In conclusion, it will be crucial for the social partners to adopt a more positive approach towards older workers. They need chiefly to develop a new culture of ageing, focusing not only on retirement itself but also on measures which will enable workers to choose freely what they want to do: retire or continue working. In Italy, possibly more than elsewhere, systematic coordination of private and public sector initiatives is required if the culture of early retirement is to be reversed. Some promising examples are provided in Box 7.6.

Box 7.6 First steps towards reversing early retirement practice

A 2003 programme promoted by the Ministry of Labour and Social Policies intends to put into place a nationwide *Welfare-to-Work Strategy*. The programme is to be tailored to the characteristics and needs of the various regions: for example, in the centre-north the focus will be on training of adult workers and the fostering of active ageing, while in the south the emphasis will be on measures to support the transition from the widespread shadow economy to regular work so that employment prospects for older workers can improve in the long-term.

Some regions provide financial resources to encourage the employment of older workers, mainly through adult training supported by cooperation between employment centres, higher education institutions, regional training systems and firms, and temporary contracts.

The economic structure is characterized by small and medium-sized firms, and retaining older workers in the labour market is particularly beneficial for small firms. A few promising examples are the following:

- Many small firms in Brescia, which is located in the industrial area of Lombardy, produce metal products. The contribution of older workers is particularly appreciated in these firms, because the productive system is based on a high level of technical expertise and the experience of the older worker is often a key success factor for the enterprise.
- In the Trentino Alto Adige Region (an autonomous and special status region) two important initiatives have been taken to keep or reintegrate older workers. In the first place financial incentives are provided to firms recruiting unemployed workers, in particular older workers. This region is particularly interested in active ageing, for example, by promoting activity through the intricate networks of small firms, associations or voluntary services. Second, the region and the social partners recently agreed to establish a 'Servizio di ripristino e valorizzazione ambientale', that is a service for environmental restoration and improvement. About 800 people are employed under this project, of whom 350 are on temporary contracts. This project has had great success, notably for example in laying cycle tracks, building parking areas and refurbishing and staffing museums.
- Other regions, such as Emilia Romagna and Tuscany, intend to set up plans to maintain senior workers in the labour market, by encouraging partnerships with local firms and employers' associations.

Mara Tagliabue – Macros Research, Milan, October 2004

Switzerland – a high employment rate

General outlook

Switzerland has one of the highest employment rates of older persons (aged 55–64) among industrialized countries (in 2002, 77% for men and 53% for women, compared to 50.1% for men and 30.5% for women in the EU15). Apart from Switzerland, only some Nordic European and East Asian countries, together with the US, have participation rates of about 60–70%. As can be expected, the general employment rate is also very high (79% in 2002) as well as that for women (71.8% in 2002); over 50% of them working part-time.

In Switzerland, the legal retirement age (men: 65; women: 63, to rise to 64 in 2008) matches the actual retirement age well. The main reason is that early retirement has so far not been promoted by public policy. In particular, the social security system does not include financial incentives for early retirement. The design of other social insurances, such as invalidity or unemployment insurance, does not encourage an early exit from the labour force. During the 1990s, however, early retirement became increasingly popular in Switzerland as well. In 1991/92, 21.8% of all individuals who were within three years of reaching the legal retirement age had already retired. In 1999/2000, this quota had increased to 29.8%. A notable increase in early retirement took place in 1997/98, when the option to make an early claim for the public old-age pension up to two years before the legal retirement age was introduced.

The Swiss pension system is a three pillar system. As in other continental European countries, public pension schemes are resourced from social contributions shared between employers and employees. But, unlike these other countries, contribution and benefit rates under the first pillar system are fairly low. On the other hand, the second pillar has been compulsory since 1985 for almost all wage earners (although optional for the self-employed). Switzerland was the first OECD country to introduce a mandatory privately funded and managed second pillar scheme. The third pillar (private savings) is encouraged by fiscal incentives.

Public policies

The recent increase in early retirement

According to data from the 2002 Swiss Labour Force Survey, the three most common grounds for early retirement in Switzerland are personal reasons, company reasons and health reasons, which together account for two-thirds of all early retirement (Sousa-Poza and Dorn, 2004a). Company reasons, such as reorganizations and mergers, rapidly gained ground during the economic recession of the 1990s. Large companies began promoting early retirement by offering employees flexible and attractive conditions for early retirement. Private and frequently company controlled pension funds have been used to set the appropriate incentives. Roughly 85% of employees insured in the mandatory second pillar of Swiss old-age provision are able to receive pensions five years prior to the legal retirement age. In addition, second pillar contributions increase with age, although in some pension schemes this rule has been changed.

Sousa-Poza and Dorn (2004b) distinguish between two basic types of employee who show different early retirement behaviours:

1. White-collar workers with an intermediate or high level of education frequently go into early retirement. These workers, who are often employed in the public or financial sectors, have a relatively high income and may also have accumulated savings.
2. Blue-collar workers with low education do not often go into early retirement. They are employed in sectors such as agriculture, construction or manufacturing. Due to their low income and an absence of personal wealth, they do not have the financial resources comfortably to bridge the gap between early retirement and the beginning of entitlement to old-age benefits.

Apart from a worker's financial situation, retirement behaviour is influenced by a worker's preferences for leisure and other activities outside the workplace (for example, relating to the employment situation of a spouse), and by the worker's attitude to work.

Recent surveys (for example, *L'Hebdo*, 29 April 2004) show that in Switzerland too the importance of family and leisure activities has increased compared to the value traditionally attached to work in the life-cycle. This survey, called the 'Swiss dream of part-time work', reveals that half of workers would like to reduce their work time.

In the building sector, the official retirement age went down from 65 to 60. This measure, long sought by the trade unions, has proved very necessary since, due to the intensely physical nature of the work in this sector, the employment rate of older workers is low and the invalidity rate very high.

The data of the Labour Force Survey also showed that more than 30% of the people who went into early retirement in 2001/02 continued working after retirement. Two-thirds of these workers were still employed by their former employers. Some companies hence allow for a more gradual transition to early retirement of their employees, which includes the possibility of working part-time, as is the case with three out of four working early retirees. Public policy should thus aim at facilitating more flexible and individualized retirement options.

According to Widmer et al. (2001), the main characteristics of Swiss 'retired' (after 65) workers are:

- they are employed frequently on a part-time basis
- they often have middle and high education
- the rate of self-employed individuals is relatively high
- older workers are primarily employed by small and medium-sized enterprises.

Bigger firms have made great use of early retirement:

- older workers are primarily employed in manufacturing and retail.
- the main reason for working later after reaching the official retirement age is not always a financial one. In a way, the higher the income of the household, the higher is the probability of working later. (In the UK, for example, financial motivation is very strong.) However, a minority of women, often lone women, and of men continue working to make ends meet.

Recent pension reforms

The first pillar system (and to a lesser extent, the second pillar system) is subject to regular revision. Rather than passing drastic reforms as in other European neighbouring countries, the pension system in Switzerland is being adjusted step by step.

The 10th (1997) revision, for example, overhauled the entire system, bringing two of the most notable changes:

- provision was made for a gradual rise in the retirement age for women from 62 to 64 years (set at 65 for men)
- a 'splitting' arrangement was introduced for couples, providing entitlement to an 'individual spouse pension' where both spouses could draw a benefit based on one half of the combined income of the couple received during the time of marriage, with an addition to cater for education and child care.

Box 7.7   High activity rate of seniors in Switzerland

Although in decline, participation in the labour force in Switzerland of 50–64-year-olds is second highest in the OECD. The main reason for this is that a flexible age for retirement was enacted in law only relatively recently. The high proportion, compared with other countries, of seniors still in remunerative work has initially resulted in a rise in wages. Three other consequences should also be noted:

First, early retirement is much more frequent among men with relatively little training than among persons with higher qualifications and on higher wages as a consequence.

Second, the higher the age, the better seniority and professional experience are rewarded. The salaries of 50–63/65-year-olds are approximately 37% higher than those of 20–29-year-olds, and here *professional experience* carries greater weight than seniority, as, for example, in the machine industry where know-how from experience is crucial to the production process. Loyalty to the enterprise also is fairly strong in Switzerland: in 2001, the proportion of persons who had been with the same employer for at least five years was 53%.

Third, the level of *social costs* also affects the situation. With men between 25 and 34 years, as also with women between 25 and 31 years, the joint compulsory contribution to the second pillar both by the employer and the wage-earner is 7%. But for men between 55 and 65 years and for women between 52 and 62 years the contribution is 18%. The age categories for women will be brought into line with those for men with the revision of the LLP or Occupational Welfare Act.

Petra Huth – Crédit Suisse (Economic and Policy Consulting), in Huth (2004)

An 11th revision, adopted by Parliament in 2003 but refused by vote by the people in May 2004, had two objectives: (i) to strengthen arrangements for financing the AHV/AVS (old-age public pension) with additional resources, derived from value added taxes (VAT), in order to make the state pension sustainable until 2015, and (ii) to equalize the age of retirement for both women and men at 65 years. Earlier proposals regarding the need to encourage flexibility and *à la carte* retirement were reserved for the 12th revision.

The OECD recommends that the official retirement age be gradually increased to 67 years of age for both men and women. But this increase has been a controversial topic of recent political debate and, following the May 2004 refusal of the 11th revision, one has serious doubts about the decision and implementation of such a reform.

Firm practice

Training of older workers

Among European countries, Switzerland has a large proportion of older workers participating in career upgrading training: whereas, for example, Belgium, the Netherlands, and Great Britain all have less than 10% of their older labour force (aged 55–64) taking part in this form of training, the corresponding figure for Switzerland is approximately 20%.

According to data from the 1999 Swiss Labour Force Survey, which included a comprehensive supplement on training, the probability of older workers receiving training is comparable to that of younger workers (Sousa-Poza and Henneberger, 2003). Thus the course participation rate of workers between the ages of 50 and 60 is high (20%), and then a marked decline occurs for the oldest workers aged 60–70 years (4%). Motivation to receive training is strongly influenced by the retirement age, and thus to a large extent by public policies.

Older workers are well represented in computer courses (word processing, database courses, general computer courses). An under-representation of older workers can be observed in language courses.

The willingness of employers to fund training does not depend on age. In fact, Sousa-Poza and Henneberger observed a slight increase in the proportion of employees receiving funding from their employers in the older age categories. These results suggest that firms do not, in general, view older workers as unsuitable for training and thus employment. Firm funding of courses is strictly gender-neutral, strongly suggesting that employers do not discriminate in this regard. But the probability of taking part in a course decreases with lower levels of education, being a foreigner, women in part-time employment, and working for a small firm. A high education level and being in management increases the probability.

The probability of training being available is highest in banking, insurance, energy and public administration.

Company examples

It is not rare to find companies that have set up flexibility measures at end of career. In Geneva, for a number of years the chemical firm Firmenich has set up a gradual retirement scheme for its employees between the ages of 60 and 65, and employees are satisfied with the flexibility the scheme affords.

LeicaGeosystems AG (in *'"La flexi-employabilité"*: un changement de paradigme pour les travailleurs âgés', *La Vie économique*, 11, 2003) also offers a transition during the last five years before the official retirement age.

For the ABB in Switzerland, a technology company with 7,800 employees and with 4.8% of workers on the workforce aged 60+, because of population ageing, human capital is becoming a main factor of company competitiveness. Thus retention of the productivity of older workers through improved motivation and more widespread recognition has become a very important part of the company's human resource management strategy.

ABB's policy towards older workers includes the following points:

- age has no effect on the productivity of employees
- ABB needs a healthy age tree-structure within the firm
- employees are responsible for their competitiveness on the labour market
- they are responsible for their old-age care
- same earnings for the same tasks/performance/experience.

In the top posts, ABB employs only employees who have to resign their position at the age of 60. The ABB model aims (i) to rejuvenate employees in high positions; (ii) to make use of the experience of older workers; and (iii) to provide the opportunity of gradual exit from work to older workers. In several cases, ABB rehires qualified employees aged over 60 as consultants.

In order to prepare employees for old age, the company also organizes seminars for workers at age 57, with a spouse, on topics such as: ageing at work and in the family; active life-design; 'young and old' generational issues; and finance and health in old age.

Several Cantonal administrations have also set in place partial early retirement measures to provide a transition between full-time work and full retirement. To date, these measures have been less successful than when applied to full early retirement.

Two experts on these questions, Dr A. Sousa-Poza and F. Henneberger, mentioned above, have developed an interesting concept: *'flexi-employabilité'*. Indeed, in Switzerland, where for the most part working conditions are not precarious, what are most needed at end of career are flexibility and employability. Both part-time work and continuing training being quite common, there is a high potential for further extension of the work-life. Two changes could, however, help greatly to develop this extension: adopting the same second pillar contribution rates for all ages and removing the need to contribute to the first pillar after the age of 65.

As in other countries, retired or semi-retired qualified workers often have voluntary or quasi-voluntary commitments. For example: at Adlatus, professionals advise small and medium-sized young firms on launch and efficient management ('coaching'); Senexpert does similar work; Senior Expert Corps specializes in helping companies from developing countries or from Central and Eastern Europe; and Sertus helps workers over 50 to find a job.

Hungary – a drastic change of direction

Pension reforms in the new EU member states

As already mentioned in Chapter 3, pension reforms promoting extension of work-life have been implemented not only in Western but also in Eastern Europe. In order to reform pension schemes according to the principles of the market economy, multipillar old-age insurance systems have been established and retirement ages have been increased in all new EU member states.

In Poland, for example, in 1992, new rules for calculating the old-age pension, disability benefits and survivors' pensions were adopted. These new rules linked more closely the level of benefits to work records, wages and salaries. In 1999, a thorough reform of the Polish old-age social security system was undertaken: a two-pillar system was established, with both pillars entirely based on individual accounts. Moreover, since 2004, measures have been implemented to reduce access to early retirement and to suspend pre-retirement transfers (these will come fully into force in 2007).

In 1995, the Czech Republic and Lithuania also started to set up new, two-pillar pension systems with, on the one hand, compulsory, pay-as-you-go pension insurance, and, on the other, a private life and/or pension insurance system. At the same time, in both countries, the retirement age has been increased (to 59–62 years for women – depending on the number of children – and to 63 years for men by 2013 in the Czech Republic, and to 60 years for women and to 62.5 years for men by 2009 in Lithuania). Similar policies also obtain in Slovenia: (i) establishment of a three-pillar pension system; (ii) gradual raising of earliest possible retirement for men from 55 to 58 years and for women from 50 to 53 years (by 1998); (iii) penalties for retirement prior to, and bonuses for retirement after, the full pensionable age of 63 years for men and 61 years for women (phased in until 2008); (iv) extension of the period for calculation of the pension base from the previous ten years to the best 18 years.

Some of these countries have also implemented policies aimed at increasing directly the labour force participation of older workers. Thus, for example, in Slovenia, an anti-age discrimination law was adopted in 2002, and in Poland and Lithuania, a programme for the labour market activation of older workers has been prepared and implemented.

In the following, we shall deal with the Hungarian situation in some detail.

General outlook

In Hungary, in 2002, 35% of men and 18% of women aged 55–64 were employed. The low labour market participation of older Hungarians reflects low life expectancy (68.4 years for men and 76.7 years for women, compared to 75.8 years for men and 81.6 years for women in the EU15), the consequences of the economic transition, and earlier experience with the retirement age and pensions. Following the broad pension reforms implemented from 1997, however, development of the fourth pillar was also begun in Hungary.

New public policies

Reform of the pension system

In the 1990s, pension reform meant adapting to the requirements of the World Bank. The main features of these reforms were:

1. *Implementation of the three pillars pension system* with the guarantee of a minimum income also for citizens not contributing to the system: The *first pillar* is still a mix of insurance and social security provision, that is, the old and new systems exist in parallel. Thus there is a need to continue with the reforms even though the first pillar could go on functioning until 2020 without major change. Among social partners there is no debate about rebuilding the old system, that is, a pension system based exclusively on social security principles. The *second pillar* is designed to provide around 30% of the pension income. However, pension benefits from the first and second pillars will be relatively lower than the pension under the old system.

2. *Increasing the statutory retirement age and bringing the female retirement age into line with the male.* The retirement age increased for men from 60 to 62 in 2002 and will increase for women from 55 to 62 by 2009. A raising of the legal retirement age to 65 years for both sexes is expected between 2015 and 2020.

3. *Prolongation of the contributory period.* Currently, the average contributory period is 38.4 years.

4. *Changes in pension indexation.* The current indexation works according to the Swiss model, that is, pensions are adjusted 50% to prices and 50% to net wages.

5. *Providing flexible retirement.* Early retirement is possible on the following terms:

   - for women five years before reaching retirement age and for men from the age of 60 and with a contributory period of 38 years (for full pensions)
   - for women five years before reaching retirement age and for men from the age of 60 and with a contributory period of 33 years (with reduced pensions) only until 2009
   - for employees doing physically demanding work or in jobs which are potentially dangerous to health, for varying periods before retirement age but with a certain contributory period defined in law (for full pensions)
   - five years before reaching retirement age and with a contributory period of at least 33 years provided the employer agrees to purchase the contributory period needed to reach retirement age (for full pensions).

6. Older workers after reaching retirement age can be economically active *without restrictions.* Moreover, retired older workers pay taxes on earnings from work only and not on the cumulation of pension and earnings.

7. *Restrictions on access to disability benefits.*

Work after retirement

According to a GKI Economic Research Co. Survey (cf. Adler, 2003), in Hungary, the reasons for the decision to retire are tiredness and health problems (40%) and the financial disadvantages of working after retirement (30%). Two out of three older workers volunteer for retirement; only one out of ten was forced into retirement by the employer. Of retired people, 2% were unemployed just before retirement.

Retired older workers work on average 6.5 years, that is, 75% of life spent in retirement. Work after retirement is performed primarily for financial reasons (80%). The intrinsic importance of work seems to be an argument almost only for intellectual white-collar workers, whether in later life or earlier. Of retired older workers, 60% earn less from work than they get from their pension. Earnings from work in retirement widen the income gap between retired Hungarians.

A high level of education seems to be a requirement for the employment of older workers after pension age.

Table 7.4 Synthesis of Part II – Working beyond 60 – how? Recent policies/measures to encourage later exit and employment of older workers

Measures, Policies	Austria	Belgium	Denmark	Finland	France	Germany	Greece	Ireland	Italy	Luxembourg	Netherlands	Portugal	Spain	Sweden	UK	Switzerland
Pensions																
1. Increase retirement age/contributory period	X	X		X	X	X	X		X			X		X	X	X
2. More links between contributions and benefits	X			X	X	X	X		X			X	X	X	X	X
3. Flexibility of retirement age	X	X	X	X		X			X		X	X	X	X		X
4. Gradual retirement	X	X	X	X	X	X			X		X		X	X		
5. Development of occupational pensions	X	X	X	X	X	X	X	X	X	X	X	X	X	X	X	X
6. Cumulation of earnings and benefits	X	X	X	X	X	X	X	X	X	X	X	X	X	X	X	X
Work Exit																
7. Reducing disability benefit access	X	X	X	X		X					X			X		X
8. Reducing early retirement access	X	X	X	X	X	X					X		X	X	X	
9. Reducing unemployment benefit access	X	X		X	X	X					X				X	X
Employment 55+																
10. Incentive for continuing training	X	X	X	X	X		X				X			X	X	
11. Reintegrate unemployed 50+	X	X	X	X	X		X	X	X	X	X		X	X	X	
12. Encourage part-time work age 55–65	X	X	X	X		X			X	X	X		X	X	X	X
13. Employment subsidies reduction of social contributions	X	X	X		X		X		X	X	X		X	X	X	
14. Anti-age discrimination legislation	X	X	X	X		X	X	X	X	X	X	X	X	X	X	X
15. Information/education campaigns						X					X			X		

Notes: Reference is made of recent (not before 1996) measures. Importance of measure is illustrated by the bold character of X. Information is complete and up-to-date (October 2004) for the countries analysed in the book (FI, DK, UK, NL, DE, FR, IT, CH).

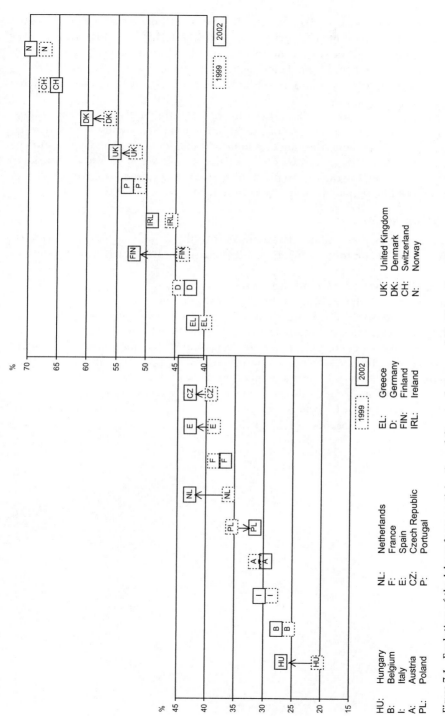

%

70 — N [N]

65 — [CH] CH

60 — DK [DK]

55 — UK [UK]

P [P]

50 — IRL [IRL]

FIN [FIN]

D [D]

45 — EL [EL]

[2002] [1999]

[1999] [2002]

%

45 — CZ [CZ]

E [E]

40 — F [F]

35 — NL [NL]

PL [PL]

30 — [A] A

I [I]

25 — B [B]

20 — HU [HU]

15 —

HU: Hungary   NL: Netherlands   EL: Greece   UK: United Kingdom
B: Belgium   F: France   D: Germany   DK: Denmark
I: Italy   E: Spain   FIN: Finland   CH: Switzerland
A: Austria   CZ: Czech Republic   IRL: Ireland   N: Norway
PL: Poland   P: Portugal

Figure 7.1 Evolution of the labour force participation of the population aged 55–64 in selected European countries, 1999–2002

Source: OECD *Employment Outlook*, 2003.

Of retired older workers, 50% work full time. Reasons for part-time work are first bad health and thereafter other interests like leisure pursuits and family responsibilities. Part-time work is not normally subject to employer pressure.

However, the number of retired older workers is decreasing. The supply of retired older labour is twice the demand. For older workers leaving the labour market there is little chance of re-entry.

According to the Time Use Survey (Hungarian Central Statistical Office, 2000), older people who are pushed out of the labour market are usually very active in the family, for example in the care of grandchildren. According to another survey carried out in 2001, the majority of Hungarians aged between 46 and 60 consider retiring before reaching the legal retirement age. However, after retirement, two out of three would be prepared to work part time (Dobossy et al. 2002).

The current debate

Political interests play the main role in reform of the pension system. There is no established regulatory tradition, the law changing with each new legislative period.

Reform and the debates about further reforms focus on the pension system itself, and not, as yet, on the employability of older workers.

Governments so far have launched neither ageing awareness campaigns nor programmes encouraging lifelong learning or lifelong employment.

There is massive age-discrimination in Hungarian society (Széman, 2004). Since April 2004, the Hungarian Democratic Forum, the opposition party during this legislature period, has promoted a programme called 'Give a Chance to Employees over 45'. The party suggests subsidies, namely lower social security contributions, for the employment of workers aged 45+. However, so far there has been no parliamentary debate of this suggestion.

8
Recent Company Measures and Best Practice in Selected European Firms

In most European countries, because of the shrinking and ageing of the population, there will probably be a steady increase rather than a sudden jump in the proportion of older workers in the labour force.

According to an important German research programme, this development will have the following consequences for companies (Buck and Dworschak, 2003, pp. 31–2):

- Phase 1: Up until 2005, companies recruiting primarily younger employees profited from the demographic situation because the under-40 age groups were numerically strong.
- Phase 2: The proportion of people over 40 increases after 2005. Human resource development is becoming an increasingly important competitive factor. The key issue here is to maintain and continue to develop the skills and qualifications of older workers.
- Phase 3: From 2010 the number of over-50s will continue to increase disproportionately. Many companies will be confronted with the reality that the average age of workforces is rising. Companies which have still not developed sustainable models for managing ageing workforces will be threatened by a loss of innovative potential and performance.

This chapter will analyse the main components of what we call 'age management', with examples of practice when available. Box 8.1 lists the main options open to companies regarding the management of ageing workforces.

However, effective models for managing people's occupational biographies should not be restricted to older workers who are already beginning to experience a decline in their working capacity.

Box 8.1   Main components of age management in enterprises

Career planning involves a number of interviews and activities designed to assess and help individual workers remain motivated and productive, and to provide them with the learning and mobility (internal and external) which will make for a better match between workers' and company needs.

Training and occupational 'recycling' and promotion need to be encouraged: workers aged 50 or above must not be sidelined. The practice of continuing training right up to the end of working life seems at last, though only gradually, to be taking root in European countries. But continuing training methods must be designed with the age of workers in mind.

Flexible work schedules and part-time work are an ideal way for firms to retain workers. Working hours should be adjusted to take into account the aptitudes and motivation of older employees; ideally, they should have some choice of where and how they work (for instance, from home for one or two days a week). Gradual retirement or reducing hours worked as retirement is approached are becoming more common.

Ergonomics and 'function identification' mean taking action to prevent, or compensate for, diminishing physical capacity of older workers. There exist not only preventive measures but also ways of improving conditions so as to avoid some of the work-related physical problems associated with certain types of job, especially those involving regular, painful and strenuous movements.

Promoting occupational health and capacity, and particularly functional capacity, which requires a tripartite approach integrating workers, employers and the community as a whole.

Age diversity means promoting the notion that the enterprise should have a mix of workers of different ages and abilities. Employers adopting this approach find that it is an advantage to have in one's work force an age pyramid that tends to mirror that of one's clientele.

Anti-age discrimination: policy makers within the countries of the European Union are at last beginning to give proper attention to *age discrimination* issues. This concern is reflected in the Treaty of Amsterdam and in a European Union programme of action, and all member states must pass legislation before 2006. Complementary to legislation, promoting best practice among the social partners – governments, enterprises and unions – is essential. A *Code of Good Practice* on 'older' workers has been prepared and disseminated in all member states. Both voluntary measures and legislation with incentives will be important in changing the drastic early retirement culture and promoting a longer work-life.

GINA and the Geneva Association (2002), The Future of Pensions and Retirement

Reduction of work time, gradual retirement, part-time work

Definition

Reduction of work time, gradual retirement and part-time work, that is, work-time adjustment, is one of the most effective policies for various categories of worker (for example, workers with stressful functions, the handicapped) or for workers at various points in their career (for example, students, adults with family or other responsibilities, older workers) and is being used extensively. It is considered to be one of the most easily implemented and cost-saving strategies for adjusting work to suit companies and workers at end of career.

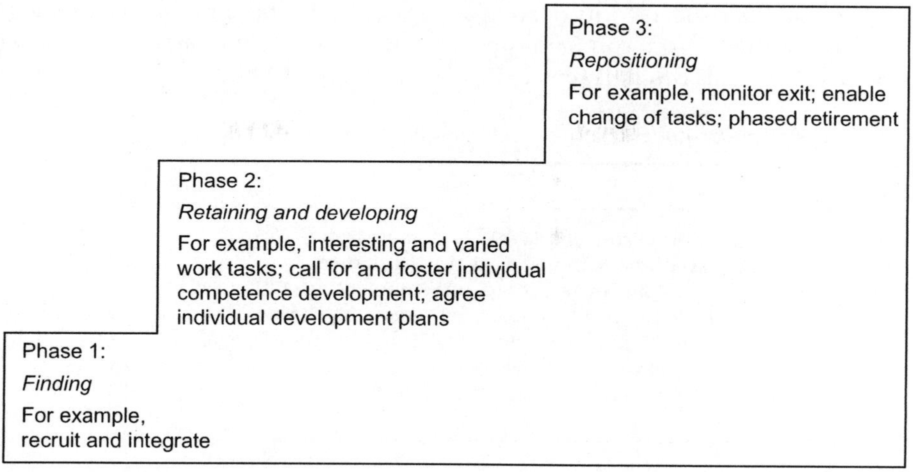

```
                                            ┌──────────────────────────────┐
                                            │ Phase 3:                     │
                                            │ Repositioning                │
                                            │ For example, monitor exit;   │
                                            │ enable change of tasks;      │
                                            │ phased retirement            │
                          ┌─────────────────┤                              │
                          │ Phase 2:        └──────────────────────────────┤
                          │ Retaining and developing                       │
                          │ For example, interesting and varied            │
                          │ work tasks; call for and foster individual     │
                          │ competence development; agree                  │
                          │ individual development plans                   │
         ┌────────────────┤                                                │
         │ Phase 1:       └────────────────────────────────────────────────┤
         │ Finding                                                         │
         │ For example,                                                    │
         │ recruit and integrate                                          │
         └─────────────────────────────────────────────────────────────────┘
```

Figure 8.1   Longer-term human resource orientation from the beginning to the end of work-life

Source: Buck and Dworschak (2003, p. 36).

Gradual retirement, often referred to as partial or part-time retirement, is the favoured formula for work-time reduction at end of career. The worker, instead of working full time one day and fully retiring the next, can reduce work hours according to graduated and agreed schedules while drawing part-time pay (and in some cases, income support).

Implementation

In most European countries, all non-standard working patterns are more frequently available in large companies and in the public sector. However, in the UK as in other countries, while early retirement is still offered by around four in ten companies, official phased retirement is less common, but often takes the form of part-time work (Table 8.1). The vast majority of such schemes have entry criteria, most usually a minimum length of service before joining. In the various country chapters, some national examples are provided. Here are some other eloquent examples.

Table 8.1   Work-time adjustments in British companies

Working arrangement offered by the employer	*% of surveyed employers*
Part-time work	83
Job share	39
Flexible working hours	5
Early retirement	37
Phased retirement	14

Source: Age Positive (2001, p. 17).

In the UK, also, the majority of companies adopt a flexible attitude to retirement age. Around half of the companies plan for the retirement of staff by assessing whether their skills could be replaced internally (Table 8.2).

Table 8.2   Policies/attitudes relating to retirement schemes in the UK

Policies/attitudes	% of surveyed employers
We evaluate the skills of retiring employees so that we know whether we can replace these within the existing workforce	55
Some employees can stay on beyond company retirement age if they wish	44
All employees can stay on beyond company retirement age if they wish	41
We offer flexible retirement schemes with a selection of retirement ages	21
We retain some retired employees as consultants	24
We offer employees pre-retirement counselling	10
None	15

Source: Age Positive (2001, pp. 18–19).

Company examples

Table 8.3 lists some examples of UK companies implementing work-time adjustments.

The main *principles* underlying the company approaches are:

- employees can continue working beyond the company's normal retirement age (NRA) subject to operational needs
- employees, irrespective of age or length of service, may apply for part-time work or job share
- changing employee and employer mind-sets, ensuring a 'culture shift' away from early retirement within the organization.

In these companies, the policy was *introduced in response to*:

- requests from employees within the organisation to continue working after the company NRA on a full- or and part-time basis
- a desire to retain skilled and valued older colleagues
- a wish to recruit older employees
- a drive to introduce age-neutral employment policies, remove age discrimination and be a 'responsible employer'.

Table 8.4 lists the companies' perceptions of the main benefits of work-time adjustments.

Career planning

Definition

Career planning means organized planning interviews and activities to assess workers and opportunities in order to create optimal conditions for older employees to be

Table 8.3 Companies implementing work-time adjustments in the UK

Organizations offering, besides extending the retirement age, additional flexible retirement options including part-time work, job sharing, reduced responsibilities, time out for sabbaticals, and volunteering:

ASDA (110,000 employees).	Introduced mid-1980s
B&Q (30,000 employees)	Introduced 1999
BT (101,000 employees)	Introduced April 2001
BUPA (36,000 employees)	Introduced September 2000
Department for Education and Skills (**DfES**) (4455 employees)	Introduced September 1999
Ford Motor Company Ltd (20,000 employees)	Policy in practice (no introduction date provided)
Marks and Spencer Plc (60,000 employees)	Policy in practice (no introduction date provided)
Nationwide Building Society (14,700 employees)	Introduced October 2001
NCH (5,500 employees)	Introduced December 2001
J Sainsbury Plc (130,000 employees)	Introduced 1985
Tesco Plc (190,000 employees)	Introduced early 1990s

Organizations which have already introduced flexible retirement by extending the companies' normal retirement age (NRA):

Age Concern England (800 employees)	Introduced late 1995, other flexible working arrangements under consideration
Imperial War Museum (650 employees)	Introduced September 2001. Other flexible working policies under consideration
Nuneaton & Bedworth Borough Council (1,300 employees)	Introduced July 2001

Organizations which are currently either considering or developing flexible retirement policies:

AMP (UK) Ltd (8,000 employees)	Considering extension of NRA and introducing flexible working arrangements
BAE Systems (130,000 employees)	Considering extension of NRA and introducing flexible working arrangements
Barclays (80,000 employees)	Considering introducing flexible retirement in two phases (Phase 1: extension of NRA from 60 to 65; Phase 2: introducing flexible working arrangements)
HBOS (60,000 employees)	Considering an extension of NRA to 70, as well as the introduction of flexible working arrangements
Innogy (10,000 employees)	Initial stages of considering flexible retirement policy options
Royal Bank of Scotland Group Plc (95,000 employees)	Considering a policy of flexible retirement from 55, as well as the implementation of flexible working arrangements

Source: 'Flexible Retirement: A Snapshot of Large Employers' Initiatives – Company Case Studies', <www.agepositive.gov.uk>

Table 8.4   Main benefits of work-time adjustment according to responses of companies

Benefits	AMP Ltd.	ASDA	Barclays	Barchester Healthcare	BAE Systems	BUPA	DfES	Ford Motor Company	Nationwide Building Society	Royal Bank of Scotland
Retain experience/ corporate culture	X		X	X	X	X	X		X	X
Tutoring of younger staff		X		X						
Improving staff morale (low staff turnover, absenteeism)		X		X			X		X	X
Cost saving (on recruitment, training, …)		X	X	X	X					X
Match consumers' age/ needs	X	X	X	X		X				X
Prevent future shortage of skilled workers	X		X		X					
Firm 'good employer' image	X		X			X	X	X	X	

Source: 'Flexible Retirement: A Snapshot of Large Employers' Initiatives – Company Case Studies', <www.agepositive.gov.uk>

productive, to learn and to improve performance, and thus remain employable until the end of their career or until they reach pension age. It is an attempt to recognize the individual differences among workers over the age of 45, some of whom may wish to reduce their commitments, or may wish simply to strive after fresh goals. The aim of career planning is to obtain the best possible match between the employees' performance and competency and the needs of the organization. Career planning meetings between managers and workers should cover possibilities (and limits), desires and needs concerning career/job changes/adjustments and vocational training/further education. Career plans are aimed not just at compensating for workers' perceived deficits but at securing the most advantageous use of their newfound strengths. In some countries, for example in France, career planning has become a regulatory right of employees.

Implementation

The priority goal of organizations should be to build age awareness into human resource management (HRM) policies to address the needs of workers of all ages. In principle, middle-aged and older employees must be given equal opportunities with other age groups. The HRM department has to identify the full range of available options for work organization, the extent to which flexibility is possible and, where necessary, how to increase it. Together with senior management and as part of the organization's business plan, the department will need to prepare an overview of the career possibilities available to older workers. It is important to bear in mind not only that people are being moved from one job to another, but also that the content of the job itself is frequently evolving. Plans need to be both vertical and horizontal in nature. HR managers need to decide which of the following options are relevant to their firm's situation: job rotation or exchange, additional training, part-time work, gradual retirement, mentor or facilitator roles, sabbatical leave, project leader or project participant roles. When working groups are established consideration should also always be given to whether there is a need for an age mix.

As important as working with career possibilities/job adjustments is the preparation of an overview of the learning opportunities and skills development initiatives available: professional and vocational courses, further education, on-the-job training or temporary assignments to other departments or organizations. In addition, all training will require a pedagogical age profile.

In seminars for HR managers, for employees in the age group 45–54 (mid-life seminars) and for workers aged 55 or over (senior seminars) the following issues should be covered:

- ageing and work, ageing and learning, potential for development of older employees
- phases of life, value changes over the life course, priorities
- upgrading of the older worker's skills and capabilities
- the 'package' of available possibilities for career/job changes and vocational training/education
- ageism and age discrimination
- the need for involving younger people in the above processes and how to achieve this.

In addition, seminars for HR managers will need to focus on the following specific issues:

- how to manage older employees, and how this differs from managing younger employees
- motivating older employees
- the age profile of the organization, changing demography and its implications for recruitment
- age-adapted work organization, occupational stress and physical well-being, work adaptability, ergonomics
- training in the process of conducting a career planning meeting with an older worker.

Specific issues for mid-life seminars for workers aged 45–54 are:

- the need for further education, the need for new skills and competencies, and vocational training (lifelong learning)
- new/alternative careers, job enrichment, changing job tasks
- focusing on career challenges in a 10–15-year perspective.

Specific issues for seminars for workers aged 55 or over are:

- the need to be professionally updated in late career
- the need to be employable up to pension age; reducing work hours; reducing job pressure
- the need for physical adjustment, ergonomics; or changing working tasks.

Country and company examples

In Europe, one of the most advanced countries in this field is Norway, where career planning for middle-aged and older workers in companies is supported by government action programmes. The semi-public Centre for Senior Planning (SSP) and the Working group for Promotion of Seniors in Working Life (ASSA), for example, prepared an 'Action Programme for Senior Policy', which began in 2001 and is scheduled to end in 2005.

This national development plan for older workers (45+) proposes six areas of activity:

- mobilizing employers and unions around good practice
- public awareness campaigns about ageing and work
- development projects in different employment sectors, in partnership with the national Work Research Institute
- research on, for example, the impact of changes in work-life on older workers; effects of working later in life; evaluation of the Action Programme for Senior Policy
- provision of education and 'competency lift' for older workers to get up to date, and for managers to understand and change their practice
- establishment of a national Centre for Competence to coordinate the plan's activities; maintain records of research and good practice; build networks and consultancies; publish a monthly newsletter. Training and better understanding on the proof of human resources managers could help the development of 'senior planning' within organizations and good practice be spread by a network of consultants.

Parallel to the Action Programme for Senior Policy, an agreement called 'An Inclusive Working Life', was concluded by the government and the social partners in October 2001. The programme aims to reduce sickness absence by 20% by the end of 2005, in particular through increased focus on rehabilitation and retraining. This must be seen in connection with proposals to restrict sickness benefits, which are rather generous in Norway (workers can remain on sick leave for up to one year with full pay, and there are no waiting days). Greater financial resources have been put

---

Box 8.2   AXA France: a new approach to career management

After years of end of career management as a function of employee age (for example, reserve management staff, gradual retirement, and so on), the company began a long debate about the issues of career development, of training throughout an employee's time with the firm and of mobility within it. In 2002, mainly because of the prohibitive costs involved, the company abandoned its 'reserve management' practice (which at the time involved some 500 employees). For its part, in 2003, the government refused to sign a collective agreement on phased early retirement.

On 16 October 2003, AXA concluded a fresh agreement on prospective employment management, called the Accord Cap Métiers 2003–05, which focused on the job functions of the future and adaptation and mobility of employees. The 'Cap Métiers' approach was about identifying the skills development that would be required and the demographic profiles of employees. Indeed, the average seniority of employees was 20 years and the average age 44 years; 30% of the staff were over 50.

According to this new approach, age was no longer the only variable. It was, quite to the contrary, considered that each employee had his or her own special part to play and any occupational expertise and experience was treated as a valuable asset in a company where 'saving' was after all the main professional focus. It is of course an established fact that the desire to 'save' increases with age and it was felt to be sound company policy to have staff and customers able to meet on common experiential ground.

Cap Métiers provides for and supervises continuing training designed to enable administrative staff who have essentially a support function to move across to a customer relation function. Continuing training and maintenance of mobility in this way become relevant and necessary throughout the employee's time with the company.

The cornerstone of this new kind of management is the interview given to each employee every three years during which the latter is given an opportunity to take stock of his or her situation within the company and to discuss the prospect of further training with a view to moving to new functions. This policy of promoting mobility within the firm is deliberately age-neutral and is designed to prevent all forms of discrimination on age grounds alone. The old type of bargaining with respect to end of career management has thus given way to a new intergenerational approach where a mixing of ages is encouraged making tutorship a standard practice. Tutors are given a crucial supervisory role in the individual training and skills development of younger employees.

Of the 12,000 employees currently working for the company in France, it is reckoned that each year 800–1,000 agree to redeployment within the firm. Continuing training is slightly lower for those in the 50–60-year age group than for younger employees, but this reflects employee rather than management preference. Indeed, AXA's management is concerned to promote career-long development of its staff.

Unsurprisingly, some AXA employees opt to leave the company and to set up as independant general agents and AXA underwrites the cost of preparing them for such a move. Part-time is also encouraged and now involves approximately 15% of staff and is gaining ground steadily. Its increase, however, is not a function of age.

Direction des Ressources Humaines, AXA France, June 2004

behind 'An Inclusive Working Life' (about €27 million for 2002), than were given to the Action for Senior Policy (€0.65 million).

Another related programme is 'The Competency Reform', introduced in 1999. This programme is designed to help establish 'lifelong learning' as a standard practice. Since 1 January 2001, employees have had a general right to three years' unpaid leave for educational purposes. This reform is not aimed directly at middle-aged or older workers, but is expected to sustain and even develop the competency of all workers to retirement age.

We follow with the example of France's biggest insurance company which recently modified its career planning policy for workers aged 45+. The changes are part of a reappraisal of human resource management, not just at end of career but throughout the occupational life-cycle (Box 8.2).

Continuing vocational training and lifelong education

Chapter 2 analysed the key importance of life-long training and education for a longer work-life in the context of ongoing technological change. Below, some additional information is provided and illustrated with examples of company practice following legislation.

According to the International Adult Literacy Survey, in the OECD, with the exception of three countries (Ireland, Italy and Switzerland) where about 50% of CVT (continuous vocational training) courses are paid for by employers, firms fully pay for more than 70% of CVT courses. Data on training rates in large and small firms from the European Continuing Vocational Training Survey show that workers in small firms usually receive less employer-sponsored training than workers in large firms.

In many countries, increased flexibility of working-time arrangements has led to the creation of working-time accounts for individual employees. In the Netherlands, for example, about one-quarter of large collective agreements establish the possibility of saving spare time for educational purposes. In a recent employer survey in western Germany, 11% of all companies that offer training and operate working-time accounts offer the option of using the accumulated working-time capital for training purposes (cf. OECD, 2003b, pp. 265–6).

The example of Sweden

As already mentioned, Sweden is one of the European countries with the highest employment rate for workers above the age of 55 (men: 79.7% for ages 55–59 and 51.6% for ages 60–64; women: 76.0% for ages 55–59 and 45.0% for ages 60–64). A concern to maintain these rates is reflected both in recent pension reforms and in policies promoting continuing competence development over the entire life-cycle. A government proposal to create 'Individual Learning Accounts' was approved in 2002. The principle behind this scheme is that the learning accounts should be more accessible to all workers, on a voluntary basis, with contributions made by both the employee and his/her employer. The state would contribute in the form of tax subsidides of various kinds. It is the individual who decides when to draw on the account in order to finance his/her competence development and also what kind of competence development to undertake, with the idea that it will be broader and more general than current staff training and less closely tied to the current job.

Box 8.3   The extent of continuing training for Swedish employees

During the first six months of 2003, 48% of all gainfully employed Swedish women and 44% of Swedish men participated in staff training. The average length of training was about five days for both men and women. Those employed in the public sector had a higher training rate (63% for government sector employees and 53% for those employed by local authorities) than those employed in the private sector (43%). This rate is one of the highest in Europe. The age pattern is also one of the best in the EU. The highest training rate for men (48%) is observed for the 25–34 and 45–54 age groups, but the rate for the 55–64 age group remains relatively high (42%). The same is true for women, where the training rate for the 55–64 age group (49%) is almost as high that for younger age groups. There is also no tendency for the training rate to decrease with length of service with a current employer. However, as in France and most EU member states, there are marked differences in training rates between different categories of worker. For example, workers with only compulsory education (nine years) have training rates of about 28%; workers with secondary education have training rates of about 44%, and those with higher education have training rates in the 55–60% range.

A comparison of the situations in Sweden and France leads us to suspect that there might be something of a vicious circle between early retirement and staff training. Expected early retirement could mean that the incentives to invest in training of older workers are small for both employers and employees, thus leading to lower productivity among older workers, which would in turn reinforce early exits, and so on.

Inga Persson, Lund University, in Training and Employment, no. 54, January–February 2004

The example of France

The example of France is also interesting since, as mentioned in Chapter 7, the law obliges companies to organize regular in-service training for employees. In the EU member states, company expenditure on continuing training represents 1–2.2% of total labour costs. Three groups can be distinguished as a function of the relative volume of such expenditure: France stands alone at the head of the list, followed by the Netherlands, Luxembourg, Italy, Germany and, finally, Spain and Belgium (the survey included these countries only). Reference to the sectors with the highest training rates is merely indicative, since they can vary from one year to another and from one firm to the next: banking and insurance (around 70%), telecommunications and post office (59%), retail trade (57%), automobile sales and repair (43%), machine and equipment manufacture (42%), and the hotel and catering industry (42%).

Since the early 1970s (and the 1971 law obliging companies to spend over 1% of wages on continuing training), the training policy in French firms has been mainly of two kinds:

- mixed training programmes (half at school or university, the other half 'in basket', that is, on a real job), destined for young people who intend to study for a diploma
- the annual training plan that provides a framework for the continuing education of employees, resulting from the global strategy and its translation into the HR policy; the time devoted to this training was automatically regarded as working time.

In order to establish a training plan, most firms have established procedures for identifying training needs, on the basis of:

- an analysis of individual training needs, with a view to improving the key job skills; this analysis generally results from an annual evaluation interview between employees and their managers
- a listing of the main components of the training policy, reflecting the goals of the firm: putting in place a quality management system, accompanying the launch of new products, and opening up new markets.

The training programme was (and still is) presented to the firm's Works Council, whose opinion is sought. Many studies have shown that a small part of training expenditure is earmarked for unqualified and older employees: 31% of private sector employees participated in some form of training, those in the 25–34 age group reported twice as much training as those over 55 (36% and 18% respectively). Training also goes to the most qualified: 54% of managers and 45% of employees in intermediate occupations participate in at least one training activity per year, as compared to only 29% of white-collar employees and 20% of operatives ('Continuing training in the private sector put to the test of age', *Training and Employment*, no. 54, January 2004). Age further aggravates the situation, since decreases in access to training begin earlier for those at the bottom of the job ladder.

Box 8.4   Continuing training in French legislation and firms

Since 2004, all employees are entitled to training by law (DIF – Droit Individuel de Formation): 20 hours/year on average, it being possible to capitalize this right up to 120 hours. Opportunities for training outside work time have also been increased; the principle being that the employee is responsible for developing his or her own skills and competencies.

In actual practice, this law does not mean that firms are obliged to set aside 20 hours/year for every employee: the latter may use public funds (financed by taxes on wages paid by employers) to finance the training.

What is the likely effect of the foregoing on the training of employees beyond 50 or 60 years? This new right would appear to suggest that older employees are trained insufficiently and would wish to receive more: nowadays many firms tend to anticipate a high number of claims coming from people (or from their representatives) who habitually are not trained.

▶

In some cases, discrimination might be involved (and the fact of not training older employees might be regarded as a proof of this).

But, above all, wider training will help provide answers to new issues in relation to the demographic evolution: if older people become globally more numerous and remain active longer (which is the aim of the 2003 French law on pensions):

- can they be kept in the same job, without loss of motivation and productivity (and an increase in absenteeism and occupational illness and injury)?
- will their skills continue to create added value for the firms, or will it be necessary to move these employees to new jobs?

Given demographic prospects, many firms will be expecting to increase the number of senior employees able to move to another job; obviously, training seniors will be one the main roads to reaching this goal, and an appropriate way of meeting their new right.

The recent law also increases the share of resources that firms have to earmark for training: the equivalent of at least 1.6% of wages.

It also requires, when the annual training plan is communicated to the Works Council, that the latter be made aware of the aim of the various training programmes: are they designed to increase the employee's effectiveness in his or her current job, to facilitate adaptation to changing functions, or to develop skills in other fields that have no obvious link with a current job (for example, preparing a future move, or gaining access to a management function)?

The DIF is supposed to depend on the employee's initiative but the employer has a duty to initiate the training programmes required to maintain people in their job. As a result, even in big firms, whose training expenditure is often over the minimum of 1.6% and where employees are trained for around 40 hours/year on average, the DIF may have an impact. Examples in banking, insurance, and the pharmaceutical industries, have shown that a high percentage of training expenditure is related to 'firm crucial' initiatives: to familiarize employees with new products, new regulations or new kinds of customer. Such training will clearly not be prompted by the DIF and the employees concerned, even though they are already receiving 40 hours/year of training, might still make a claim under the DIF.

This is one of the main reasons why this law encourages firms to look ahead carefully, especially as regards identifying priorities and making economic choices, when planning and investing in training.

Jean-Michel Brunet, expert in company senior issues – CEGOS Consulting, Paris, October 2004

A few examples of training by companies in the UK

SeniorNet (www.seniornet.org), for example, is a non-profit organization of computer-using adults, aged 50 and older. SeniorNet's mission is to provide education and access to computer technologies for older adults, thereby enhancing their lives and enabling them to share their knowledge. SeniorNet claims that it has assisted millions of older people since it was founded in 1986. It supports over 240 learning centres throughout the UK and in other countries, publishes a quarterly newsletter, holds regional conferences and collaborates in research on older adults and technology.

Another example is *Better Prospects*, an independent recruitment and training company, which has been actively encouraging the training and employment of people of all ages for some time. It introduced a 'silver surfers' learning club which is a specialist IT learning club for the over-55s.

Ergonomics and mobility

Definition

Age-friendly work design should have three objectives:

1. adapting the workplace, premises, equipment, working hours and processes to the employee's changing capacities
2. taking the capacities of older employees into consideration by selective organization of qualification opportunities
3. promoting possible substitution functions by selective promotion of special work throughout work-life (beginning with young employees with a view to reducing any slowing down in their ability to process information).

As a rule, older workers should not be regarded as being of reduced capacity but as having changed capacities. Biological age is the individual state of capability and behaviour reached by ageing, but does not necessarily correspond to chronological age. As shown in Chapter 5, interpersonal differences are regarded as considerably more significant for the capacity ageing process than personal diminution. Individual factors (such as professional activity and experience, training, education and general life-style) have at least the same amount of influence on capability as the biological ageing alone.

According to this point of view, it is important to adjust work systems and working processes to the capacities of older employees. An employee can function more easily and longer when his/her work is planned to be age and health friendly, differentiated, flexible, participation orientated, preventative and with more prospects. Theoretically, an integrated design process should take into consideration the differences between individuals (so-called differential work design) and the changes within an individual occurring over time (so-called dynamic work design).

Favourable working conditions are those which encourage older employees to adapt to their changing capacities to the best advantage. The need for planning is required, especially at workplaces which are subject to the following particularly unfavourable demands for older employees:

- short cycle, repetitive work, continuous heavy manual work
- extreme, changing demands in the absorbing and processing of information
- high, changing demands in accurate motor activity and coordination
- working in forced positions
- working in unfavourable environmental climates (for example, heat, noise)
- working with several stress factors.

Implementation

To overcome the age critical problems of work requirements the following measures need to be taken simultaneously:

- problem-preventive (active) measures
- problem-reducing (passive) measures.

Problem-preventive measures reduce the occurrence of problems concerning age critical working demands or directly address the possible causes of the problem. Problem-reducing measures, on the other hand, can be resorted to when a cause of age-critical working conditions (for example, the introduction of new technology or changed economic circumstances) cannot be avoided by an organization.

The basic strategy should be redesigning existing workplaces rather than transfer to another. Where transfers are unavoidable, the employee should be offered a workplace of an equal standard.

Company examples

An Age Positive study shows that in the UK requests to change an employee's role, hours of work or make ergonomic adjustments are considered by the employers on the basis of need, not age (Age Positive, 2001, pp. 37–38). However, many examples can be identified of employers making an adjustment to accommodate issues around an employee's age. For instance:

- shift work: employers using shift work systems are willing to accommodate requests from older workers to change to different shifts if circumstances permit
- working week: employers endeavour to support requests from older workers to adjust the length of their working week
- role adjustment: where tasks are quite physically demanding, older workers are provided with opportunities to increase the supervisory element in their work, or move to new positions within the organization.

In several cases, employers have made ergonomic adjustments to accommodate specific needs of older employees. These adjustments have frequently required minimal investment by employers. For example:

- office design and furniture: employers modify the design of their workstations to accommodate issues raised by older workers, and review the office seating, and where necessary, provide seating with greater lumbar support and/or seats with arm rests to assist older workers to rise from a seated position
- hearing related adjustment: older workers have been supplied with an amplifier for a 'hands-free' car phone to overcome a hearing difficulty
- annual medicals: employers provide annual medicals for all staff aged over 50. These consider what the employee may be able to do to combat issues around physical decline. The results of the medical remain confidential to the employee, but the procedure allows individuals to identify with their employer.

Box 8.5   Ergonomics at John Crane Safematic Oy

This medium-size manufacturing company (200 employees in Finland, but part of a large British corporation) has invested substantially in the health of its workers (around half in production functions, the other half in white-collar jobs) and their productive capacity.

Main recent improvements have been in ergonomics and in the protection equipment of dangerous machines, eye protection, safety shoes, and so on. Problems raised by workers are examined and solutions found. John Crane Safematic Oy is certified according to a specification of OHSAS18001 on 18 February 2003 by DNB. The certificate is valid for all the functions.

Maintaining health and satisfactory work ability are felt by managers to be very important. The median age of workers is 43, and there is no early retirement. Employees are also encouraged to stop smoking and practise sport or fitness activities.

A questionnaire is filled up each year and shows that the work atmosphere and team spirit have improved and remain satisfactory.

John Crane Safematic Oy measures its work atmosphere (including senior management skills) regularly once a year to find out where improvements are needed to maintain good team spirit, a good working environment and atmosphere, and superiors' managing skills. Part-time work is not much developed but not impossible. So far, a couple of blue-collar workers have opted for part-time work rather than taking gradual early retirement.

The firm is also planning continuing training until end of career, something that is not always evident for workers over 50 who have been with the company for a number of years.

Ritva Hyytiä – Human Resources Department, John Crane Safematic Oy, October 2004

Aérospatiale, in Toulouse, France, has had well-documented experience of ergonomic improvements that have kept qualified blue-collar workers, technicians and engineers in work until retirement age and thus considerably reduced early retirement (and with it of course the loss to the company of work experience and know-how). In this large industrial firm, there has been an attempt to attenuate the arduousness of certain work functions and to promote function sharing by mixed-age teams within strict observance of the parameters established under collective agreements. Tutoring has been much developed as a way of formalizing the handing-on of knowledge and expertise. The company has also been at pains to educate its production engineers to an awareness of the problems of ageing in the workplace with a view to their being better able to understand and cater to the specific occupational and functional needs of each age-category of worker.

Seniority wages

Definition

Traditionally, older workers have been more expensive because of the seniority rule, which has existed in most firms worldwide. In many countries, for example, in Belgium, France and Germany, there has been an implicit contract between the generations: young workers are paid below their level of productivity, knowing that their wage will follow a positive evolution with time. In actual fact, young workers have been subsidizing the higher wages of older workers. In principle, there is nothing wrong with this rule; it is an incentive for higher productivity and has led to the life employment we have known for decades in large corporations and in the public sector. However, it causes problems when the average age of the workforce increases and when workers approach the end of career. To the extent that older workers are paid more than their effective productivity, enterprises will have an incentive to get rid of them or, when redundancy occurs, to shed them first. That is the reason why the seniority rule has thus far been, and will remain until abandoned, an obstacle to any extension of work-life.

Current practice

For example, OECD data shows that the average pay of a 55-year-old in France is 40% higher than that of a 45-year-old, while 10% lower in the UK. In the UK, in April 2004, *Personnel Today* published a survey reporting that experienced staff earn less money. Managers over age 50 in accounting earn £10,000 less than those under 50, a discount of one-third. In IT and banking the differential is much the same. Figure 8.2 shows how different male wages are according to age in four countries.

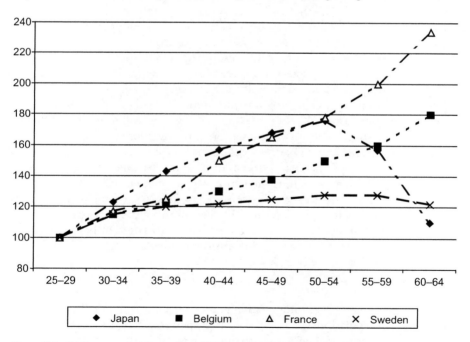

Figure 8.2   Male wages by age in four OECD countries (age 25–29 = 100%)

Source: Pestieau (2003, p. 690).

It can be seen that in two of the countries employers have to encourage early retirement programmes in order to rid themselves of expensive labour – costly, above all, in relation to productivity. Moreover, in a few countries (such as Switzerland), pension rules cause pension contributions to increase with age. Furthermore, in some countries there is a widespread belief in political and trade union circles that any early retirement of older workers creates vacancies for younger ones. This belief rests on the hypothesis of perfect substitutability between jobs for older and younger workers. That hypothesis is however debatable, and it is now widely recognized that sending older workers into retirement in order to promote employment for the young does not work and may even be counter-productive. Indeed, certain recent empirical studies show that this type of policy has usually failed.

Implementation

These two observations would suggest, therefore, that if the trend towards early retirement is to be reversed a revolution is needed in the mentality of actors in the countries concerned. Economic agents, employers' organizations, trade unions and governments must be persuaded to adopt wage scales which more closely match productivity, and they must give up the belief that there is a direct link between early retirement and jobs for the young unemployed.

It would indeed be naive to think that a drastic reduction of implicit taxes on postponed activity would suffice to increase the activity rate of older workers. Such a reduction would have to be accompanied by active employment policies in a number of areas: training of ageing workers, legal barriers to age discrimination, employment subsidies and, as already mentioned, a better adjustment of wages to productivity. On these matters the successful experience of countries such as Japan, the United States, Sweden and more recently Finland could be used as guidelines for countries plagued by too-early retirement. The new performance-based remuneration, especially for professional categories, will promote a different wage profile and should thus make the senior employee more competitive.

There have been profound changes over recent years in adapting pay profiles to performance, first in American and British firms and subsequently, although to a lesser extent, in German, Dutch, French and even Japanese firms.

In the Netherlands, for the vast majority of workers, wage progression occurs during the first half of the career (until 30–45 years). Supporters of the new system include the trade union confederations, and it is generally felt to be hardly punitive for those who continue to work full time until retirement.

Pension regulations

One important variable of employment at end of career is undoubtedly the whole issue of pension regulations. In many countries, pension benefits have long been calculated on the basis of the final salary or of the salary of the last five years. This system, common in countries like the UK and the Netherlands, has been an obstacle to the reduction of work time at end of career and has therefore adversely affected the employment of senior workers.

However, over recent years pension regulations have been modified. In the Netherlands, for example, the basis for pension calculation now reflects the recent decision to make greater use of prudential techniques. In most collective agreements it is now the entire range of contribution years that are taken into account rather than just the final salary. It should be noted that this latter development is very much in line with a reduction of work time at end of career. As Ruud Fux of the FNV Confederation stresses, computation of the pension on the basis of occupational life in its entirety obviates the financial drawbacks, in terms of pension entitlement, of moving from full-time to part-time work during the latter years of occupational life. The new system is now gaining considerable ground. According to estimates by the Dutch Ministry for Social Affairs and Employment, in 2002 almost 60% of wage-earners belonged to a system based on wages throughout the career as opposed to 32% in 1999, and 23% in 1995.

Another feature of pre-retirement reform has been the support given to mobility at end of career, the possibility, that is, of transferring from one firm to another pre-retirement funded entitlements, something that was impossible under the old voluntary pre-retirement system.

Another crucial factor is age-neutrality with pension contributions. In Switzerland, for example, second pillar contributions increase with age in a number of occupational schemes, but have now been changed in several pension funds in order to facilitate employment at end of career. Current debate and proposals suggest that there will be further progress in this area before long.

In Finland, in February 2004, a working group convening representatives from employer and employee organizations agreed to abolish the link between age and pension contributions by 2007. This will apply to large firms for 'TEL' pension contributions, that is, contributions governed by the Employees' Pensions Act (TEL). This means that, by 2007, TEL pension contributions will be the same for all employees, regardless of age and the size of the firm. As a result, pension contributions will be rising for young people and falling for older workers.

Anti-age discrimination legislation

Definition

Age discrimination against older workers means discrimination, either direct or indirect, at various stages during the end of career. It takes, among others, the following forms: early exclusion from the workforce (for the older unemployed, re-entry into the market is virtually impossible) and lack of training opportunities. Discrimination against older workers involves differential treatment based upon prejudices or stereotypes. These include the view that older workers are more expensive, less productive and less adaptable than younger ones. Such prejudices may be held by employers, the public, policy makers and even by older workers themselves. Thus, in society, age discrimination has a relatively lower saliency compared to other forms of discrimination. It is generally considered to be less of a problem than other types of discrimination, most notably discrimination on grounds of gender and race. To some extent, it has been rendered less evident by a belief among older people themselves that they should make way for younger people, particularly in relation to promotion.

Implementation

At an EU level the member states have acknowledged the importance of combating age discrimination in Article 13 of the Treaty of Amsterdam, which came into force on 1 May 1999. Subsequently, the Community Action Programme to Combat Discrimination 2001–06 and the EU Directive on Equal Treatment in Employment were adopted in October 2000. According to the European Directive, all EU member states are required to introduce equality in employment legislation, including age discrimination, by December 2006 (see also Chapter 6). As a consequence, most member states have already adopted such legislation.

Country and company examples

Among current national age-discrimination legislation in the EU, the Dutch law has perhaps the widest scope. The Equal Treatment in Employment Bill makes it illegal to distinguish according to age in recruitment and selection as well as vocational training and promotion, and permits age discrimination only in cases in which setting an age limit is objectively justified (see also Chapter 7). From December 2006, this also applies to provisions in collective agreements concerning pension-related dismissal at certain ages below the pension age of 65 years. However, in some cases, age limits are still allowed: for instance, dismissal on grounds of reaching retirement age, or the employment promotion of youth (separate minimum wage levels for youth will remain).

In the UK (where the new age-discrimination legislation in line with the EU Directive is currently under preparation), the final evaluation of the Code of Practice on Age Diversity in Employment shows that, since the code was introduced, there has been a reduction in the use of age as a criterion in company policies relating to recruitment and selection, training and development, promotion and redundancy. In the companies surveyed, the use of age in selection has halved, from 27% in survey wave 1 to 13% in wave 3. However, the older person's survey and the company case studies provide some evidence of age discrimination, even in companies with good practice guidelines. Often managers were unaware that their behaviour could be deemed discriminatory. Thus nine out of ten older people believe that employers discriminate against older people in the workplace. However, a much lower proportion – one in four older people – report that they have personally experienced age discrimination in relation to an actual or potential job at some point in time. Discrimination was experienced most frequently in relation to getting a new job and/or obtaining a job interview (Table 8.5).

Codes of practice

Definition

A Code of Practice contains guidelines intended to assist employers and others responsible for recruitment and training to productively manage the ageing of

Table 8.5   Age discrimination in British companies – experienced in relation to an actual or possible job (as a percentage of older workers surveyed)

Age discrimination experienced regarding:	% of older workers surveyed
Getting a new job	12
Obtaining a job interview	11
Being offered a promotion	5
Being offered training and development	5
Obliged to take early retirement	4
Offered early retirement	4
Prevented taking early retirement	1
None	75

Source: Age Positive (2001, pp. 22–3).

the workforce. This is voluntary, and helps to promote an age-neutral approach to employment and avoid the unnecessary exclusion of workers as they age, as well as to ensure better employment prospects for older workers. The Code of Practice is not necessarily an alternative to legislation against discrimination but provides guidelines on how to avoid such discrimination and, therefore, could be very useful alongside such legislation.

Good practice on age and employment has been defined as a combination of (i) specific measures to overcome or minimize age barriers; and (ii) general employment or human resource (HR) policies which provide a work environment in which individuals are able to achieve their potential without being disadvantaged by their age and which therefore enables companies to retain a highly motivated and diverse workforce, reflecting a flexible approach and greater understanding of customers' needs. The six universal dimensions of HR management in the cycle of employment underpin the Code of Good Practice:

1. job recruitment: recruit on the basis of the skills and abilities needed to do the job
2. learning, training and development: encourage all employees to take advantage of relevant training opportunities
3. promotion and internal job changes: base promotion on the ability, or demonstrated potential, to do the job
4. flexible working practices and the modernization of work
5. workplace design and health promotion
6. employment exit and the transition to retirement.

Employers who replace unnecessary age criteria with objective, job-related ones, will:

- have a wider choice of applicants from which to recruit to get the best person for the job
- manage resources more effectively by minimizing staff turnover
- be better able to build a more flexible, multiskilled workforce

- have access to a wider range of experience and expertise to provide business solutions that meet market needs
- develop a better-motivated workforce which feels valued and is willing to contribute to business success
- reduce costs through increased productivity and reduced levels of absenteeism.

Implementation

Codes of Good Practice in the employment of certain groups of workers (for example, women, ethnic minorities, disabled people) already exist in several EU member states. Not many countries, with the exception of the UK, have a national Code of Good Practice on age (Code of Practice for Age Diversity in Employment, since 1999). However, as we saw in Chapters 5 and 7, national governments have taken action also in other EU countries. For example, Finland has anti-discrimination legislation and had a national programme for ageing workers running from 1998 to 2002; Ireland introduced anti-age discrimination legislation and special measures for older workers in October 1999; the Netherlands proposed a ban on age discrimination in employment in 1999 and, in September 2000, a special Taskforce on Age and Employment was established by the Minister for Social Affairs and Employment to develop a national action programme to promote the labour market participation of older workers. In a number of cases, employers have developed their own 'business case' for ending age barriers and creating equal opportunities in the labour market. However, so far evidence of good practice has been demonstrated mainly in large organizations.

Country and company examples

Among the European countries, the UK is the most advanced in this field. Its Code of Practice has already helped many employers to change their employment practices for the better since 1999. Results from the last evaluation of the Code of Practice show that awareness of the code among employers has been increasing (37% currently compared to 23% in the course of the previous evaluation). Awareness is significantly higher in large companies: only one-third of small companies have been aware of the code, compared with half the medium-size companies and six out of ten large companies. Awareness is more widespread in the service and public sectors (cf. Age Positive, 2001, pp. 26–7).

One must also mention that a European Code of Good Practice – Ageing in Employment has been prepared by Eurolink Age in 2000, with financial support from the Employment and Social Affairs Directorate-General of the European Commission. The code was prepared with representatives of eight countries (Germany, Spain, France, Italy, the Netherlands, Finland, Sweden and the United Kingdom), under the leadership of Alan Walker and Gerd Naegele, assisted by Elizabeth Drury. The code involved extensive consultation of social partners and companies. Its main objective is to help countries, firms and professional organizations to prepare their own code on age and employment. To illustrate the company measures described in this chapter, Table 8.6 lists 10 best practice firms in industry and services.

Table 8.6 Best practice of 10 firms in industry and services

Sector					
			Company		
Industry	**Arcelor** Branch: Steel industry Location: France & EU	**Ford Motor Company** Branch: Car Industry 20,000 employees Location: UK	**Novo Nordisk** Branch: Medicinal production 15,000 employees Location: Denmark	**Laboratoire Boiron** Branch: Homeopathic medicine 2,200 employees Location: France	**Safematic Oy** Branch: Manufacturing 200 employees Location: Finland
Working time	Since 1994, employment of blue-collar workers aged 50 and over on part-time basis	Official retirement age is 65. From age 58, employees can choose a preferred retirement date. Some flexibility is allowed also after 65. Since 1994, the Ford *Community Volunteer Scheme* has worked to link employees with organizations which need their skills. Retirees are particularly encouraged to participate		Since 1976, preparation for retirement: 6 years before retirement, employees can reduce their working time, by at least 3 hours per week in the first year, and by one third at the end of the career	
Career planning					
Continuing training until end of career	Pay for skills – no departure, improvement of skills		Utilizing the necessary resources to education and training	Older workers have the same rights to continuing training and promotion	Plans to develop it
Ergonomics, mobility			Adapting workplaces to the individual needs		Protection against heat, noise, machines, etc. Better positioning

185

Table 8.6 *continued*

Sector	Company				
Age diversity				Company insists on age diversity as one aspect of good balance and team spirit	
Evaluation/ benefits	Increase of retirement age from 50 to 60; decrease in absenteeism; improvement of health condition; higher satisfaction with work	Well-being of the older worker, both pre and post-retirement; Ford: socially responsible employer	Development and maintenance of qualifications, competencies, productivity, flexibility and satisfaction at work	Transition between employment and full retirement; development of spontaneous system of tutorage between the senior worker and the younger employee who will be replacing the former; increase in productivity	Better work climate; less sickness leave
Services	AXA Branch: Insurance Location: France	Carl Bro Branch: Consulting Location: Denmark & worldwide	Munich Transport and Tariff Association Branch: Public Transport Location: Germany	BUPA Branch: Health and care services 36,000 employees Location: UK	J Sainsbury Plc Branch: Food retail 130,000 employees Location: UK
Working time		Gradual withdrawal is possible		Since 2000, older workers are offered the choice to continue working beyond the regular retirement age (60 years) to a max. age of 65. Employees working beyond 60 retain all earlier benefits	Official retirement age is 65 years for men and women. Since 1998, workers may retire at any time between the ages of 50 and 75 ('25-year window')

Career planning	Regular assessment of qualifications; reorientate career paths, second and third career possible in the firm	At the age of 50, information meeting with the employee and his/her spouse; at 55 a senior course is offered; from the age of 55, it is planned individually. Main points: future job possibilities; knowledge and experience transfer; educational needs; job diminution possibilities; exit point	
Continuing training	In coordination with career planning; improvement of qualification; no decrease in access with age	Lifelong learning is supported	Training relevant to the employees' needs provided to all regardless of age
Ergonomics, mobility	Mobility is encouraged to increase motivation	Since 1993, Human Resources Development and Workplace Health Promotion Programme with the aim of reduction of psychical load and stress among underground drivers aged 50 and over. The programme consists of 20 working days per year. The aim of the programme is to improve drivers' physical conditions through gymnastics, and to	

187

Table 8.6 continued

Sector	Company		
	teach them how to cope with stress by means of relaxation exercises. Exchange of experience also plays an important role	Retention of key nursing skills; removing age discrimination; employees reflect better the age profile of society	
Age diversity	Important to reflect the customer age profile		
Evaluation/ benefits	Increase of motivation, satisfaction with work and productivity	Improvement of health condition; reduction in stress at work, back and heart problems; reduction in absenteeism; better team spirit and company atmosphere; fewer problems with customers	Retention of key nursing skills; removing age discrimination; employees reflect better the age profile of society	Increased staff retention; advantage of age diversity regarding better communication, and understanding of the needs of customers of all ages

Part III

Working Beyond 60 – For Whom?

The Need for Fairness, Diversity and Flexibility

9
Who Can and Would Wish to Work Beyond 60?

This chapter will address the third main aspect of working beyond 60. We now know much more about why we need to extend work-life, as well as how such an extension beyond 60 can be of benefit to employers and employees alike. The question we must now address is: for which categories of worker exactly would working beyond age 60 be desirable? The issue was of course touched upon when in Chapter 4 we looked at the changes that occurred as the traditional industrial state evolved into the new service economy with its modified set of physical and mental work requirements. We shall examine in this chapter two important and interdependent aspects of this issue: first, the crucial need for diversity and with it the importance of fairness, and second, the all-important need for flexibility and informed choice.

The need for diversity and the importance of fairness

The need for diversity is crucially important whenever policies for extending work-life are adopted and implemented by firms. This is because workers enter the labour market at different ages and in differing personal circumstances, and with a wide range of life expectancies.

Extended study and training

Over the last two generations, a revolution has taken place in education and training in all developed countries, and overall young people now have access to much longer study and training, and to better qualifications. They enter the world of work later than in the past. Although it varies from country to country, the age of entry is often at 20 years or even later. In France and Germany, for example, the average age of entering work is among the highest in the EU at respectively 21 and 22 years. In the UK it is slightly younger at around 20, and in Denmark, the lowest in the EU, it is close to 18 years. This is in stark contrast to the age at which many workers leaving their job today started work, often between the ages of 14 and 17. The age at which young people enter the labour market varies not only from one generation to the next but also within the space of a single generation and depends mainly on the educational level of the individuals concerned. When pension systems, as is already the case in many countries, require 40 or more contribution years, the age of entering work will of course be critical. It is precisely for this reason that many social scientists consider a single age for retirement for all a socially unfair criterion. Moreover, tasks also differ greatly from one branch and from one category of worker to the next. The building industry, for instance, is an obvious example of a branch where most workers simply cannot work for 40 years, and where diversity of end of career is absolutely essential.

Retirement age, a function of the arduousness of work?

Should therefore the age of retirement be a function of the arduousness or of the inherent stress of a job? Yes, in principle, and it is precisely for this reason that different ages for retirement have already been put in place, for people, among numerous others, like firemen, military personnel and airline pilots. Nowadays all countries have a number of specific retirement conditions for specific categories of worker.

In Switzerland, the retirement age for women is currently increasing and, following advice by the OECD, an increase to 67 years for all workers is now contemplated. And yet a few years ago the retirement age for builders was reduced from 65 to 60 years in recognition of the difficult conditions builders have to face but also in order to bring down the high disability rate among workers in that sector.

If the factor just described accounted for retirement at an early age in some branches in the past and to some extent still today, in many occupations things have improved. Coal miners, who in times past performed extremely hard jobs, are, in most if not all European states, pretty well extinct, and driving a modern train, though in many respects involving greater responsibility, is not as physically arduous as driving a steam locomotive 50 or 60 years ago. Must the privileges and special concessions of the past be maintained when conditions have changed? Almost certainly not. And yet the second halves of many careers need reassessment and extensive redesign to include functions which are less active and more sedentary in nature. Alternatively, for example, firemen or nurses who need to retire before their peers could be found other part-time tasks in other fields. Education, cultural pursuits and training, for instance, offer numerous opportunities for 'second careers'.

Examples are common. A few are given as illustrations of our purpose, and the reader will have additional examples in mind. Hospital nurses from the age of 55 often find it difficult to continue working full time. However, they possess experience, knowledge and often empathy. They can be assigned to other tasks, such as call centres in hospitals (for example, for emergencies), work in schools, organization of long-term care services for elderly people in urban areas, visits to sick elderly persons who need a quality of contact and moral comfort, or mobile blood transfusion units. Teachers also find it difficult to teach after the age of 55 or 30 years of teaching. They often could reduce their working time and be employed at other paid tasks (libraries, book shops, private tuition, work in non-governmental agencies, and so on).

On the other hand, in France also, a recent survey (*Le Monde*, 9 June 2004), pointed out that professional employees from the private sector increasingly move to teaching in order to benefit from a more culturally oriented and stable job, and one which entails transmitting one's experience to young people. These persons represented 15% of new applicants for teaching vacancies in 2003. Teaching is a typical job which can perhaps be better performed as a second career, bringing to it a vast professional experience. In Switzerland, in a number of German-speaking towns, retirees have started helping teachers at both primary and secondary levels: in Winterthur over 60 retirees and in Zurich over 230 are already performing jobs in various schools and this successful new experience is developing fast (*Le Temps*, 26 November 2004).

When freed from physical duties, firemen could well continue working later than at present by having a second shorter career, for example, in first aid care and road safety. Civic jobs in town halls and municipal councils are well performed by experienced persons from various backgrounds and would therefore constitute valuable second careers.

According to a decision taken by the French government in November 2004 (*Le Monde*, 13 November 2004), in the near future teachers from primary and secondary schools will be able to move from teaching to other responsibilities in the public service. Indeed, following the 2003 pension reform which will extend working life, teachers had expressed their difficulties in remaining active after 30 or 35 years of teaching. The decision has therefore been taken to allow them (after a minimum of 15 years' teaching) to move to other public service activities. Teachers leaving their first career will need to have their qualifications assessed and undergo additional training (up to six months with full salary) in order to qualify for new jobs and embark on new career paths.

Different life expectancies

But can the *arduousness* of a job or function actually be measured? Measurement is certainly difficult to do especially when working conditions are changing constantly. One more obvious approach to the problem is to examine life and health expectancies where data for the latter exist. In France, on average, at 35 years the remaining life expectancy of a domestic employee is 36.5 years and that of a qualified blue-collar worker 37 years. On the other hand, civil servants, artists and intellectual workers all have a life expectancy of around 46 years. These significant differences in life expectancy from one category of worker to the next are twice as great for men as for women. At 60 years, in France, over the period 1982–96, men in general had a life expectancy of 19 years, agricultural labourers an expectancy of only 15.5 years, while professional workers (civil servants, intellectual workers and artists) at the same age could expect to live for another 23.5 years. At the same age over the same period, women in general had 23.5 years before them – blue-collar workers 23 years and professional workers (civil servants, intellectual workers and artists) 27.5 years (Conseil Economique et Social, 2001, pp. 54–5).

For these reasons, according to many social policy makers, the notion of retirement age should be gradually replaced by that of the number of contribution years to pension systems. They feel it essential that, in future, pension schemes be based on more objective and fairer criteria than hitherto. Reforms like those adopted in Sweden have been very much on these lines. It has been suggested, incidentally, that, save for special cases where early exit is a compensation for certain recognized disadvantages, the situation of public sector workers should now be brought into line with those in the private sector. Most countries, and Italy is one example, have already been able to meet these criteria. Others like France suffer from wide disparities in the age and conditions of pensions which confer, in the opinion of some, unacceptable privileges on civil servants and certain special categories such as SNCF train workers and the employees of the Electricité de France and the National Postal Service.

If, then, for sound economic and financial reasons, society expects workers to remain longer in the labour market, the need for a diversity of ends of career must equally be accepted so as to avoid the negative impact of the kind of long-lasting strike that Europe has recently experienced with firemen and truck drivers. The public debate on this issue and the policies to which it gives rise must therefore accommodate a limited number of exceptions to a later exit age which will help to confirm the new rules and consolidate future practice. In other words, if major resistance to the new measures is to be avoided, employers and the public authorities must ensure that the new policies pave the way for a wide range of end-of-career options and modes of transition into retirement. Such diversity would no more than reflect the characteristics of the sectors, professional branches, categories of worker and individual and cultural preferences involved. Finally, financial incentives must be used to encourage flexibility towards the end of occupational life while not ruling out the possibility of a downward trend in the retirement age for some.

The need for flexibility and the importance of informed choice

In most European countries, labour market flexibility has increased considerably over the last quarter-century. The new functions of our service economies have greatly contributed to promoting and broadening this trend and, as we saw in Chapter 4, atypical work has now gained enormous ground. Flexible work time is crucial not only for young parents who need to combine work and family responsibilities but also for end-of-career employment: it makes the extension of work both possible and necessary. However, extension of work-life *full time* is likely to be possible only for a few categories of worker, for example, the self-employed whose work patterns are in any case inherently more flexible, and workers who are in very good health and personally very committed to what they do. Meanwhile, the average employee will in all probability be more ready to work later if he or she can work *part time* and thus enjoy the benefits of more leisure and more time for activities outside the workplace. Employers also stand to gain since it is now established that part-time work reduces absenteeism (which often increases with age) and the cost of the senior worker (see Chapter 5). In short, such an arrangement, for both the employee and for the company concerned, will make for a smoother transition between work-life and full retirement. Firms all over Europe that have in this way developed an extension of work-life part time have been found to be highly satisfied with the results.

Working longer – an unavoidable obligation

A high proportion of workers of the baby-boom generation will need to work later because of pension reforms. Moreover, a fair proportion of those working part time for a good part of their career – this mainly concerns women but increasingly men as well – will need to work longer to improve their second pillar pension. It may be helpful at this point to remind ourselves of Figure 2.1 which showed the trend towards a new distribution of activity across the life-cycle. It implies that, in the long term, we shall all, willy-nilly, be working differently.

But for the time being, not only are women more accustomed to part-time, and flexible and temporary work patterns, but because of their smaller contribution and careers that are often interrupted for family or care reasons, their pension rights are frequently poor when compared to those of men with the same level of qualification. In spite of the gradual convergence of national pension systems across the EU, the Commission acknowledges that 'significant coverage discrepancy in pension entitlements, particularly under second pillar schemes, of women atypical workers will persist for a long time to come'. As a consequence, in the UK, for example, a recent publication (Age Concern England, 2003) shows that one in four single women pensioners lives in poverty, and twice as many women as men rely on means-tested benefits in retirement. Fortunately, the rates in most other old EU member states are not as alarming. However, the majority of women, in particular those ageing alone (whether divorced, widows or single) will need to work beyond the pension age in order to bring their income and pension benefits up to acceptable standards.

Given that women's life expectancy is definitely longer than men's in most countries, is it fair that women should work longer than men? Whatever answer we give to that question, it is our belief that both women and men should be encouraged to work later (and to continue to train until the end of their active life), in particular on a part-time basis, so as to continue to contribute to economic life and to optimize their pension benefits. It is, however, also a fact that women, as a general rule, bear a greater load than men in terms of being primarily responsible for the care of children, of the elderly and sick persons within the family and community. It is not rare, for example, for women around 60 still to be responsible for ageing parents or in-laws and it is they who in practice perform most of the caring. As grandmothers, they also play a key role in assisting with the bringing up and education of young children and are often the only way their daughters and daughters-in-law can combine a family with work. It is also recognized that women often make up the majority of workers in voluntary organizations. Indeed, worldwide, it is women who still perform by far the main bulk of unpaid (that is, non-monetarized, however essential to the community) work, while men do most of the paid work. In spite of encouraging convergence with work cycles, the roles of men and women remain essentially complementary. And for these reasons, if for no others, the European Commission is promoting gender-neutral pension systems and schemes.

Importance of informed choice

Flexibility is also crucially important at end of career because, if workers are to remain later on the labour market, they must be motivated and productive, and they will be neither of these things unless they have freedom of choice – an all-important modern value – in the matter. They must be made perfectly aware of the alternatives on offer: basically, leaving earlier on a reduced pension or staying on so as to benefit later from a more generous one. Hence the need for workers to receive regular *statements* of their pension benefits as a function of the number of years worked (for example, the 'orange' annual Swedish pension bulletin).

Over recent decades, retirement as a specific period in the life-cycle has acquired much greater and altered significance for most persons. Increasingly, seniors are thinking about it, planning and preparing for it and looking forward to a time of good health and of family and personal achievement. Having, for the most part, worked extremely hard throughout occupational life (though probably not as hard as in the past), they look upon retirement as a time of rest and unpaid activity they have richly deserved. But the realities of an individual's everyday life cannot and should not change from one day to the next. It is important therefore that they extend work-life for a few more years than they do today to optimize pension benefits and to provide for a smooth transition from full-time work to full retirement. But in turn, it is important also that this extension be flexible and, for the most part, part time, and that its terms and conditions be freely consented to and fully desired by the individual concerned. In short and in other words, retirement should become *a process* rather than the event it still is most of the time.

Part IV

Working Beyond 60 – Key Policies and Recommendations

10
Working Beyond 60 – Key Policies and Recommendations

This last chapter is divided into three sections: (i) a comparative country synthesis, with strong factors and needed improvements (Box 10.1); (ii) key policies for working beyond 60, which include our main recommendations; and (iii) suggested additional policies needed in facing the overall demographic challenge.

Box 10.1 Comparative country synthesis, with strong factors (+) and needed improvements (–)

1. Countries with *global* policies

- **Finland**
  - ++ Information and age awareness campaigns of all actors, *Experience – a National Treasury*
  - ++ Models and practice in firms of improved health at work and work ability/ capacity
  - +   Pension reform linked to life expectancy and including partial pensions
  - –   Develop more part-time work and transitions to retirement

- **Denmark**
  - ++ Reduction of exit roads, in particular disability (now *working capacity*)
  - +   Adaptation of working time and conditions, for example, *soft* jobs
  - +   Incentives to employers and employees

- **The United Kingdom**
  - ++ Campaigns to convince employers, for example, *Age Diversity, Age Positive*
  - +   Flexible retirement and working time
  - +   Incentives to employees (employment credit)
  - –– Improve state pension benefits

- **The Netherlands**
  - ++ Reduction of exit roads, in particular early retirement (public) and disability

  ▶

++   Promotion of part-time and atypical work
+   Legislation against age discrimination
−−   Encourage more full-time work

2. Countries with *partial* policies

*   **Germany**
    +   Pension reform will reduce first pillar and extend second pillar
    +   Studies on age management and experimental firm practice
    +   Ergonomics, continuing training, especially in large firms
    −−   Insufficient practice

*   **France**
    +   Pension reform will extend work-life
    +   Improvements in career planning, training and part-time work, especially in large firms
    −−   Early exit still in practice
    −−   Insufficient debate and age awareness campaigns

*   **Italy**
    ++   Drastic pension reform
    −−   Early retirement still the norm
    −−   Insufficient debate and age awareness campaigns

*   **Switzerland**
    ++   High level of employment and continuing training
    +   Part-time work common
    −   Early retirement being currently developed
    −   Lack of policies and of incentives, insufficient flexibility

*   **Hungary**
    ++   Drastic pension reform
    −−   Low employment and no age management.

Author's compilation

Key policies for working beyond 60 and main recommendations

Successful extension of occupational life requires that certain preconditions be met. All new policies, any measures taken by the authorities, any significant change in enterprise culture, will need to be preceded by a coherent, thoroughly democratic, broad-based and informed debate of the issues involved. In this regard, there are lessons to be learned from the example of the Nordic countries. It is also essential that all regulations governing pensions, social insurance and tax arrangements be made to serve the same end: that of extending occupational life. Within the enterprise, such extension must be accompanied by an adjustment of work schedules, and countries with high rates of qualified part-time workers will find the going a lot easier. Similarly, continuing training until end of career will be crucial in keeping productivity and motivation at optimum levels. And lastly, part-time work will exercise downward pressure on the cost of senior employees.

In what follows we shall briefly examine four main recommendations regarding the need for (i) an holistic approach, (ii) coordinated social and economic policies, (iii) a lively and well-informed debate, and (iv) an effective and rapid plan of action.

The need for an holistic approach

Countries such as Finland, Denmark and the UK, which have been so far successful in flexibly extending work-lives, are all countries that have adopted a global approach to healthy and active ageing and end-of-career management. Most actors today, at almost all levels – the European institutions, national governments, companies and the trade unions – are convinced of the wisdom of this approach. And this is now seen to be especially true of countries like Germany, France, Italy, Austria and the Netherlands where the early retirement culture has been particularly pronounced. It is only when all variables – pension reforms, social welfare regulations, employment and company policies – start to change that attitudes, norms and behaviour will progressively alter with all actors of economic and social life. And let us remember that long-term issues need global policies sustained *over time* to be successful. Figure 10.1 shows not only that social and economic policies need to be properly coordinated, but that they need to take into account company age management

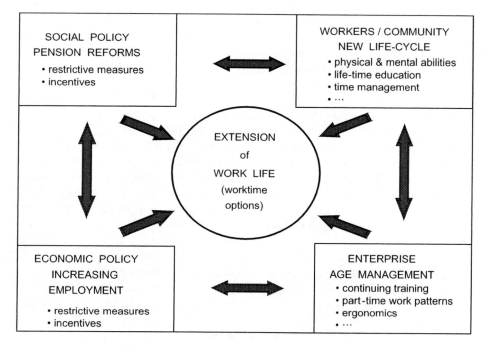

Figure 10.1 The model of working beyond 60

Source: Reday-Mulvey (2002).

and new life-cycle patterns. It now becomes clear that if we need pension reforms, we need to accompany them by a root and branch reassessment of the overall end-of-career and retirement contexts within which they will need to operate.

The need for coordinated social and economic policies

As early as 1996, a Japanese expert, I. Shimowada, concluded: 'One can hardly overstress the importance of properly integrated public and company policies for promoting the employment of older people' (Delsen and Reday-Mulvey, 1996, p. 162). Indeed, in the 1990s most Western countries adopted pension reforms, but it is only more recently that governments realized that to encourage longer working lives, social reforms had to be accompanied by employment measures at the state and company levels.

Public policies: the need for restrictive measures and incentives

What stands out as essential is that public policies need to be sufficiently comprehensive and accompanied by incentives at various levels (Figure 10.2). In order to reduce exit roads from work at an early stage, it is essential to accompany pension reforms by other welfare changes, in particular to make early retirement options as well as disability and unemployment routes more difficult, more costly and their terms more stringent. But restrictive changes of this kind clearly need to be accompanied by government-funded financial incentives. Both carrot and stick are needed in order to stimulate new attitudes and behaviours. Changing the deeply-rooted mind-sets of the early retirement culture requires drastic redesign, a good partnership between government and enterprise in the *gradual* implementation of new age-management policies.

Company policies: the need for comprehensive working-life measures

Four areas at least, among the many that require attention, should be a particular focus for this integrated policy approach. First, training. In order for older workers to remain competitive, continuing training should not terminate at 45 or 50 years but should persist until end of career and be better adapted to experienced workers. Countries where such company policies already exist are in a much stronger position. In Sweden and Switzerland, the extent of training is impressive throughout work-life and there seems to be little discrimination towards older workers. In France and Germany, especially in bigger companies, a similar policy approach is now gaining ground. What is required is an extensive redesigning of the second part of the career in order to give new shape and identity to work-life between 45 and 65.

Second, a key variable is pay policy. It is clear that seniority-based pay policy, by raising the wage costs of workers at end of career, has constituted a real obstacle to all forms of extension of work-life. The growing trend in wage calculation today towards reducing the weight of the seniority factor and increasing that of performance must be encouraged. The financial needs of senior workers are usually lower than those of workers in their 40s. Moreover, changes in pension calculation mean that wages at end of career no longer need to be the highest. This will enable companies to link pay to performance and not exclusively to age. The difficult situation in this

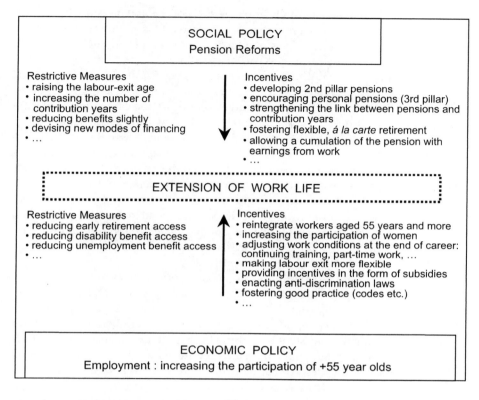

SOCIAL POLICY
Pension Reforms

Restrictive Measures
- raising the labour-exit age
- increasing the number of contribution years
- reducing benefits slightly
- devising new modes of financing
- ...

Incentives
- developing 2nd pillar pensions
- encouraging personal pensions (3rd pillar)
- strengthening the link between pensions and contribution years
- fostering flexible, *á la carte* retirement
- allowing a cumulation of the pension with earnings from work
- ...

EXTENSION OF WORK LIFE

Restrictive Measures
- reducing early retirement access
- reducing disability benefit access
- reducing unemployment benefit access
- ...

Incentives
- reintegrate workers aged 55 years and more
- increasing the participation of women
- adjusting work conditions at the end of career: continuing training, part-time work, ...
- making labour exit more flexible
- providing incentives in the form of subsidies
- enacting anti-discrimination laws
- fostering good practice (codes etc.)
- ...

ECONOMIC POLICY
Employment : increasing the participation of +55 year olds

Figure 10.2 Coordinating social and economic policies

Source: Reday-Mulvey (2003).

regard in Switzerland should serve as a lesson that social contributions now need to be made age-neutral.

Third, part-time pay is obviously an important variable in helping to reduce the cost of the senior worker. Part-time work must be accompanied by better social protection and in-house promotion. Most companies have improved conditions of part-timers, and some countries – France and the Netherlands are examples – have modified legislation to this end.

Fourth and finally, occupational pensions have to be adapted to longer and more flexible life-cycles. Although there has been progress, particularly in the UK and the Netherlands, in modifying them to make them average-salary based, pension funds in a few other countries are still final-salary based.

The need for a lively and well-informed debate

Another factor crucial to the effectiveness of policies promoting a longer work-life is the extent to which their purpose has been communicated to, and accepted by, the public through a well-informed, broad-based debate of the issues. The experience of countries so far that have successfully implemented policies and measures in this area shows that the issues must be properly communicated to, and thoroughly debated by, all parties concerned – employers, employees, trade unions – in intelligible terms. They must, moreover, be perceived as part of a medium- to long-term exercise, since in this sort of area little or nothing can be achieved over the short term. Enterprises, for example, need a *long-term approach* to investment and to changing mind-sets and attitudes. Hence the importance of targeted information campaigns, of raising public awareness and of organizing an open debate within firms, trade unions and the general public. And the media have of course an essential part to play in conveying a new message: that today the onset of old age is retreating, occurring later, and that the way we manage our lives between the ages of 50/55 and 70 needs serious reappraisal. Firms must now initiate democratic debate of these issues and encourage wider discussion with decision making bodies and the press. The ideas that underpin the new thinking on ageing must be couched in new language which is both intelligible and innovative. *Experience – A National Treasure* (Finland), *Active Ageing* (worldwide) or *Age Positive* (UK) are all examples of this and important first steps in changing people's prejudices and attitudes.

One is, even so, bound to admit that the current context is far from ideal for the discussion and widespread acceptance of pension reforms. The general public still has a perception of ageing that is fairly remote from current sociological reality. Not only do these reforms provide for an increase in the number of contribution years (which is perfectly consistent with rising life expectancy in good health, albeit difficult for people to accept), but, above all, they are being adopted at a time when early retirement is still widespread and until very recently was seen by many as a new social *right*. The fact that governments almost everywhere have some time ago ceased encouraging the practice has not yet really affected people's attitudes.

Codes of Employment focusing on a reassessment of occupational mid-life and the position of senior workers, with examples of best practice, would certainly help in a number of countries, as, indeed, has successfully been done in the UK. For its part, the European Commission has shown the way by preparing its own Code of Employment to be used as a model.

The need for an effective and rapid plan of action

Some experts believe that it is only when the labour market has experienced acute manpower shortages – depending upon the country, this will occur in four to ten years' time – that the majority of enterprises will move their policies towards retaining workers later than they do today and adapting work conditions accordingly. In many of the Danish and UK companies that are models in this area having adopted a new approach, the change was triggered by experience of manpower shortages. It is our contention, however, that it is now time that governments plan for and anticipate this kind of contingency as part of *a global strategy on ageing and work* rather than waiting for shortages to occur before taking action. Dramatic changes in the dependency ratios mean that in most countries the well-being of the population overall will soon depend on fewer workers. By 2010, workers over 45 will account for 40% of available manpower in the EU. Workers in general – not just young workers – will be in short supply and in some places already are. All ages will need to lend a hand.

Ageing workers will therefore hold a *key* position, because of their number, quality and experience. Moreover, public and company policies need to be implemented on a certain scale and over time before change can come about. Interdepartmental cooperation is essential because of the broadness of the issues involved and because of the need for cooperation between employer and employee organizations. A well-briefed media can also play a very positive role as a catalyst of the new mind-set that will facilitate subsequent acceptance of the new policies and measures. And one lesson the examples of the Nordic countries and the Netherlands teach us in this connection is that, however generous social policies remain, financial incentives of various kinds are required if extension of work-life is to meet with wide acceptance.

Additional policies

As shown in Figure 4.10 (p. 73), increasing the participation of older workers is essential if we are to be equal to the challenges posed by demography, changing labour market conditions and the mutating life-cycle. In Chapter 3 we saw how crucial pension reforms were in meeting these challenges. In what follows we shall be looking at some additional policies we feel to be desirable. These latter fall into three distinct categories.

The need for increasing employment participation overall and for controlled immigration

The first measure concerns an increase in employment overall, but on this occasion by raising the participation rates of three specific categories of potential worker: women, the unemployed and the disabled. As we have seen, there are important differences in the labour market participation rates for these three categories in the EU member states. The Nordic countries, for example, are doing better than the EU southern states, but in the long term the convergence principle should help to improve these rates almost everywhere. Part-time work is here also a key factor in particular for women and disabled persons. Not only is part-time an excellent transition between non-activity and activity but it also allows a better combination of work with family responsibilities and so may contribute to a higher birth rate for women.

This change calls for more active employment measures and less passive social protection. Countries such as the Netherlands, Finland, Denmark, Sweden and others have set up excellent special measures to help disabled persons to enter the market, which include 'soft' jobs, frequently on a part-time basis. Other member states (Austria, France, Germany, Ireland and the UK) have set national targets for employment of the disabled.

Another solution, much debated in recent years, is to increase, where realistic, immigration into EU member states. The UN and the OECD have both estimated the number of new migrant workers required to compensate for demographic change and for a future shrinking of the labour force. According to a UN estimate in 2000, for example, the number of migrants needed to keep constant the size of the population in labour force age in France and the UK is about double the level recorded for the early 1990s. For the same purpose, Germany's requirement would be about 3.4 million migrants per year, that is, more than ten times the annual number of migrants entering Germany between 1993 and 1998. In the case of Germany, for example, the sheer number involved would cause severe social and political problems with, in all probability, very negative financial consequences on both sides of the frontier of migration. This is why in Germany's and in many other cases, we would advocate as a complementary solution some form of controlled immigration. In Germany's case, for example, the number of new migrant workers might be kept down to the levels of the 1980s.

The need to reinforce family policies

The second kind of measure or solution, in our view much more important than immigration, is family policy aimed at a stable increase in fertility rates over the long term in Europe. Various surveys (Godet, 2003) have shown that in some member states women do not have the number of children they would like to have. We believe that there is a correlation, both direct and indirect, between appropriate family policies and the fertility rate.

Appropriate family policy must include, among many other things, generous family allowances, a tax system that encourages large families, the availability of adequate care provision for children and other dependants and a better work-life balance. The differences in women's employment rates with and without children are particularly pronounced in Ireland (16.3%), in Germany (21.4%) and in the UK (22.8%). In these countries, as well as in others like Spain or Greece where the differences are by comparison more modest, the care services available are woefully incapable of meeting demand. In countries with better care facilities such as Sweden or France fertility rates (respectively 1.7 and 1.9) are higher than in the EU southern states.

The example of Norway is in this connection rather interesting. It is one of the countries with the best fertility rates in Europe (1.8) but also with one of the best rates for female employment. All very intriguing until we learn that, in Norway, companies attract women workers by offering them excellent child care facilities (Credit Suisse, June 2004).

In short, family policy will be crucially important if Europe is to secure higher fertility rates over the long term and so avoid the pitfalls of an 'old' society with a diminishing population and workforce.

Measures to reconcile work and family life have been put in place in most EU member states (COM 2003 728 final, Brussels 26.11.2003). They include: more flexible work and work time organization (Germany, Belgium and France); part-time work facilities (Sweden, Luxembourg and Ireland); development of parental leave (Denmark, France, UK, Spain and the Netherlands); new measures, quantitative targets and deadlines on child care provision (Belgium, France, UK, Ireland, the Netherlands, Greece, Spain, Portugal and Sweden). Nevertheless, child care provision is still far from the 2003 Employment Guidelines targets which require that child care be provided by 2010 to at least 90% of children aged between three years old and the mandatory school age, and for at least 33% of children under three years of age. 'Therefore,' concludes the EC Communication 'a greater effort should be made in providing more accessible and high quality care services for children and other dependants, and in facilitating a choice between part-time and full-time work' (COM 2003 728, p. 17).

The need for improving the quality of work

The new definition of old age we proffered in Chapter 2 is, in our opinion, crucial and should not only inform the process of pension reform and any reassessment of employment, but also guide the new design for work and its place within the life-cycle, allowing for a 'mix' of concurrent activities, reflecting changes in the life-cycle itself.

The three post-war decades of rapidly increasing prosperity were followed by a 20-year period during which leisure pursuits, the family and free time acquired increasing significance while work values tended to decline. European countries have reduced work time, work conditions have been personalized and made more flexible, holidays are longer than they were, and travel and leisure time are now standard for the vast majority of the population. Many have acceded to *the right of free time* (a phrase coined by Jean Viard, a French sociologist).

If active ageing is to become a widespread phenomenon, then work and its place in our lives need to be reconsidered. We need at all costs to improve the quality of work if we want more people in their 50s and 60s, and perhaps even their 70s, to modify their work/leisure balance in favour of more work. The International Labour Office has had an extended programme on Decent Work (ILO, 1999 and 2001). As mentioned earlier, workers in low-quality jobs withdraw from the labour market two to four years before workers in good quality employment. The *cohort effect* – with more and more workers being better qualified, working flexibly in service activities and benefiting from continuing training and lifelong education – will allow more easily than in the past later exit patterns and more flexibility.

Health and safety in the workplace constitute another key issue – many workers currently describe work conditions as more stressful than ten or fifteen years ago. The short-termism of our 'just in time' society, as some have described it, is inimical to those who wish to bring balance and harmony to their occupational lives and to plan for the future.

Perhaps one of the greatest challenges facing us today is that of better organizing our service society where the demand for so many of 'traditional' services remains unmet. We need to be rethinking work and retirement as parts of an integrated continuum where reform of the one calls for transformation of the other. Raising the number of contribution years to our pension schemes is simply inconceivable without a thorough reappraisal of work and employment. Requiring that companies provide an employee with sufficient work until 65 or later is simply not enough. The activities and functions provided, whether paid or unpaid, must involve work that is satisfying and fulfilling and this throughout the occupational span from entry into the labour market until exit.

Our societies should not have to choose between leisure and work but be able to opt for a satisfactory balance between the two. What is true at the individual level is also true at the society level between welfare and workfare. This new reassessment is urgent so that, in a few years or decades, work will almost naturally last a few more years.

Today, facing both the demographic challenge and the coming shrinking of the workforce, we need to rediscover the value and the taste of working. As stated by O. Giarini (Giarini and Liedtke, 1997), we probably are more what we produce than what we consume. Of course this means rethinking and improving working conditions. More and more firms will soon offer better conditions to maintain older workers later than today. But conditions need to be humanized for all by encouraging more flexible rhythms, adequate education, ergonomics and health at work, and making working life more compatible with care activities and voluntary commitments important for the community, in particular an older one.

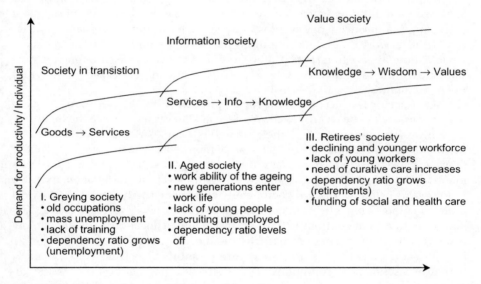

Figure 10.3   Three ageing waves of the workforce

Source: Rantanen (1999).

As can be seen from Figure 10.3, our societies have evolved from manufacturers of industrial produce to communities where the service information economy predominates and where, as a consequence, the organization of work is changing radically. Progressively, and increasingly in future, our societies will be marked by an older population whose maturity will gradually replace today's cult of youth to give the values of solidarity and social utility the place they deserve.

Bibliography

Adler, J. (2003) Consequences of raising the retirement age with regard to possible further increase of pensionable age as well as to labour market situation (Hungarian), GKI Economic Research Co., <www.celodin.org/read.php?lang=hu&pid=5082>

Age Concern England (2003) One in Four – A quarter of single women pensioners live in poverty: this scandal must end, <www.ageconcern.org.uk>

Age Positive (<www.agepositive.gov.uk>) (2001) *Age Diversity: Summary of Research Findings*, Department for Work and Pensions, London

Age Positive (<www.agepositive.gov.uk>) (2004) *A Snapshot of Large Employers' Initiatives*, Company Case Studies, Department for Work and Pensions, London

Auer, P. and Fortuny, M. (2000) *Ageing of the Labour Force in OECD Countries: Economic and Social Consequences*, Employment Paper 2000/2, Employment Sector, International Labour Office, Geneva

Avenir Suisse (2002) Verbreitung und Profil der Altersteilzeitarbeit in der Schweiz: eine empirische Analyse, in R. Widmer, A. Sousa-Poza, H. Schmid, *Zusammenarbeit mit der Stiftung*, Avenir Suisse

Baker, D. and Price, M. (2002) Financing the Future: Mind the Gap! The implications of an ageing population – key findings and proposed actions, Financial Services Authority (FSA), London, <www.fsa.gov.uk/pubs/other/financing_future.pdf>

Börsch-Supan, A. (2003) From Public Pensions to Private Savings: The Current Pension Reform Process in Europe. Paper presented at the Conference on the Economics of an Ageing Society: 'The Future of Funded Systems', Rüschlikon, Switzerland, 28 November 2003

Buck, H. and Dworschak, B. (2003) *Ageing and Work in Europe: Strategies at Company Level and Public Policies in Selected European Countries*, in the series Demography and Employment, Stuttgart

Confederation of German Employers' Associations (BDA) (2003) *Proage – Facing the Challenge of Demographic Change*, Berlin, November 2003, <http://Abt_04@bda-online.de>

Conseil d'Analyse Economique (2000) *Retraites choisies et progressives*, Rapport D. Taddei, La Documentation Française, Paris

Conseil Economique et Social (2001) *Les personnes âgées en France*, Conseil Economique et Social, Paris

Credit Suisse Economic & Policy Consulting (2004) Marché du travail en Suisse – salaires élevés et faible réglementation, Economic Briefing, No. 37, <http://research.credit-suisse.ch/fr/publications>

Dalen van, H. and Henkens, K. (2002) Early-retirement reform: can it and will it work? *Ageing & Society* 22, 2002, pp. 209–231

Dang, T.T., Antolin, P. and Oxley, H. (2001) Fiscal Implications of Ageing: Projections of Age-Related Spending, Working Papers No. 305, OECD (ECO/WKP 2001/31).

Davis, P. and Li, C. (2002) *Demographics and Financial Asset Prices in the Major Industrial Economies*, Brunel University, West London, 23 October 2002

Delsen. L. (2002) Active strategies for older workers in the Netherlands, in M. Jensen, D. Foden and M. Hutsebaut (eds) *Active Strategies for Older Workers*, European Trade Union Institute, Brussels, pp. 299–344.

Delsen, L. and Reday-Mulvey, G. (1996) *Gradual Retirement in the OECD Countries*, Ashgate, Aldershot

Delteil, V. and Redor, D. (2003) L'emploi des salariés de plus de 55 ans en Europe du Nord, Etude réalisée pour la DARES (Ministère des Affaires Sociales) par le GIPMIS (Mutations des Industries et des Services), <www.gip-mis.fr>

DGB (Deutscher Gewerkschaftsbund) (2004) *Demographischer Wandel: Schritte zu einer alternsgerechten Arbeitswelt*, Berlin

Direction régionale du travail Rhône-Alpes (1998) *La Préretraite Progressive – Un dispositif au service de l'emploi et de l'enterprise*, Ministère du travail et des affaires sociales, Paris

Dobossy, I., Molnár, E. and Virágh, E. (2002) Ageing – retirement – retired life – old age, in, Zs Spéder, *Demographic Development and Social Environment* (Hungarian), Budapest

The Economist (1996) All our tomorrows: A survey of the economics of ageing, 27 January 1996

The Economist (2004) A survey of retirement, 27 March 2004

European Commission (1999) Work, Employment and Welfare in 2010, *Demographic and Social Trends Issue Paper*, No. 09, May 1999

European Commission (2001) Making a European Area of Lifelong Learning a Reality. Communication from the Commission, COM(2001) 678 final, Brussels (21 November)

European Commission (2003a) *Adequate and Sustainable Pensions*. Joint report by the Commission and the Council, Directorate-General for Employment and Social Affairs, Unit E.2, Brussels

European Commission (2003b) Recent Reforms of Pension Systems: An Assessment Framework, ECFIN/440/03-EN, Brussels

European Commission (2003c) Communication from the Commission to the Council, the European Parliament, the European Economic and Social Committee and the Committee of the Regions, COM(2003) 728 final, Brussels

European Commission (2004) Increasing the Employment of Older Workers and Delaying the Exit from the Labour Market. Communication from the Commission to the Council, the European Parliament, the European Economic and Social Committee and the Committee of the Regions, COM (2004), 146 final, Brussels

European Employment Observatory (2000–04) Newsletter No. 12–17, <www.eu-employment-observatory.net/en/newsletter>

European Foundation for the Improvement of Working Conditions (2000) *Active Strategies for an Ageing Workforce*, Conference Report, Turku, 12–13 August 1999, Dublin.

European Foundation for the Improvement of Living and Working Conditions (2003) *A New Organisation of Time Over Working Life*, Office for Official Publications of the European Communities, Luxembourg

Eurostat (2004a) *European Social Statistics – Labour Force Survey Results 2002*, Luxembourg

Eurostat (2004b) *Population Statistics*, Luxembourg

Fouarge, D., Grim, R., Kerkhofs, M., Román, A. and Wilthagen, T. (2004) *Trendrapport Aanbod van Arbeid 2003*, OSA-publicatie A205, Tilburg, Organisatie voor Strategisch Arbeidsmarktonderzoek

Gallenberger, W. (2002) *Weiterbildungsabstinenz älterer Beschäftigter in einer alternden Erwerbsbevölkerung*, Opladen, Leske und Budrich

Gaullier, X. (2003) *Le temps des retraites – Les mutations de la société salariale*, Le Seuil (coll. La Républiques des idées), Paris

The Geneva Association (1999, 2001, 2003) *Studies on the Four Pillars*, *Geneva Papers on Risk and Insurance*, Special Issues (G. Reday-Mulvey, editor), October 1999, 2001 and 2003, International Association for the Study of Insurance Economics, Blackwell, Oxford

The Geneva Association (2000–04) *The Four Pillars* (G. Reday-Mulvey, editor), Newletters 26–35, International Association for the Study of Insurance Economics, Geneva

The Geneva Association (2002) *Etudes & Dossiers* No. 270, Papers prepared for an international symposium 'Public Policy, Ageing and Work', Cambridge, December 2002, International Association for the Study of Insurance Economics, Geneva

The Geneva Association (2003) *Etudes & Dossiers* No. 271, Contributions given at the 'Work Beyond 60 Conference', Vienna, March 2003, International Association for the Study of Insurance Economics, Geneva

The Geneva Association (2004) *Etudes & Dossiers* No. 288, Contributions given at the 'Health, Work and Ageing Conference', Trieste, October 2004, International Association for the Study of Insurance Economics, Geneva

Giarini, O. and Liedtke, P. (1997) *Wie wir arbeiten werden*, Hoffmann und Campe, Hamburg

Giarini O. and Malitza, M. (2003) The Double Helix of Learning and Work, *Studies on Science and Culture*, UNESCO, Bucharest

GINA and The Geneva Association (2002) *The Future of Pensions and Retirement – 10 Key Questions*, International Association for the Study of Insurance Economics, Geneva

GIPMIS (Groupement d'Intérêt public Mutations des Industries et des Services) (2004) *Newsletter*, No. 21, July 2004, Paris

Glover, I. and Branine, M. (2001) *Ageism in Work and Employment*, Ashgate, Aldershot

Godet, M. (2003) *Le Choc de 2006: Pour une société de projets*, Odile Jacob, Paris

Guillemard, A.-M. (1990) Les nouvelles frontières entre travail et retraite en France, in *La Revue de l'IRES*, 2, hiver, pp. 41–98.

Guillemard, A.-M. (2003) *L'âge de l'emploi: Les Sociétés à l'épreuve du vieillissement*, Armand Colin, Paris

Hashimoto, R., Mondale, W. F. and Pöhl, K. O. (2002) *Meeting the Challenge of Global Ageing*. A report to world leaders from the CSIS Commission on Global Aging, Washington

He, Y. H., Colantonio, A. and Marshall, V. W. (2003) Later-life career disruption and self-rated health: an analysis of general social survey data, *Canadian Journal on Aging*, 22(1), Spring, pp. 45–57

Henkens, K., Remery, C., Schippers, J., and Ekamper, P. (2003) Managing an ageing workforce and a tight labour market: views held by Dutch employers, *Population Research and Policy Review*, No. 22, pp. 21–40

Hornstein, Z. (2002) Outlawing age discrimination: Foreign lessons, UK choices, in Transitions after 50 Series, Joseph Rowntree Foundation, <www.jrf.org.uk/bookshop>

Humphrey, A., Costigan, P., Pickering, K., Stratford, N. and Barnes, M. (2003) Factors Affecting the Labour Market Participation of Older Workers, DWP Research Report 200, <www.dwp.gov.uk/asd/asd5/rports/2003–2004/rrep200.asp>

Hungarian Central Statistical Office (2000) *Time Use Survey*, Budapest

Huth, P. (2004) Marché du travail en Suisse – salaires éléves et faible réglementation, *Economic Briefing* No. 37, June, Credit Suisse (Economic and Policy Consulting)

Huth, P. and Beck, A. (2002) Die Bedeutung der Altersteilzeitarbeit im Spiegel einer alternden Gesellschaft. Paper prepared for the project '4. Säule: Potentiale einer erhöhten Beschäftigungspartizipation älterer Arbeitnehmer', Crédit Suisse, Economic Research & Consulting, Kompetenzzentrum Wirtschafts- und Sozialpolitik

Illmarinen, J. (1999) *Ageing Workers in the European Union: Status and Promotion of Work Ability, Employability and Employment*, Helsinki

Illmarinen, J. (2001) Ageing Workers in Finland and in the European Union: Their Situation and the Promotion of Their Working Ability, Employability and Employment, *Geneva Papers on Risk and Insurance*, Vol. 2, No. 4, October, pp. 623–41

ILO (1999) 87th Session of the ILO, Report Decent Work, Geneva.

ILO (2002) *An Inclusive Society for an Ageing Population*, Geneva.

Initiative Neue Qualität der Arbeit & Bundesanstalt für Arbeitsschutz und Arbeitsmedizin (2004) *Mit Erfahrung die Zukunft meistern! Altern und Ältere in der Arbeitswelt*, Dortmund

Jackson, R. and Howe, N. (2004) *The Graying of the Middle Kingdom – The Demographics and Economics of Retirement Policy in China*, CSIS (Center for Strategic and International Studies), Washington, DC, and Prudential Foundation, Newark, NJ

Jaumotte, F. (2003) Female labour participation: Past trends and main determinants in OECD countries, OECD Working Paper, <www.olis.oecd.org/olis/2003doc.nsf/linkto/eco-wkp(2003)30>

Jensen, M., Foden, D. and Hutsebaut, M. (2002) *Active Strategies for Older Workers*, European Trade Union Institute, Brussels

Jensen, M., Foden, D. and Hutsebaut, M. (2003) *A Lifelong Strategy for Active Ageing*, European Trade Union Institute, Brussels

Jensen, P. (2002) Fostering longer working lives: Best practice policies, in G. Reday-Mulvey, *Encourager une vie professionnelle prolongée – Nouvelles politiques et bonnes pratiques en Europe*, Avenir Suisse, Zurich, <www.avenir-suiss.ch>

Jolivet, A. (2002) Allonger la vie professionnelle: état des lieux, in G. Reday-Mulvey, *Encourager une vie professionnelle prolongée – Nouvelles politiques et bonnes pratiques en Europe*, Avenir Suisse, Zurich, <www.avenir-suiss.ch>

Jørgensen, Klaus (1997) *Aeldre og arbejdsliv – Tilbagetraekningsmønstre og seniorpolitik*, Kobenhavn, Udviklingscenteret for folkeoplysning og voksenundervisning

Karoly, L. and Zissimopoulos J. (2004) *Self-Employment and the 50+ Population*, Public Policy Institute, AARP, March 2004, <www.aarp.org/ppi>

Kessler, D. (1990) Les quatre piliers. Rapport pour l'Association de Genève, *Etudes & Dossiers*, No. 144, March, Geneva.

Kohl, J. (2002) European Public Opinion Concerning the Extension of Working Life. First results of a recent Eurobarometer survey. Paper prepared for the seminar 'Extension of Working Life. Gradual and Flexible Retirement Systems', Lanzarote, 4–5 February 2002

Kolikoff, L.J., Smetters, K. and Walliser, J. (2001) *Finding a Way out of America's Demographic Dilemma*, NBER Working Paper, No. 8258, 2001

Kuhn, K., Taylor, P., Lunde, A., Mirabile, M. L. and Reday-Mulvey, G. (1998) Career Planning and Employment of Older Workers, Action Research Report, *Re-Integration of Older Workers into the Labour Market*, Driekant, The Netherlands

Latulippe, D. and Turner, J. (2000) Partial Retirement and Pension Policy in Industrialized Countries, *International Labour Review*, 139, (2), pp. 179–95

Liedtke, P. M. (2003) Pension Economics: The Relativity of Time and Risk, in *Geneva Papers on Risk and Insurance, Studies on the Four Pillars*, Vol. 28, No. 4, October, Blackwell, Oxford

Lissenburgh, S. and Smeaton, D. (2003) Employment Transitions of Older Workers: The Role of Flexible Employment in Maintaining Labour Market Participation and Promoting Job Quality, in Transitions after 50 Series, Joseph Rowntree Foundation, <www.jrf.org.uk/bookshop>

Maltby, T., de Vroom, B., Mirabile, M.-L. and Øverbye, E. (2004) *Ageing and the Transition to Retirement: A Comparative Analysis of European Welfare States*, Ashgate, <www.ashgate.com>

Mantel, J. (2001) The Impact of Aging Populations on the Economy: A European Perspective: From Baby Boom to Baby Bust?, *Geneva Papers on Risk and Insurance*, Vol. 26, No. 4, October, pp. 529–46

Mercer, S. (2004) Extending Working Life: UK Experiences, *Etudes et Dossiers* No. 288, International Association for the Study of Insurance Economics, December

Michel, J. P. and Robine, J. M. (2004) A 'New' General Theory on Population Ageing, *Geneva Papers on Risk and Insurance*, Vol. 29, No. 4 October

Molinié, A. F. (2003) *Age and Working Conditions in the European Union*, European Foundation for the Improvement of Living and Working Conditions, Dublin

Moynagh, M. and Worsley, R. (2004) *The Opportunity of a Lifetime: Reshaping Retirement*, Tomorrow Project & Chartered Institute of Personnel and Development, Cromwell Press

Nordheim, F. von (2002) EU Policies in Support of Member State efforts to Retain, Reinforce and Re-integrate Older Workers in Employment. Contribution to the international workshop 'Ageing and Work', organized by Institut Arbeitswirtschaft und Organisation at the Internationales Kongresszentrum, Bundeshaus Bonn, 2 September 2002

Nordheim, F. von (2003): European Policies on Age and Employment, in: *Etudes et Dossiers* – Working Paper Series of the Geneva Association, No. 271, pp. 191–6

OECD (1998) *Maintaining Prosperity in an Ageing Society*, Paris, OECD

OECD (2000) *Reforms for an Ageing Society, Social Issues*, Paris

OECD (2002) Increasing employment: The role of later retirement, in *OECD Economic Outlook 2002*, pp. 137–54

OECD (2003a) *Coping with Ageing: A Dynamic Approach to Quantify the Impact of Alternative Policy Options on Future Labour Supply in OECD Countries*, Economics Department, Working Papers No. 371, Paris

OECD (2003b) Towards more and better jobs, *Employment Outlook*, Paris

OECD (2004) *Reforming Public Pensions: Sharing the Experiences of Transition and OECD Countries*, Paris

Pedersen, L. and Tranaes, T., eds (2004) *Det danske arbejdsmarked* (*The Danish Labour Market*) Socialforskningsinstituttet (Danish National Institute of Social Research), Kobenhavn

Pestieau, P. (2003) Raising the Age of Retirement to Ensure a Better Retirement, *Geneva Papers on Risk and Insurance*, Vol. 28, No. 4

Phillipson, C. (2002) Transitions from Work to Retirement: Developing a New Social Contract, in Transitions after 50 Series, Joseph Rowntree Foundation, <www.jrf.org.uk/bookshop>

Proage (2003) *Facing the Challenge of Demographic Change*, Berlin

Rantanen, J. (1999) *Työelämä ja Kestävä Kehitys: Työ vuonna – näkymiä suomalaiseen työelämään*, Työterveyslaitas, Helsinki

Reday-Mulvey, G. and Giarini, O. (1995) *The Green Document*, summary of The Four Pillars Research Programme, Geneva Association

Reday-Mulvey, G. (2000): Gradual Retirement in Europe, *Journal of Social Policy and Aging*, Special issue 2000, US

Reday-Mulvey, G. (2002) Report prepared for Avenir Suisse, *Encourager une vie professionnelle prolongée*, Avenir Suisse, Zurich <www.avenir-suisse.ch>

Reday-Mulvey, G. (2003) Encourager une vie professionnelle prolongée: Nouvelles Politiques et Bonnes Pratiques en Europe, Report prepared for the Avenir Suisse Foundation in Zurich, *Etudes & Dossiers*, No. 268, International Association for the Study of Insurance Economics, Geneva

Reday-Mulvey, G., with Taylor, P. (1998) *Career Planning and Employment of Older Workers*, Report for the European Commission, Euroworkage, Driekant, Maastricht

Sarfati, H. and Bonoli, G. (2002) *Labour Market and Social Protection Reforms in International Perspective*, Ashgate, Aldershot

Schuller, T. and Walker, A. C. (1990) *The Time of our Time*, IPPR Institute for Public Policy Research, Employment Paper, London

Schumacher J. and Stiehr, K. (eds) (1996) Retirement in the 1990s and Beyond. Documentation of a European Seminar in Frankfurt, 1996 June 20–21, Frankfurt a.M., Institut für Soziale Infrastruktur

Sigg, R. (2004) *Social Security and Extending Working Life: Policy Challenges and Responses*, International Social Security Association, Geneva

Sousa-Poza, A. and Dorn, D. (2004a) *Motives for Early Retirement: Switzerland in an International Comparison*, Discussion Paper No. 99, Department of Economics and Research Institute for Labour Economics and Labour Law, University of St Gallen

Sousa-Poza, A. and Dorn, D. (2004b) *The Determinants of Early Retirement in Switzerland*, Discussion Paper No. 98, Department of Economics and Research Institute for Labour Economics and Labour Law, University of St Gallen

Sousa-Poza, A. and Henneberger, F. (2003) *The Determinants and Wage Effects of Course-Related Training of Elderly Workers in Switzerland*, Discussion Paper No. 94, Department of Economics and Research Institute for Labour Economics and Labour Law, University of St Gallen

Stepczynski, M. (2003) *Les Vrais Enjeux de la Retraite*, Slatkine, Genève

Széman, Z. (2004) Ageing and the Labour Market in Hungary, in T. Maltby, B. de Vroom, M-L. Mirabile, and E. Øverbye (2004) *Ageing and the Transition to Retirement: A Comparative Analysis of European Welfare States*, Ashgate, <www.ashgate.com>

Taylor, P. (1998) *Projects Assisting Older Workers in European Countries: A Review of the Findings of Eurowork Age*, European Commission, Employment and Social Affairs, Brussels

Taylor, P. (2002) *Improving Employment Opportunities for Older Workers – Developing Policy Framework*, Report to the European Commission, mimeo, Brussels

Taylor, P. (2003) New Policies for Older Workers, in Transitions after 50 Series, Joseph Rowntree Foundation, <www.jrf.org.uk/bookshop>

UNICE (2003) Commission Communication on the Future of the European Employment Strategy, 'A Strategy for Full Employment and Better Jobs for All', UNICE Position, <www.unice.org>

United Nations Population Division (2000) *Replacement Migration: Is it a Solution to Declining and Ageing Populations?*, New York

Velladics, K. (2004): The Need for an Extended Working Life in Europe, in *Etudes & Dossiers*, No. 285, Follow-up of International Symposium in Cambridge and Related Papers, Geneva Association

Verband Deutscher Rentenversicherungsträger (2003) *Arbeitsmarkt und Alterssicherung*. Papers prepared for 'Jahrestagung 2002 des Forschungsnetzwerkes Alterssicherung', Dresden, 5–6 December 2002

Walker, A. (1999) *Managing an Ageing Workforce – A Guide to Good Practice*, European Foundation of Living and Working Conditions, Dublin

Walker, A. (2002) A Strategy for Active Ageing, *International Social Security Review*, Vol. 55, No. 1, pp. 121–40

Walker A. and Hagan-Hennessy, C. (eds) (2004) *Growing Older – Quality of Life in Old Age*, Open University Press/McGraw-Hill Education.

Walker, A. and Wigfield, A. (2003) *Older Workers Skills and Employability: A Guide to Good Practice in Age Management*, Working Paper, University of Sheffield

Warr, P. (1994) Research into the Work Performance of Older Employees, *Geneva Papers on Risk and Insurance – Issues and Practice*, Vol. 19, No. 73, Geneva

WHO (1999) *A Life Course Perspective of Maintaining Independence in Older Age*, Geneva

WHO (2001) *Men, Ageing and Health, Ageing and Life Course Unit*, Geneva

WHO (2002) *Active Ageing: A Policy Framework*, Geneva

Widmer, R. and Sousa-Poza, A. (2003) *Verbreitung und Potential der Alters(-Teilzeit)-Arbeit in der Schweiz*, Avenir Suisse Foundation, Zurich

Widmer, R. and Sousa-Poza, A. and Schmid, H. (2001) *Verbreitung und Profil der Altersteilzeitarbeit in der Schweiz: eine empirische Analyse*, St Gallen University

World Economic Forum (2004) *Living Happily Ever After: The Economic Implications of Ageing Societies*, Geneva

Index

Compiled by Sue Carlton